Prophets of the Hood

Politics

and

Poetics

in

Hip Hop

· · · · · **Prophets of the Hood**

Imani

Perry

Duke University Press Durham & London · 2004

© 2004 Duke University Press

All rights reserved

Printed in the United States of America

on acid-free paper ∞

Designed by C. H. Westmoreland

Typeset in Scala with Stone Sans display

by Tseng Information Systems, Inc.

Library of Congress Cataloging-in-Publication

Data appear on the last printed page

of this book.

- For Freeman Diallo

Contents

Acknowledgments

This project was nurtured, supported, and fueled by many people. Abundant thanks to J. Reynolds Smith, my editor, and Sharon Parks Torian of Duke University Press for commitment, encouragement, and careful reading over the years in which this project developed.

Thank you to the institutions, foundations, and programs that have supported this work: The Minority Summer Research Exchange Program at the University of California, Los Angeles, the Ford Foundation, the Mellon Foundation, the American Studies Association, Harvard University's Black Graduate Network.

Thank you to the mentors, teachers, motivators, and opportunity creators: Robert Bellinger, Hazel Carby, Fr. Thomas Clark, Michael Denning, Gail Dines, Michael Eric Dyson, Janet Eisendrath, Ann Fabian, Henry Louis Gates Jr., Herman Gray, Farah Jasmine Griffin, bell hooks, Cesar McDowell, Phillip McFarland, Reneé Neblett, John Szwed, Cornel West, and Thomas Wilcox.

Thank you to those with whom I have broken bread over hip hop analysis and the vagaries of popular culture at various points over the last thirteen years, colleagues, students, acquaintances, friends, and loved ones: Michele Alexandre, Anthony Almeida, Terence Barrett, Alvin Bragg,

Jean Ann Brown, Tammy Brown, Daphne Brooks, Illya Davis, Jeremi Duru, Farah Griffin, Michael Hill, Larry Johnson, Larry Jackson, Shani King, Darryl Rick Lane, Tammy Mack, Stephen Marshall, Sydney Todd Ellis Murray, Onitara Nelson, Mtu Pugh, Maurice Rabb III, Saleem Washington, Simone White, Cheryl Jones Walker, Noland Walker, Ivy Glen Wilson, my students at Suffolk, and many others.

Also, in loving, memory of Okokon Okon III. Thank you for your friendship and insights on hip hop and otherwise.

Thank you to the multitudinous, but not yet enough, scholars who have written and who will write on black popular culture.

Thank you to my family:

The beautiful, brilliant, and numerous Perrys, led by the incomparable Neida Mae Perry. Writers, thinkers, contrarians all!

To my parents for teaching me the gorgeousness in the ordinary and the ongoing nature of the struggle.

My mother, Theresa Perry, my friend and hero, who believes in me above all others, who taught me to love books and black folk, and who thinks, writes, and acts with a fierce intellectual rigor.

My father, Steven Whitman, my greatest cheerleader, my friend and funnybone, and my role model for impassioned social justice scholarship, who listened to Run-DMC and Public Enemy with me in the car.

My husband and partner, Christopher Murphy Rabb, who imagines with me days of laughter, film, art, sunshine, music, books, and doing our part for the world, and with whom I share a cross-cultural house head/hip hop head love.

My son, Freeman Diallo Perry Rabb, the most beautiful person I have ever met in my life. Thank you for choosing me to be your mother.

Introduction

We gathered together, a group of black students from Harvard law school, the day after our final examination period was completed. The examination for Property law had been a rigorous one, an eight-hour take-home. A young man announced, "I wouldn't have been able to get through it without that Biggie." In that particular group of hip hop heads, the logic of the statement was clear: The generated energy, the adrenaline rush, and the rhythm of the Biggie Smalls music he listened to while writing his exam all motivated him as he expressed his knowledge and skills of argumentation in text. Many of Biggie's music videos celebrated the trappings of wealth, while scantily clad women surrounded men as testimonies to the latter's affluence and charisma. There were lyrics of hustling and lyrics of sexual exploitation. But there were also lyric narratives of endurance, ones describing the alienation of the impoverished and the depression of marginalization. Regardless of the content, the poetry was lyrical and elegant and the beats were hot. To listen to hip hop is to enter a world of complexity and contradiction. In the midst of a consumer culture that glorifies violence and eschews intellectualism, hip hop has both spewed American vices on the airwaves and aggressively introduced progressive politics, compelling artistic expression, emotion, and beauty into popular culture. It makes us uncomfortable, frustrated, and perhaps even confused that all of these contradictions should exist together in one musical form, sometimes in one artist. Yet hip hop has become a form reflecting both the beauty and the belly of the beast in American society, refracted through the lens of black American culture. As John Szwed has written of rap: "All those elements of black folk culture that had been denied by the elegance and pretense of the ballroom or the club came back with a vengeance on the avenues and in the parks. Performers were free again to talk that talk, to insert curses, blessings, and jokes into their raps, and to return to the funky, individually grained voices that disco had made to seem gauche."[1]

Hip hop is an iteration of black language, black music, black style, and black youth culture. Hip hop music, or rap, the subject of this book, is an art often culturally rich and economically impoverished, and, sometimes recently, artistically impoverished but backed by huge corporate dollars. At its best, it is compelling art and culture. It is at once the most lucrative and culturally oppositional musical force in the United States, and it demands a literary and musical criticism, a criticism in the tradition of Henry Louis Gates's *Signifying Monkey*, which uses the vernacular as a theoretical foundation of its analysis.[2] The present book ventures to be such a critical enterprise, an analysis of the art, politics, and culture of hip hop lyrics and music as revealed by the words and gestures of what I call the "prophets of the hood."

If the book title were lyrics, the double entendre would be obvious: prophet/profit. Textuality and orality bear a strained relationship. However, *Prophets of the Hood* aspires to use text to illuminate and examine an oral and auditory art form. Although written language can never fully explain other media, my efforts at theorization and elucidation will hopefully not be in vain. The homophones at play in the title constitute, for my purposes, a perfect idiosyncrasy of the English language and American culture. Hip hop artists are often self-proclaimed contemporary prophets, their work constructed of truth-revealing parables and pictures. That truth may be spiritual, cultural, personal, beautiful, and it may resonate with inspiration or tragedy. And even as the soul of the music resonates with marginalized people of various nationalities and ethnicities, in its American form, it is overwhelmingly and fundamentally black American—and expressive of that experience.[3] Moreover the black Americanism of the music forms part of its international appeal, given the resonant power of black music and culture globally. Recall the biblical quotation, "A prophet is without honor in his own country."

Hip hop has, at various times, served as fodder for conservative and racially biased agendas, but it nonetheless continues to maintain a core of artistic integrity and has grown enormously as an art form over the years it has been under attack. Simultaneously, it is fraught with dilemmas and inundated with the crises of urbanity, consumerism, and late capitalism. Disney, McDonald's, and numerous other global corporate entities have adopted the forms of rap as a marketing tool. Hip hop music sells clothes, fast food, soda, shoes, and films. The commodification and commercialization of hip hop has forever altered the art form, at times challenging its integrity. Nevertheless, it is far from a demented music produced by damaged people, nor is it, despite the frequent testimonies of political pundits, violence without art. This book will not read as an apologia for, or a crisis text about, the destructive forces in hip hop. Instead I attempt to justly treat the difficult political and cultural issues presented in hip hop, and to examine its artistic value as a style of music.

This work stands amid and relies on the body of scholarship already extant on hip hop: the distinguished and landmark examinations in book and article form by authors such as Michael Eric Dyson, Houston Baker, Tricia Rose, Robin Kelley, Mark Anthony Neal, and many others. Throughout *Prophets of the Hood*, readers will see references to their work and arguments, although my discussions of their work are not nearly exhaustive, and I encourage those interested in hip hop to read the growing body of academic literature treating the music. What is distinct about the present book is that it departs from the primacy of historical and sociological interpretations of hip hop and concentrates instead on the aesthetic, artistic, theoretical, and ideological aspects of the music, working from the premise that it has been undervalued as an art per se, even as its cultural influence has often been noted. While mine is certainly not the only work that concentrates on this theme, it is unique in its analytical framework of beginning with artistic and aesthetic analyses that then move into cultural inquiry. I am interested in exploring the artistic requirements for hip hop as an art, in understanding what philosophies and assumptions one finds in the spaces between the poetry of the lyrics and the music of the beats, and in examining what philosophies interplay between the artists and an audience that receives the music as one deriving from its own community and experience, and what role record companies play in mediating this relationship. In this book I use lyrics which I have transcribed from recordings for purposes of explication and example. The process of transcription is humbling yet critical to providing nuanced interpretations of the music.

Reunion

> And behold, the veil of the temple was rent
> in twain from the top to the bottom; and the earth
> did quake, and the rocks rent.
> —Matt. 27:51

Gospel in church and blues in juke joints. Rosa Parks and the unwed teenage mother, Claudette Colvin, who refused to move from her seat on the bus two weeks before her. Public oratory and the dirty dozens. Motown and the rougher, funkier Stax. The division between the respectable and funky stuff has existed throughout African American history. Most Americans rooted in African American cultural experience have sophisticated relationships with both the sacred and the profane, in black culture—or with their secular corollaries, the respectable and the rough. The division of the sacred and profane constituted an important civil rights strategy for a number of generations. "Clean" Negroes, in the black dialectic sense of being well-heeled and dressed sharply and neatly, but also in the sense of respectability served as civil rights models. Being impeccable, moral, and well-spoken stood as evidence of the unjustifiability of white American racism and brutality.

Recall many of the images of the civil rights movement: student activists at lunch counters, clean-cut, with clothes starched and hair trimmed. As models of respectability, they, in their impeccable presence, highlighted the brutality of the segregated South. Joseph Lowery, former president of the Southern Christian Leadership Conference (SCLC), stated in 1996 that in the civil rights era, black people had served as the moral conscience of the nation, and he lamented the fact that in the age of hip hop that was no longer the case.[4] By "moral conscience" he meant that African Americans threw into sharp relief how the promises of the nation had been denied, and I would argue that we did so in part by demonstrating models of respectability. For example, two weeks before Rosa Parks famously resisted the law of segregated public transportation in Montgomery, Alabama, Claudette Colvin had done the same. Colvin was certainly not the first to do so, but the activist community had been seeking an event that could serve as a rallying cry for a bus boycott, and it considered Colvin's gesture. Colvin was passed over, however, because she did not, as an unwed teenage mother, provide the respectable image that the civil rights establishment desired to make its point, and so Parks was ultimately selected as the symbol of the boycott.

But let's recall the music of that era as well: Harmonic ballads sung by suited men and cocktail dress–wearing women—neat, clean, and terribly respectable. But there was other music as well. Beside the nice image of Motown stood the funky rough sounding tunes of Stax. The divide between respectable music and funkier stuff was a long-standing one in black music, going back to the early divisions between spirituals and jook music, gospel and the blues. The division between the sacred and the secular transitioned into one between that presented as the face of respectability, often marketed to the mainstream, and that which was music for dark, smoky nightclubs. Again, this division in part served as a civil rights strategy; it was necessary to have a clearly demarcated space of respectability that could provide an unmarred example of the denial perfect citizens experienced in a racist society.[5]

The neat fades of the 1950s gave way to bushy afros, big jewelry, fatigues, and raised fists in the late 1960s, heralding the denial of the cults of sanctity and respectability as a political strategy for the post–civil rights generations. In what Mark Anthony Neal terms "the post soul" generation, the community of participants in hip hop culture, "the hip hop nation" has embraced a holism in music and culture in contrast to the earlier divisions. More than postmodern blending, it signals a novel culturo-political era in which the traditional dividing line between various forms of expression no longer appeals to the sensibilities and aspirations of vast numbers of young and black people.

Discourse

The signature element of the reunion in hip hop is the discursive space provided within the artistic and cultural community. Ideologically, hip hop allows for open discourse. Anything might be said, or, for that matter, contradicted. The juke joint has gone public. In the world of hip hop, holy and well-behaved gestures sit next to the rough and funky. Violence, sexuality, spirituality, viciousness, love, and countless other emotions and ideas all form part of the discursive space. Part and parcel of the refusal to serve as the moral conscience of the nation any longer has been the development of a music that allows for a wide range of expressions and positions, even within the music of one artist. For example, the slain hip hop artist Tupac Shakur, born of a mother who was a member of the Black Liberation Army, recited lyrics that alternately cherished and degraded women. This dynamic only has a logic in the context of a space where the high and low sit next to each other holistically, a space in which one can act a number of roles and play out intense moral and psychic dilemmas on wax. Battles, conversations, and competition all exist within hip hop. It hosts a marketplace of ideas, and it sometimes brings them together in a heteroglossic mélange. When emcees (MCs) critique each other, these critiques are more readily and better found in song than in interview form.

In contrast, generally speaking, the mainstream press categorizes and creates dichotomies of good and bad. It does not foster debate when it comes to hip hop, but rather encourages the censorship of ideological diversity through condemnation or praise. Mainstream media efforts at morality often appear more disingenuous and controlling than conscientious. In *Aesthetic Theory*, Theodor W. Adorno defined art as a critique of praxis.[6] Hip hop critiques the division of that characterized as clean and that characterized as dirty or evil as both social and artistic praxis. Hip hop calls for a radical honesty concerning the complexity of black communities and art, even in the public eye. While news media attempt to reinstitute the divide, trying to sift through the sea of MCs and searching for "good Negroes," they face a difficult and inorganic task. None of hip hop exists in a vacuum; each artist provides but one orientation within a diverse community, to be understood within the context of that community.

The reunion marks a democratic space in which expression is more important than the monitoring of the acceptable, a space, rather, that suppresses the silencing impulse extant in various segments of American popular culture, both within and outside black communities, be it the silencing of certain politics, ideologies, sexual preferences, or some other matters of personal choice possibly verging on the taboo. Hip hop may be democratic, but it is not, as a musical community, inherently liberatory. There are particular artists with liberatory agendas, who by their words protest racism, sexism, classism and thereby enlighten. But hip hop is not "liberation music." The ideological democracy inherent in hip hop prevents the kind of coherent political framework necessary for it to be characterized as such. That is not to say that the music lacks conscience or is amoral. Rather, there is abundant space for moral expression as well as critique. When Posdonus of De La Soul said, "Fuck bein' hard Posdonus is complicated!"[7] he critiqued the popularity of thug narratives about how tough you could be, and how many guns you toted, and instead offered the idea that it was more important to be intellectually complex. In forming this critique within the context of the musical community, rather than in a mainstream media outlet, the author avoids the perception that he is begging to be differentiated from the "bad ones" under a mainstream moralistic gaze. He avoids the mediation between different sorts of MCs by the gaze of white America, instead offering the choice up to hip hop heads, whether the better argument exists for being hard or being complex.

I recall an interview with Snoop Doggy Dogg after he had signed with Death Row Records, in which he endearingly questioned why so many prominent black leaders critiquing his work went to the networks in order to castigate him, rather than speaking to him personally. In the interview he spoke highly of congresswoman Maxine Waters because she had done just that. He explained how she came to him personally to offer loving critique. Hip hop cherishes engaged discourse within the community and balks at being offered up for scapegoating, particularly by other black people, regardless of the good intentions behind that gesture.

And yet the combination of democracy ("speak your piece") and meritocracy ("be the best MC") that exists in hip hop is threatened at every turn. The manipulations of capital, media, and record company distribution, the ruthless promotion of some acts to the disadvantage of often musically superior ones, the commodification of black female bodies, and the grotesque marketing of racist images of black male violence threaten to completely overwhelm the public face of hip hop. Warning labels and lawsuits have forever altered the face of hip hop in the United States. In the late 1990s, it became possible for a hip hop artist to become rich and acclaimed with very little skill or participation in the community discourse of hip hop, feeding from it, contributing to it, or being sustained by it. Maintaining the discourse-reunion community in the face of the categorization and manipulation that forms part of the recording industry and American consumer culture in general stands as one of hip hop's central challenges. The discourse continues, however, particularly among underground independent artists, but also on the part of many successful artists who maintain a dedication to urban, poor, and working class communities of color, the core hip hop community.

Moreover, hip hop still constitutes a form that can be referred to as a form, a specific kind of music defined by rhyming lyrics and a multitextual collage-style composition. Despite its uniqueness, hip hop does exist on a continuum of black music forms and is indebted to several of them, most especially blues and jazz. However, hip hop has several features that appear to be particular, if not exclusive, to it in terms of content. Discussion of these features will appear throughout the *Prophets of the Hood*, but I would just to highlight a few here. First, there exist far fewer depictions of idealized romantic love, or even painful and deep romantic love, than in any other black music form. Conversely, there are far more explicit expressions of rage and more intimate expressions of psychological pain. Finally, detailed explications of the criminal underworld, and of interpersonal conflicts and dysfunction, are unique in their predominance in the musical form. The present book seeks to both analyze the music on an anesthetic level and as a site of cultural production with cultural consequences. The distinctive features of hip hop are products of both. Often these features distinguishing hip hop and its reunion ethos make it an uncomfortable music to listen to, yet it also allows for brilliant insights into human relationships and into existence in a society mired in difficult race and gender politics and often economically exploitative and exclusive.

1

Hip Hop's Mama

Originalism and Identity in the Music

Good music often has a beauty identifiable across the boundaries of nation and culture. And yet a musical composition, and musical forms in general, have identities rooted in community. The community might be as small as an artistic collective or as vast as a continent. While the individual artist and the individual composition provide compelling subjects for analysis, the validity of that analysis in part depends on knowledge of the community from which it emerges. To know that community means that the critic possesses both a historic and an aesthetic body of information relevant for understanding the music's original context. Of course, isolating the relevant community that is the source of knowledge forms part of the critic's work, and such discernment fundamentally shapes the critical process. Here I would like to posit an argument as to what community rap/hip hop music belongs to in the United States. The arguments that follow in later chapters will rely on this foundational argument.

Hip hop music is black American music. Even with its hybridity: the consistent contributions from nonblack artists, and the borrowings from cultural forms of other communities, it is nevertheless black American music. It is constituted as such because of four central characteristics: (1) its primary language is African American Vernacular English (AAVE); (2) it has a political location in society distinctly ascribed to black people, music, and cultural forms; (3) it is derived from black American oral culture; and (4) it is derived from black American musical traditions. I argue that to describe rap or hip hop music as black American is not inconsistent with an understanding of its hybridity, a characteristic that will be elaborated upon later in the text. While I will rely on Afro-Atlantic theory to put forth this argument, I will also suggest that the manner in which the Afro-Atlantic model has been used to consider hip hop in its transnational rather than multiregional focus with respect to an analysis of American hip hop is flawed, although the model does offer great benefits when analyzing hip hop as a global phenomenon.

The assertion that hip hop is a form of black American music is in some ways radical (and unpopular) given current trends in hip hop scholarship that emphasize the multiracial origins of the music, in particular the significant contributions of Caribbean, white, and Latino communities and artists. Many critics have resisted the description of hip hop as black American music because they quite appropriately contest any suggestion that it is "100 percent black" given the active participation of other groups in the world of hip hop since the nascent days of the music. Critiques of the description of hip hop as black music also often stand as critiques of racial essentialisms, or critiques of the way in which culture is marketed through race at the same time that it is fundamentally hybrid. I caution, however, that taking issue with essentialisms should not occur at the risk of failing to understand politics or cultural frameworks, and hip hop does exist within black American political and cultural frameworks. The accuracy of the assertion that hip hop has multiracial and multicultural origins does not suggest that it is not black. Only a worldview that subjugates blackness marks the phrase "it's just black" as an offensive designation. Why can't something be black (read, *black American*) and be influenced by a number of cultures and styles at the same time? The idea that it cannot emerges from the absurd reality that blackness in the United States is constructed as a kind of pure existence, a purity, to most, of the negative kind, defined by a pure lack of sophistication and complexity and a pure membership in a group of undesirables. To deem something French or English rarely implies that there were no Germanic cultural influences, or Irish, or even Algerian. Why, then, is it so troubling to define something as black? Color consciousness that allows for an understanding of both the political implications of the category of race and the cultural forms that have emerged under that category is useful and progressive, and certainly not essentialist.

I would argue that while critics have good intentions when they pay attention to the numerous nonblack American influences in the music, and nonblack audiences for the music, there is an inconsistency between that side of the argument and their concurrent alignment of rap to the sociology of black America and the politics of black existence. The paradigm effectively applied to a music drawing on hybrid influence yet also having a black political and social existence is one that understands hip hop as existing within society as black music, but also one that assumes that black music is and has always been hybrid, drawing on influences from other cultures and places. In fact, music is never compositionally pure, even as it exists within a culture and is identifiable with a community.

Part of the resistance to the description of hip hop music as black music results from an emphasis on "originalism," that is to say, a fixation on who made the first records or created the first dances and what ethnic groups they came from. This focus on originalism, while important for historical acknowledgment, seems to fail with respect to identifying an art form as a cultural project. Certainly, although hip hop was born in the multiethnic, colored melting pot of New York and has become a national form with dominant voices emerging from the three other major geographical regions of the United States (the south, the midwest, and the far west), it is far more identifiable in the American imagination and in American practice as particularly black American in terms of what group rappers are constituted from and which communities push forward the music's artistic growth. Ethnomusicologist John Szwed, with respect to originalism, asks,

> Does rap have a beginning? Where does the credit or (some might say) the blame lie? The quick answer is to say that it's an African-American

form, for which, on a diasporic flow chart, you could plot an unbroken line from African to the Caribbean and on to the United States. Or maybe bypassing the Caribbean altogether, but in any case ending with the youth of the black working class. Yet things in the United States have never been that simple. Or that pure. The origins of everything American twist and shout their way through history, giving and taking as they go, inventing and reinventing themselves, praising their authentic beginnings about as often as they deny them.[1]

Szwed locates the music as African American, and yet he also understands that this categorization cannot refute hip hop's *créolité*. Paul Gilroy, who in his outstanding critical work resists the identification of hip hop as black American music, nevertheless acknowledges the danger of relying on originalist sensibilities for discussions of hip hop. He writes,

> No straight or unbroken line of descent through either gendered line can establish plausible genealogical relations between current forms and moods and their fixed, identifiable and authentic origins. It is rather that the forbidding density of the processes of conquest, accommodation, mediation, and interpenetration that helps to define colonial cultures also demands that we re-conceptualize the whole problematic of origins. . . . Our difficult object: black performance culture and its social and political forms is a profane practice. It has been propagated by unpredictable means in non-linear patterns. Promiscuity is the key principle of its continuance.[2]

Gilroy and I part ways, and therefore reach divergent theoretical conclusions, because he takes as his unit of examination for black performance culture the Afro-Atlantic, rather than any national community. Nevertheless, I agree with his argument concerning the nonlinear and promiscuous course of cultural production within the African American context in particular. And certainly it is the case that at critical moments in the development of hip hop the participation of nonblack Americans was paramount. Yet I argue that the promiscuous composition does not destroy cultural identity. The manner in which the music became integrated into the fabric of American culture was as a black American cultural product, through an overwhelmingly black American audience (no longer the case), and using black American aesthetics as signature features of the music. As Szwed has also written, "Having noted rap's broad affinities, its American-ness, its creole emergence, and its lack of exclusive rights to be offensive, no one would be fooled into missing the fact that it finally is also very much an African American form."[3]

Although I am asserting that hip hop is black American music, I do not want that to be mistaken as a nationalist glorification or simplification. It is the very fact of postmigration fragmentation and reintegration that explains much of the music's beauty, as well as its various regional and international variations and interactions. It is black, and yet it is certainly "impure." What is southern hip hop without the tension between the urban and the rural South? What is New York hip hop without the Caribbean and African American blend, the memory in text of experiences of adolescents who returned to ancestral homes for summer vacations or to get away from the negative influences in the city? What is West Coast hip hop without the shadow of Hollywood and the history of the Black Panthers, funk, and blaxploitation? These questions are impossible to answer because the cultures in question are constituted by a postmigration mosaic at once plagued by the feeling of loss, by constant efforts to recover, and by the celebration of the current hybrid self. Russell Simmons once noted that hip hop was about doing the unexpected. That unexpectedness constitutes the par excellence feature of hybridity: unexpected encounters lead to unexpected productions.

The most powerful critiques of the construction of hip hop as black American music have come from people who understand how critical the influences of the English-speaking Caribbean have been, in particular in the early days of hip hop formation and in the creation of DJ technique. Jamaican deejaying techniques directly influenced DJ styles in hip hop, yet, while the technology proves significant, I agree with Szwed that the musical sound is what makes hip hop compelling and that the technology was simply used to reproduce sounds already deemed aesthetically pleasing to a black American audience. It was a point of cultural consistency. Szwed writes, "Much has also been made of the technologically sophisticated context in which rap emerged—the use of sound processing, sampling, mixing, drum machines, and the panoply of studio apparatus typically used with today's raps—as a means of showing that rap is radically new and only secondarily beholden to folklore and tradition. But sophisticated as these productions may be, the artful logic that lies beneath them has been part of African-American aesthetics for at least a century."[4] He references sounds from earlier black music that resembled those of scratching, delay, and even those of sampling: "Even drum machines were anticipated by scat singing (and in case anyone forgot, human beat box imitations of drum machines also remind us that drums were once used to imitate voices for sending messages)."[5]

Hybridity in rap takes place on a cultural plane, and the terms on which it exists depend on that plane. The moments at which nonblack American cultural influences take root in hip hop often occur at crossroads of sorts, at which the aesthetics of two cultures are in concert with one another. For example, we can observe this phenomenon in the discursive space using tricksterism, an Afro-Atlantic folk cultural practice with rich roots in West Africa. The storytelling of a Barbadian MC, which emerges from his linguistic and cultural tradition, might resonate with a black American audience with has similar storytelling traditions, as well as with other Afro-Atlantic listeners.

It is, however, important to recognize the substantive contributions of non–African American cultures on hip hop music. I would argue that there are at least three principal areas of English-speaking Caribbean influence on hip hop that are consistent with Gilroy's conception of transcultural and transnational cycles of cultural flow.[6]

I will critique the employment of this concept by some critics later in this chapter. Each area of influence is primarily Jamaican, although a number of hip hop artists clearly have other Caribbean ancestries. These influences are:

> 1. The use of DJ techniques and recording technology as it would be fully embraced in hip hop. Much as the R & B melodic form influenced reggae, hip hop was influenced by a form of Jamaican deejaying that would eventually develop into a black American version in the United States.
>
> 2. The imagery of the black outlaw. While heroic images of the black outlaw exist in African American tradition, the specific practice of using mainstream, and particularly white, heroic figures in the process of self-defining the self-proclaimed outlaw originated in the practices of Jamaican folk culture. This likely resulted from the appropriations of second-run cinematic images to postcolonial identity. The outlaw language in hip hop is often traditional black American language, but the use of identities such as Dirty Harry or figures from the *Godfather* movies likely derives from Jamaican employment of such imagery.

3. The presence of reggae music in hip hop compositions, which I would argue found a formative entrée into black American musical culture through Stevie Wonder's appropriation of reggae beginning in the late 1970s and the global popularity of Bob Marley during the same era.

Similarly to the Caribbean influence, the Latino influence on hip hop resulted from crossroads moments. As Nancy Guevara has argued, "The appropriation and dissemination of rap by Puerto Rican DJs like Charlie Chase were facilitated by the similarity in verbal dexterity and rhythmic use of voice prized in these black traditions to those common to such Latin musical styles as the Puerto Rican *décima* and *plena*."[7]

However, that crossroads space became defined through politics and the cultural identity of the form by its blackness, not its crossroad nature. Mandalit del Barco has noted that "as rap began in the 1980s to develop a more political focus on black nationalism with the advent of Public Enemy, Boogie Down Productions, Brand Nubian, XCLAN, and other groups, the visibility of Latinos in hip hop faded."[8]

The African aesthetic origins of hip hop, as with all black American music, allows for it to have a shared resonance among a wide range of diasporic and continental Africans. As Jon Yasin has written, "the spoken word of African-American music has its origins in Africa and survived the middle passage to the Western hemisphere."[9]

And at the same time, the history of black power movement talk, and its impact on the development of hip hop, located it as a musical form at best revolutionary and at least rebellious for young listeners across the globe. According to Yasin, "During the black power movement the original rappers of the 1970s were adolescents. As teenagers, these rappers had been exposed to revolutionary poetry and the spoken word of the traditional African-American secular and sacred music."[10]

Of course, U.S. global domination, and the power of the American culture industry, also play a significant role as a means by which the music of black Americans has become music of the world at large—embedded with both the possibilities of the history of black American resistance and struggle and the vacuousness, conspicuous consumption, and negative "-isms" of American culture.

One of the challenges resulting from the fact that hybridity emerges at points of aesthetic sympathy or compatibility is that it leads to some strange claims of ownership. As part of a panel on black American, Caribbean, and African relations at Harvard University in 1997, Orlando

Patterson, noted professor of sociology at that institution, commented that black American music only became political with hip hop, and that this was due to the influence of Caribbean music. Numerous black American members of the audience reacted with insult and astonishment at the ignorance the statement revealed. The words of a well-regarded scholar of African American studies had performed an erasure of the Last Poets, Gil Scott Heron, Curtis Mayfield, Marvin Gaye, and numerous political folk ballads and movement music. They put into relief the problem that often occurs when those unfamiliar with certain features of African American experience, history, and culture see similarities between those fields and their previous knowledge of other Afro-Atlantic cultures, assuming ancestry in those locations and dismissing possible roots in the national origin of the music. DJ Kool Herc, one of the grandfathers and originators of hip hop deejaying, has notably rejected any suggestion on the part of interviewers that the central source of rap lies in the form of toasting popular in the Caribbean, rather than in the American version: "Jamaican toasting? Naw, naw. No connection there. I couldn't play reggae in the Bronx. People couldn't accept it. The inspiration for Rap is James Brown and the album 'Hustlers Corner' by the Last Poets."[11]

The authors of *Reggae Routes*, a work tracing the history and impact of Jamaican popular music, argue that rap was a direct descendant of Jamaican deejay music. As a caveat, however, they say, "Of course some would say that Jamaican deejay music evolved from the southern black R & B radio disc jockeys who in turn developed their style from jazz scat singers. And they may be right. But it was the Jamaican deejays who first turned chanting/toasting/scatting into a commercial musical form that stood on its own and pushed all accompaniment into the background— where people bought the records because of the rhythmic talking."[12]

The difficulty with their authenticating claim of course lies in the fact that scatting as part of recorded music has early twentieth-century roots in black America and that poetry records became popular in the 1960s during the confluence of the black arts and black power movements in the United States. And of course the spoken word courses through local and commercial black music throughout the twentieth century as well, even during the mellifluous doo-wop era said to have been the early inspiration for reggae.

These examples serve two purposes: to explicate the hybridity of black music and to demonstrate how external influences enter at aesthetic crossroads but do not dismantle the cultural unity of the form. They also serve to demonstrate that a rigorous understanding of the history of black American culture and music is necessary before one denies the location of a form within the black American cultural universe.

An alternative trend in the critique of the idea that hip hop is black American music comes in what I would term a romantic Afro-Atlanticism. This romantic Afro-Atlanticism appears without conflict in the academic world, but it is deeply conflicted in the actual interaction between peoples of African descent in the "new world." Conflicts between African Americans and Caribbean people, Haitians and Dominicans, Haitians and Jamaicans, and Dominicans and Puerto Ricans all trouble the shared political and aesthetic culture identified in much academic scholarship. In fact, conflicts created by beleaguered histories, economic competition, the effects of white supremacy, and a classist social structure threaten what is shared. Psychologist Mary Waters has described the efforts Caribbean Americans make to distinguish themselves from African Americans, often with visual triggers of identification.[13] At elite universities, Caribbean students have reportedly excluded African Americans from organizations and study groups, claiming, as part of their immigration narratives, that the latter group lacks the appropriate work ethic to participate. Young Caribbean people learn from their parents the stories of their exploitation at the hands of African Americans, or other Caribbean people who had been here longer, when they newly arrived in the United States, and those stories become warning narratives. Most black Americans have minimal contact with black immigrants and derive their information about them from imperialistic and Eurocentric media constructions of third world, black-populated countries. Hence, immigrated blacks are taunted by them with racist terms like "African booty scratcher" or references to AIDS.

This phenomenon proves all-significant because it sets a framework against which to understand the point of communion taking place in hip hop. At these moments of cultural meeting over hip hop, the young non–African American participants are often seen by the adults in their community as becoming too American. Rather than being identified as a moment of hybridity, this moment is often interpreted as a time of crossing over to the American side, or, in the case of Puerto Ricans, to the black side. For years, I listened to the stories of friends teased by their black immigrant families for adopting the clothing and musical preferences associated with hip hop and therefore it was thought they were becoming "too American." And such a characterization is not without its merit. One day, as I came home to an apartment in Silver Spring, Maryland, I heard loud rap blasting from the apartment next to mine. From behind the door came a young teenaged boy recently arrived from Colombia. In the handful of months since his arrival, his afro had been cut down low, his gait had shifted from tentative to a strut with a bop, and he had a new leather jacket. Hip hop culture figured prominently in his Americanization.

The centrality of race as a signifier in U.S. culture results in the reading of black immigrants with the same assumptions and metaphors as black Americans, unless a vigorous self-distinguishing process takes place. For those readily identifiable as immigrants, it may be easier to obtain a small business loan or a job in the service economy, but once the accent has faded and American cultural assimilation takes place, that party begins to be identified as black American and becomes subject to the dangers of a racist society, as horrifically testified to by the experiences of Abner Louima and Amadou Diallo. In his article "(E)racing the Fourth Amendment," British legal scholar Devon Carbado describes how encounters with policing were critical to his acculturation into becoming black American.[14] A consciousness about this status as policed people is critical to hip hop and its resistant voices. The representative consciousness of hip hop is black American in its relationship of alterity to American power and race politics.

The Afro-Atlantic theory—with Paul Gilroy as its central proponent and many, including cultural critic George Lipsitz, supporting his ideas —while compelling and insightful on many planes, often falls short in its application to hip hop in the United States. In particular, despite its appropriateness for the discussion of hip hop's global presence, in centralizing the experiences of the black Caribbean, it imagines a kind of fluid structure between countries and people that mimics the immigration and migratory patterns of Caribbean people. This can serve as an appropriate metaphor through which to understand Caribbean music, but not African American music. Black American people's migration from country to city certainly differs from international migration, and it also does not manifest the same continuous loop of movement from place to place. Black American presence in other nations is generally an artistic or vanguard presence, not one of traditional migration.

What does this mean? First, it means that while African Americans in their home communities sometimes encounter other Afro-Atlantic forms of cultural production, it overwhelmingly occurs through the lens and mediation of those who share their own cultural experience, the black American artistic vanguard. Second, it opposes the postcolonial critical fantasy of a united ideology in the Afro-Atlantic world manifest through fluid musical forms. Arguments proposing such unity fail to engage with seriousness how deeply African Americans are Americans, their existence fundamentally different from Afro-Caribbeans, Africans, or Afro-Latinos and their identities profoundly shaped by black American double consciousness, whereby one is both American and black, two identities inextricably linked and yet at times in conflict. It is this "two-ness," to use W. E. B. Du Bois's term, that enables rapper Mystikal, through the metaphor of a jazz funeral, to use the bounce-back of black American experience to provide emotional uplift in the aftermath of September 11 with a profoundly patriotic sensibility.[15] Our engagement with what it means to be black and American far exceeds that of any Afro-Atlantic identity, despite the aspirations of many throughout history including Martin Delany, Marcus Garvey, Ron Karenga, and Molefi Asante.

Black American music, as a commercial American product, is exported globally. Its signifying creates a subaltern voice in the midst of the imperialist exportation of culture.[16] But the imperialist relationship of a flow of import and export does not work neatly with the black American experience. Black Americans as a community do not consume imported music from other cultures in large numbers, although other countries import enormous amounts of black American music. The imported music black Americans hear is either mediated through the tastes of the black avant-garde, artistic communities, or record labels as they trickle down to the masses, often in diluted or reinterpreted form, through sanitized popular culture, or through American-based encounters with other cultures. But outside of the Northeast and Miami, substantial interactions between black Americans and other black Atlantic people are few and far between and where they do exist, they are often fraught with territorialism, which makes borrowing less substantive that it would otherwise be. The postcolonial Afro-Atlantic hip hop community is, unfortunately in many ways, a fantastic aspiration rather than a reality.

The above, however, does not mean to deny that cultures from the

Caribbean and Latin America have an important presence in hip hop; quite to the contrary. But one must remain aware of its location. As an example, it is my observation that black American youth dance to reggae or dancehall productions that dovetail with black American aesthetics, and that have become part of the world of hip hop deejaying, they often enjoy it, but by and large they fail to comprehend the range of deep cultural, political, and linguistic symbols embedded in the music. Rather, they respond to a rhythmic structure, not unlike what occurs when most white American listeners to black American music.

Despite my critique of romantic Afro-Atlanticism to understanding American rap, I would argue that that mode of analysis holds genuine power and importance for explicating why hip hop has global influence. As Michael Dyson notes, "[Toni] Morrison argues that what unifies hip-hop throughout the world is its emergence from 'the "others" within the empire' . . . who ring profound changes in the nation's discourse."[17] Hip hop does provide a politically unifying force that proves central to any interpretation of the music's transnational presence. Its identity of double consciousness in fact speaks quite effectively to the global postcolonial participant in hip hop culture for its centralization of the voice of "the other." If a global politics could emerge, with flows in more directions and with a more informed American population, the prospect of a genuine Afro-Atlantic youth identity might be viable. Certainly any project that considers the global influence and presence of hip hop should be indebted to the creation of Afro-Atlantic theory, and such projects are of critical importance to the body of hip hop scholarship. The mischaracterization of hip hop that at times occurs in such work in part results from the attractiveness and richness of postcolonial theory. Yet applying it to hip hop can prove difficult because while postcolonial critics concern themselves with international and transnational identities emerging from the so-called postcolonial condition, hip hop is far more concerned with region and local specificity. In many ways, it is arrogantly American. Speaking of the South, Tony Green writes, "We don't need to be reminded where the Afro-Atlantic verbal tradition calls when it wants to talk to its mama."[18] He continues, "Imagine the rise of the low-riding West Coast and the East's glossy R & B reaction without the funk injection of the Sun Belt (or, for that matter, the northeastern school without all of those southern soul-jazz instrumentals). Snoop's Karo Syrup drawl, E-40's game-spittin' and Too Short's lyrical pimpology are, despite their purveyors' geographical location, unmistakably southern, all products of a West Coast scene whose members make no bones about their roots. Ditto for the Midwest."[19]

Gilroy argues that West Coast artists Ice Cube and Tim Dog borrowed substantially from the Caribbean, an argument I am not yet convinced of. I believe the more compelling story of the music of Ice Cube and many other West Coast MCs is the current of southern language through their mouths, even in a context in which regional affiliation is deeply important. The question is not, "Are you black American?" but rather, "What kind of black American are you?" Where an artist comes from proves incredibly important in hip hop, but more so as a symbolic affiliation rather than as a clear and specific historical truth. In the notorious East Coast/West Coast divide, regional affiliation was a causal element in the murders of both Biggie Smalls and Tupac Shakur. One has to wonder why such powerful media-generated geographical affinities took hold among a widespread hip hop audience. Certainly, identity is always multifaceted, and regional identity, as a kind of mini-nationalism, is subject to symbolisms that take on great meaning. The East Coast/Coast West coast dichotomy found in hip hop was preceded by that of college and professional basketball conferences, as well as of the all-star game. In that context, the affiliation of the player proves more important than his or her specific origin. Just as the Philadelphia-reared Kobe Bryant would be booed by hometown crowds when he played for the Lakers, and seemed to identify with Los Angeles sensibilities, the New Jersey–born Ice-T and the East Coast–raised Tupac both became powerful West Coast symbols because they "played" for that region.

We find another example in Biggie Smalls, who self-identified in his lyrics as a child of the East Coast. Yet he also took part in a broader national black identification as well. He rhymed:

If I got to choose a coast I got to choose the East.
I live out there so don't go there.
But that don't mean a nigga can't rest in the West,
See some nice breasts in the West
Smoke some nice cess in the West
Y'all niggas is a mess
Thinkin' Ima stop givin' L.A. props.[20]

Redman and Method Man's lyrics are peppered with southern sayings, revealing their family roots. A popular radio station in Montgomery, Alabama ran an ad in the summer of 1999 that had Redman proclaiming, "I love Alabama, my people from Alabama, I'm from Alabama." These roots creep into distinctly New York voices. OutKast, by contrast, rhyme with the unmistakable drawls of the contemporary urban South:

> Throw your hands in the air
> And wave 'em like you just don't care
> And if you like fish and grits and all that pimp shit
> Let me hear you say oh-yeah-er . . .
> Well it's the M.I. crooked letter
> Ain't no one better
> And when I'm on the microphone you bets to wear your sweater
> Cause I'm cooler than a polar bear's toenails
> Oh hell there he go again talkin' that shit.
> Bent corners like I was a curve
> I struck a nerve and now you 'bout to see the southern player serve
> I heard it's not where you from but where you pay rent
> Then I heard it's not what you make but how much you spent.[21]

Riffing on a classic hip hop call and response, OutKast alert us to their southern frame of reference with food, style, and dialect. It is the contemporary urban South that animated their first several albums, that unique meeting ground of the traditional, the old and the new, plus the "same old, same old." Goodie Mob., also from Atlanta, include a "slumtionary" in their 1997 CD, which includes definitions for words used by poor black and young Atlantans.

In the summer of 2000, I went to a movie theater in Boston, Massachusetts to see *Mission Impossible II*. It proved an uncanny experience because I felt as though I had crossed the threshold and entered the Deep South. Young men at the candy counter were speaking in drawls, their speech inflected with the words *y'all* and *holler* and *baby girl*. It wasn't until I left the theater that it occurred to me that this phenomenon of southern language entering Boston might have something to do with the massive success of hip hop artists from the South such as the Cash

Money Millionaires, Master P, and the 504 Boys. That region had taken center stage nationally.

For MCs of each region, the particular rituals and vocabulary of their home emerges in the text of the music. For New Yorkers, it might be the subway train and references to women as earths and men as gods, a feature of the parlance of members of the Five Percent Nation, an offshoot of the Nation of Islam.²² In California, low-riding cars and calling sexy folks "freaks" act as referents. There exists a constant dynamic of specificity, even as hip hop creates a national youth culture with clothing, speech, and ideological positioning, and as it has international reverberations. The specificity of a home, that of the artists, constitutes a critical element of creation. It both roots the music in a historical, cultural, and linguistic community and educates the listener about that specific community. Sean "Puffy" Combs, producer and entertainer, and the retired Mase, both enormously popular in the mainstream, often reminded listeners in their songs that their paradigm is a "Harlem world." KRS-One has said that to understand hip hop one must go to the place of its origins, the South Bronx. Depending on one's perspective it is either a wasteland or a garden. Concrete as far as the eye can see, piercing the sky and covering the earth. And yet the smells, sounds, tastes, and the smaller frames of vision encase blacks and browns, piecing together their roots in this seemingly uprooted place. It is easy to see both the hardness and imagination of hip hop being born there as part of the process of making new and hybrid roots.

Contrast that to South Central Los Angeles, where transplanted Louisianans and Mississippians are nestled in the shadow of Hollywood, conspicuous consumption, and "the beautiful people." Poverty and police brutality have an eerie quality in the midst of greenery and pastel-colored houses. When the Dogg Pound made their regional dis record attacking New York, they subverted Grandmaster Flash's refrain about New York, "too much, too many people," a socially conscious anthem of urban depression, into a critique of big city East Coast life. In the music video, larger-than-life California MCs stand above the New York City skyline rhyming in syrupy California tongues, Snoop's long, straightened hair blowing in the wind. The hook for a song that celebrates New York, from Blahzay Blahzay, "When the East is in the house, Oh my God, danger!" is composed of three separate samples, New York speech, and a gospel hum refrain. To the extent that Caribbean ancestry is asserted in hip hop music, it is often within the fabric of a New Yorker's identification and speech, the medium through which the international landscape of New York emerges. A quick pace and complex rhymes are characteristic of classic New York style.

The regional conflicts in hip hop escalated in the mid 1990s due to a potent combination of record company interest and MC macho. What could have been healthy competition over style, substance, and listeners turned into a war over capital and ownership of the art form. *East Coast* and *West Coast* became rallying cries, even for those who had lived in both regions or those who lived in other regions (Midwest, Southeast). Magazines and news reports fed the regional conflict, but many MCs and listeners also bought into it. After the deaths of Tupac and Biggie, which shook the hip hop world at its core, regional dis records largely disappeared, and collaborations between artists from various regions began to flourish. Hip hop survived that tragic moment and continued to grow economically without conflict as its central theme, hence the MTV declaration of 1998 as the "Year of Hip Hop." And yet, even as the music became further hybridized and mainstreamed, the oral and cultural regional identities remained present in the music.

This previous discussion of the relevance of region means to lend evidence to a kind of national identity in the music that proves far more powerful and constitutive than international or transnational identifications, as well as evidence to a kind of racial identity.

Black English

African American vernacular English, black English, or Ebonics— whichever name one gives it, it constitutes the central form of linguistic communication in hip hop, although it absorbs singular words or phrases from other cultural communities as well, such as *Big up!* as an affirmation from Jamaican patois, or *Papi Chulo* as a Puerto Rican/ Nuyorican term for a sexy man. Biggie Smalls, who had a Caribbean mother, on his first CD used a woman speaking southern black English to play the role of his mother. He spoke exclusively in black American English, and yet the album also featured a song put to a reggae beat. The second album, released after his murder, featured West Coast artists speaking in their distinct regional dialect. There are some popular artists of diverse national origins who use their home languages more extensively, however, such as Wyclef Jean. Although he uses English-Caribbean patois more frequently than his native Haitian Creole, he nevertheless uses it as a marker of international flow in the way described by Paul Gilroy. And then, of course, there is an entire Spanish language body of rap music. Frequently, however, popular Latino artists who rhyme in English do so with the language of black America and make it distinctive by integrating Spanish phrases or words. Widespread recognition of Latino MCs only began to emerge in the late 1990s, with the successes of Fat Joe and Big Pun. The refrain to Pun's "Still Not a Player," which was "Boricua, Morena, Boricua, Morena," was an ode to Latinas and black women. Pun rhymed, "From butter pecan to blackberry molass I don't discriminate."[23] The cultural admixture of black and Puerto Rican communities in New York, and at the inception of hip hop in the South Bronx, has resulted in songs that integrate Spanish into lyrics, as well as celebrate identities, such as the party anthem "Puerto Rico" with the refrain "Puerto Rico, Black People."[24] The language of commonality used is English, more specifically black English.

Frequently phrases or words from other languages in hip hop are used to express the desire to remain incomprehensible to a widespread audience. Coded language, in the form of other languages or increasingly obscure dialect have become an essential element in maintaining a private hip hop community, particularly given the frequency with which popular hip hop slang moves into mainstream parlance. And so artists coming from various backgrounds pepper their lyrics with brand-new terms from Ebonics, patois, Spanish, and other new world creoles. However, the extent to which the integration of Caribbean patois and creoles occurs in hip hop not from the northeastern region or Miami remains relatively small because those members internal to the hip hop community in most parts of the South, Midwest, or even the West Coast do not experience the same degree of cultural interaction and crossroads moments of aesthetic compatibility with nonblack American populations. The language of the music in those areas tends to be more exclusively black American, unless the artists making the music have developed a multiregional or multinational artistic community personally or within the recording industry.

To fully understand the linguistic additions to black English present in hip hop requires a fluency in black English, whereby new words are understood by context. As Jon Yasin has written:

"Certainly not detracting from rap's success in the African American community is that much of it is in African American Vernacular English (AAVE), the language of most African Americans. The language of rap is primarily AAVE not only in a grammatical sense, but also in the broader sense of language that includes discourse, what people actually use language to say and the verbal routines they use in saying it."[25]

And hip hop's appeal to black American ears and tongues also translates into an appeal for a white mainstream that has historically and with consistent enthusiasm consumed black language. Over the course of American history, black English, both in turn of phrase and style of presentation, has consistently been adopted piece by piece into the American mainstream. Its alterity, and its attention to aesthetics, make it appealing to a larger population. *Dis*, once an exclusive term of hip hop language, has become entirely mainstream, even used by candidates for public office and sexagenarian talk show hosts. This word, while derived from standard English terms in which *dis-* functions as a negative prefix (e.g., *disrespect*, *dismiss*, etc.), gathered its meaning in the social context of interpersonal rejection, or what another generation might have referred to as "putting someone down" not in the white American dialect sense of insulting, but in the black American sense of getting rid of someone as though setting someone on a table and walking away.

Orality and verbal dexterity are highly appreciated skills in black American culture, and that appreciation has spilled over into the mainstream through black American voices since the civil rights era. Charismatic black leadership of the past forty years has largely depended on the spoken word. Hence it is not surprising that black Americans would respond positively to the creation of a musical form based on talk, nor is it surprising that a larger American audience socialized through the media to appreciate the language of black America would respond to this music.

Political Location

In one of the earliest works of criticism to take up rap, the literary scholar Houston Baker Jr. wrote that "the black urbanity of the form seems to demand not only a style most readily accessible to black urban youngsters. But also a representational black urban authenticity."[26] That is to say that it was not only aesthetics but also identity, and I would argue a politically charged identity, that characterized rap music. Rap music has a complex relationship to American society, but a relationship ambivalent in a manner characteristic of black experience. Of course it has been used as a scapegoat for social ills and is reviled for its negative messages from both the Right and the Left. Violence, sexism, and criminal activity are all depicted as horrifying features of rap music, despite the enormous levels of violent, sexist, and racist imagery all over American media forms and the glorification of criminal behavior on television and film. In considering the relationship of rock music to hip hop, one critic notes that "they could mingle, steal, and borrow from each other, but when it came time for judgment, it was always rap that was left holding the bag. When Time Warner went ballistic over 'Cop Killer,' a hardcore rock song by Ice-T's heavy-metal band Body Count released on its Sire label, it was rap music (not rock) that was vilified for glorifying violence."[27] This is of course a result of its racial identification. Yet it is also true that the borrowing of rap by white rock acts smacks of a performative inauthenticity because it occupies neither the political nor the cultural space of rap. As the same critic writes, "As alternative rock has waned, bands have taken to rapping—using it for more jokey rhymes in the tradition of Anthrax and Faith No More—including Limp Bizkit, Bloodhound Gang, Soul Coughing, Insane Clown Posse, and Barenaked Ladies, all of whom have voices and deliveries that would get them laughed out of a hip hop club."[28] When white performers sincerely adopt hip hop, and become adored by hip hop audiences, it takes place in part as a result of their embrace of both the aesthetic and political location of blackness and their sharing spaces with black bodies, such that their racial privilege becomes at least somewhat obfuscated.

The isolation of black bodies as the culprits for widespread, multiracial social ills is not unique to rap. It has occurred in critiques of the welfare state, in the demonization of early release programs from prison, in the image of drug trafficking, and in the symbols of sexist aggression (Mike Tyson for date rape, Clarence Thomas for sexual harassment, O. J. Simpson for domestic violence, etc.). What really makes hip hop music black American is America's love-hate relationship with it. Even as black men (and some black women) were lynched throughout the South, ragtime emerged as the most popular musical form in the early twentieth century. Throughout the period of Bill "Bojangles" Robinson and Amos 'n' Andy's celebrity, Jim Crow was in widespread practice. The love of black culture with the simultaneous suspicion and punishment of black bodies is not unusual. Nor is the public fascination with the perceived depravity or dangerousness of black artists, who are simultaneously loved: Think James Brown, Rick James, and Jimi Hendrix. Or imagine the supposedly naturalistic, hypersexual constructions of blackness that drew white audiences to Harlem Renaissance–era performers. Or the racist images of shiftlessness and stupidity that brought white audiences to minstrel shows. Rappers frequently find themselves in the news presented as dangerous figures who live out the violence of their lyrics. That image often does not correlate with the actual lyrics or the personality of the artist; rather, it reflects the music's perception as violent ghetto expression. Sean Combs's trial for gun possession turned into a media circus in which he was reported to have been charged with attempted murder, which was untrue, and as living out the violent image of his music, although his music was mostly a lighthearted and simplistic celebration of conspicuous consumption and wealth. The love Combs appeared to receive from the mainstream media and celebrities prior to the trial seemed to have expressed an appreciation of his aggressively capitalist and good-natured rhyming, but that public adoration soon cooled following the accusations.

Moreover, hip hop is located politically as black music not merely because of the look from the outside in but also due to perspectives from within the music. In the late eighties and early nineties, politically conscious rap music flowered that vociferously critiqued white supremacy, classism, and racial exploitation. To a lesser extent, this trend still exists. Even though some of these performers are no longer releasing albums, the legacy of artists like Public Enemy, Lakim Shabazz, KRS-One, A Tribe Called Quest, De La Soul, and Nas continues to resonate through hip hop, although now most frequently among underground artists or embedded within musical texts outwardly dealing with other issues. As one critic writes, "If Public Enemy resurrected late-'60s black militance, De La Soul expressed a form of liberal humanism."[29] The political consciousness within rap traverses the range of political perspectives to include nationalists, leftists, humanists, Afrocentrists, and a combination of any of the above as well. Even for those MCs not explicitly political in terms of the content of their work, one still at times finds a politically motivated relationship between the music and mainstream society. For example, rap provides ample evidence of what

I would term "Jack Johnsonism" or "Shine-ism," that is, in-your-face examples of black masculinity and excess that frighten the mainstream, exploiting its fears and simultaneously challenging the economic disenfranchisement plaguing black American communities. This has been a long-standing strategy in black cultural politics. Or one finds tricksters, those who use the oral tradition to subvert their own relative lack of power through trickery and verbal dexterity. Finally, there are the "bad niggas" as well, a role that descended from slavery days, characterizing the black person who refuses to submit to the rules of society, who is fearless and unruly, and who laughs at rules of appropriateness and social regulation.[30]

Hip hop is situationally black, that is to say that the role it occupies in our society is black both in terms of its relationship to other segments of the black community and of its relationship to the larger white segment of the country and of the "global village": it is that strange blend of voices of resistance and otherness marketed through the channels of American imperialism; it is the space where the passion and anxiety of adolescence are all engaged through the consumption of black music. As William Perkins writes, "So as white-bread America searches for a new identity in a post-Soviet, postindustrial, globally interconnected new world order, hip hop speaks to youth's desire for identity, for a sense of self-definition and purpose, no matter how lawless or pointless. As long as youth culture is dominated by the cult of commodity, there will be a desire for the 'real.' "[31] It is the music that incites fear in the hearts of the arbiters of respectability. Those arbiters are not only white but black as well, and the divide between sacred and profane, the politics of respectability and ostentatious blackness, is well depicted through the vocal criticisms that rap has received from black religious figures and members of the black civil rights establishments. Today, these sorts of criticisms take place on a national scale, but in earlier generations they remained confined to discussions of the sins of the jook versus the blessings of the church. Hence they are subject to manipulation and mediation by powerful mainstream interests, fueling the scapegoating of hip hop.

The brief preceding discussion has simply meant to locate some of the central ways in which one might identify rap music as a black political project and in which rappers occupy the position of black political subjects. That the latter holds true at times even for those who are not "ethnically" black American, to conclude the verbal-ideological range of expression in the music, perhaps stands as the most powerful testimony to hip hop's political blackness.

The Black Oral and Literary Tradition

Storytelling traditions are directly adopted in narrative rap—one of the earliest forms that rap lyrics took and a form that while not overwhelmingly popular, continues as one of the basic forms in which MCs write their songs. The exhortation of oneself and one's greatness present in many hip hop lyrics derives from the toasts of an earlier era, the songs of Shine and Dolemite, for example, and the competitive orality of the dozens is at work as well, as is the use of women's bodies as the basis of competition and insult between men.

The trickster consciousness passed down from African American oral traditions in folktales and folk ballads lives on in hip hop. Tricksters such as Brer Rabbit and Anansi the Spider, or even Shine and Dolemite, represent the superiority of intelligence and cleverness over brute force. For example, think of the time when Brer Fox thought he had outfoxed Brer Rabbit. Brer Fox had fashioned a Tar Baby, to whom Brer Rabbit had gotten stuck trying hard to get the inanimate object to respond to his greetings. Completely trapped, Brer Rabbit quaked to hear Brer Fox's proclamations that he was going to barbecue him for dinner. Brer Rabbit begged and pleaded: "Whatever you do, please don't throw me in that briar patch. Drown me, hang me, cook me, but please don't throw me in the briar patch." Brer Fox had been duped by Brer Rabbit so often that he wanted to get him as bad as possible, so of course he threw him in the briar patch. The clever rabbit was able to use the briars to release himself, and the folktale ends with Brer Rabbit's joyous song, "Born and bred in the briar patch!" Hence wit triumphed over the violent predator.

Breaking, the original dance form to emerge out of hip hop culture, is intelligent dance. Mythologized for replacing fighting with dancing battles, it represents the triumph of wit over force. Breaking depends on the isolation of body parts and the ability to shift between broad acrobatic movements and minutely detailed gestures, robotic or fluid. And of course, cleverness and the unexpected are appreciated in both lyrics and beats in hip hop. Take for example the comedic thrill of hearing Jay-Z's sample from the Broadway show *Annie*, "It's a Hard-Knock Life," and having it sound funky. The trickster creates dramatic contrast.

The contrast is apparent all over our popular culture: hip hop artists appear at the Grammy and American Music Awards despite protestations that hip hop is not music, but merely talking over already recorded hit songs, and that it is disturbing. Easy listening stations advertise their quality by stating that they play no rap. More than any other contemporary music form, hip hop brings dramatic contrast to the accepted music world. It is not "done" in the same way as other music, nor is it "done" in a way that is comfortable for many. Training in traditional music forms is not required here. To *use* (rather than *create*) traditional forms, the rapper does not have to learn how to play blues or jazz, but only how to use the technology to insert it into the montage. Further, the heterogeneous sound ideal's particular technological manifestation in hip hop creates an internal dramatic contrast. As "trickster music," it inserts itself into the traditional by borrowing and reconfiguring texts in service to the authority and artistry of MC and DJ.

The trickster also always maintains a subtextual discourse. It is what enables him or her to trick; it constitutes the element of surprise. In hip hop, several levels of discourse often coexist, each level revealing greater intimacy with the performer. Knowing the slang might be one level, knowing a lot about hip hop music in general might be another, knowing the performer's home city or neighborhood yet another, and knowing the artist as a member of one's own community is another again. Many mainstream listeners of hip hop believe that knowing current slang makes them understand the songs, but there are always a number of other points of reference. Frequently, a more thorough understanding of the songs and the artist reveals a subtextual critique of society, and particularly of white supremacy. Naming at times functions as a key element signaling this subtext. Big Boi of OutKast, on the group's first album, gives an explication of the group's name: "Operatin' under the crooked American system for too long / OutKast, pronounced outcast / adjective meaning homeless or unaccepted in society / but let's dig deeper than that." With this introduction, he alerts listeners to a subtext in the pair's naming, and then guides them to it: "Are you an outcast? / If you understand the basic principles and fundamental truths contained within this music / you probably are. If you think it's all about pimpin' hoes and slammin' Cadillac doors / you probably a cracker / or a nigga that think he a cracker / or maybe just don't understand." He tells us that one's epistemological framework determines one's ability to understand the music. It is connected to race, though not essentially, given the use of the word *probably*, but effectively "crackers"—a word generally reserved for vindictive and unsympathetic American-born Southern white folks with a fundamental disdain, acknowledged or not, for black folks—will not understand. They, in fact, will translate the message of the music into two-dimensional stereotypes of black materialism and exploitative sexuality instead of an ethic of resistant cool and alternative economies of style and wealth in the face of dispossession and an active legacy of racism and oppression. The speaker provides a means of assessment: "An outcast is someone who is not considered to be part of the normal world / He's looked at differently / He's not accepted because of his clothes, his hair, his occupation, his beliefs, or his skin color / Now look at yourself, are you an outcast? / I know I am / As a matter of fact, fuck bein' anything else." This self-test leads to an affirmation of being an outcast. Despite the undemocratic means of dealing with those not imagined to reside within the framework of normalcy, the status of an outcast is celebrated. The implication here is that the critical gaze provided by otherness, that greater sense of reality afforded by the epistemological advantages of otherness—as theorized in Du Boisian second-sight—makes being an outcast worthwhile and enables Big Boi's concluding insights: "It's only so much time left in this crazy world / Wake up, niggas, and realize what's goin' on around you / Poisonin' of the food and water, tamperin' of the cigarettes / disease engineering control over your life / Take back your existence or die like a punk, this is big Rube / sayin' right on to the real and death to the fakers."[32]

It is also possible to look at signature features of the black literary tradition and see their pop cultural resonances within hip hop. Certainly, the naturalism in Richard Wright's construction of Bigger Thomas, the thrill of his kill that results from desperation and frustration, appears in hip hop character construction. And yet there are also "invisible men," humanist philosophers emerging from a distinctly masculinist experience in the tradition of Ralph Ellison who embrace universalism through the specifically vernacular black male experience. Robert Stepto's literary critical work, which looks at the importance of mobility as a sign of freedom in the African American tradition, also resonates in hip hop music.[33] Rap lyrics frequently reference "breaking out," "being out," and being in cars, on the road, or on the run.

The Black Musical Tradition

Albert Murray, distinguished music critic and writer, wrote the following of the blues: "the improvisation that is the ancestral imperative of blues procedure is completely consistent with and appropriate to those of the frontiersman, the fugitive slave, and the picaresque hero. The survival of each of whom depended largely on an ability to operate on dynamics equivalent to those of the vamp, the riff, and most certainly the break, which jazz musicians regard as the Moment of Truth, or that disjuncture that should bring out your personal best."[34] That a similar statement might be made of rap as well, at least in the eyes of those centrally concerned with the best of the art form, proves instructive as to the extent to which it constitutes a black musical form. The improvisational aesthetic occurs in hip hop through freestyling (spontaneous rhyming rather than the recitation of rotely memorized lyrics). Like jazz and blues musicians, freestylers know pieces by heart, but in the moment of improvisational composition, they blend them into a collage or assemblage, altering and reconfiguring them. Moreover, rap's fascination with and deep reliance on the break and its repetition constitutes it as a music built on the central drama of traditional black music.

Black music scholar Sam Floyd developed an interpretive theory of black music inspired by the literary critical work of Henry Louis Gates Jr. on what he calls "Signifyin(g)." This practice lends further evidence to the intertwining of the black musical and literary traditions, and the special place hip hop occupies as an art form at the crossroads of literature and music. In fact, while the hip hop community refers to the poetry of the music as lyrics, it might better be described as verses and the subsections as stanzas. That aside, Floyd's theory, which is useful for this examination, employs as its principle tool the "Call Response." Floyd tropes the black musical tradition of the call and response and turns that into an interpretation of discursive intertextuality—the literary and musical relationships between different pieces of music, between artists, and between artists and audiences. He writes, "Call Response, the master trope, the musical trope of tropes, implies the presence within it of Signifyin(g) figures (calls) and Signifyin(g) revisions (responses in various guises) that can be one or the other, depending on their context."[35]

Rap music fits within the call-response trope in a number of critical ways. First, the intertextuality of black musical texts lies at the heart of rap on both an oral and musical level. Hip hop's great dependence on the music of an earlier generation, the music artists often recall from their youth, combined with the reconfigurations of that music and its offering back to the general public, constitutes a kind of conversation with the black musical tradition. It is to say, "this is what makes it beautiful to us in this post civil rights, technological, fast paced, urban blight era." In *Soul Babies: Black Popular Culture and the Post-Soul Aesthetic*, Mark Anthony Neal has termed the workings of this kind of music the "post-soul aesthetic" of those with no lived memory of the movement but to whom it exists in iconographic form refracted through the 1970s. It also makes for a kind of mimicry of the montage of memory: here, phrases and riffs exist inside the artists to be expressed in unique form, emerging within the fragmentary mosaic of memory. Afro-Atlanticists might argue that intertextuality also occurs in other national discourses. I would agree with that argument as what I earlier termed crossroads moments. Rob Kenner claims that "there's no denying that the basic concept of deconstructing a familiar track, and then chatting over this remixed version to make something new—rap music, by any other name—started in Jamaica."[36] But rather than making a convincing argument about origins per se, the evidence shows that the Jamaican practice of deconstruction fit within the call-response trope and therefore became acceptable as part of the construction and development of hip hop music.

Further evidence of this call-response trope comes in the manner in which hip hop forms part of a broader contemporary music culture. reggae and hip hop blend into dancehall, and R & B cross-fertilizes with hip hop. While most of R & B, reggae, or soca does not contain elements of hip hop, the musical forms are in conversation with each other. For a time it seemed as though almost every popular R & B song boasted a miniature rap interlude. In many ways, R & B functions as the alter ego of rap—it is romance music, whereas hip hop only sometimes delivers love, seduction, or heartbreak songs and more often focuses on sex. That is not to say that contemporary R & B does not frequently talk about sex;

it simply addresses it in a smoother, sweeter, and frequently romantic manner. Together, they afford a greater breadth of emotional and sexual interaction than either one of them could alone.

Costuming, as well as cross-genre musical collaboration, give further evidence of the close relationship between hip hop and R & B. Father MC fancied himself a romantic and often rhymed over R & B songs attired in the sparkly threads of an R & B artist with a smooth style, one first popularized among hip hop artists by Big Daddy Kane. Jodeci always courted a visual aesthetic that blended the bagginess and athleticism of hip hop with the silkiness of R & B. There are a number of producers and entertainers who work in both styles, including Teddy Riley who, besides singing with the groups Guy and Blackstreet, developed a musical style he called New Jack Swing—light, danceable, swinging, and funk-inspired music. Yet he also produced a number of hip hop albums. Sean "Puffy" Combs and Jermaine Dupree combine producing hip hop and R & B acts with their own performing ventures. The prevalence of people who participate in both sorts of music is to be expected given that hip hop and R & B emerge from the same aesthetic foundation of black music, even if their composition styles differ quite markedly. And both kinds of music spring from the communities out of which most of the artists emerge. Several hip hop artists sing as well as rhyme. Missy Elliot (who also produces) and all three former Fugees may serve as examples. Interestingly, women artists in general seem to be more successful at straddling the fence between the two art forms.

In terms of orality, the use of black English is only the most basic level on which the intertextuality of the call response appears. Charles Johnson writes of poetry, "In words we find the living presence of others, . . . language is not—nor has it ever been—a neutral medium for expressing things, but rather . . . intersubjectivity and cross cultural experience are already embodied in the most microscopic datum of speech."[37] One can apply his thoughts to the presence of the culturally charged and shaped black language within the poetry of hip hop. Certainly, as black language is made into art, similar to the way in which Zora Neale Hurston, did in her storytelling or Langston Hughes wrote in his poetry, a conversation is established between culture and art. Moreover, a conversation exists between rap and other popular cultural phrases, contemporary and historical, so that the numerous riffings on Muhammad Ali's rhyming or Richard Pryor's comedy routines constitute another level of the oral call-response presence in hip hop. Finally, when artists take turns of phrase or structures of rhyme from other MCs, and then reconfigure them into their own texts, recognizable and yet new, still another level of call-response intertextuality emerges. Rakim's classic phrase, "I'm the R to the A to the K-I-M / If I wasn't then why would I say I am," becomes a point of reference when Nas says, "I'm the N to the A to the S-I-R / if it wasn't it must have been Escobar" (Escobar is Nas's last name). The phrase depends both on the structure of spelling the name and the conclusion with a rhyme of the last letter of the name, although that rhyme is in fact different. That Rakim has emerged as a very popular artist for such references is part of what establishes him historically as one of the greatest MCs, similar to the manner in which jazz musicians reference the greats within their improvisations and compositions in a manner recognizable only to listeners of jazz. This internal conversation between hip hop artists—combined with external conversations with black musical and oral traditions, and nonblack popular cultural forms as well—give evidence to the multilayered discourse of hip hop. Multiple registers of discourse of course lie at the heart of "Signifyin(g)" both in the traditional forms and in the literary critical form Gates describes.

The community of listeners proves central to the way hip hop fits into call response. As Sam Floyd notes, within call response, "aesthetic communication takes place when resonant contact is made between listeners' social, cultural, and psychological histories, on the one hand, and, on the other, the struggle-fulfillment configurations idealized in the music. . . . the most complete musico-aesthetic experience requires that listeners possess the knowledge, perceptual skills, emotional histories, and cultural perspectives appropriate to the various genres."[38] This community knowledge required for the deepest understanding of the music is constitutive of the form's aesthetics. To make something good in hip hop means in part to effectively employ the call-response trope on several levels, and, just as important, to know what is good requires a sophisticated, albeit not necessarily conscious, understanding of the symbolic references and cultural history from which the music derives. This includes postmigration consciousness, a sense of urbanity, awareness of the music of the 1960s and 1970s, and knowledge of contemporary struggles of black America. As Floyd argues, "The execution of Call-Response tropes opens up the symbolic field, where reside the long-standing sublimated conflicts, taboos, and myths of personal and group emotional experience and our relationships to them. On this level—the symbolic field—reside the musical instincts and intuitions that drive the creative impulse, and it is from this level that we interpret the appropriateness and effectiveness of the works and performances of Call-Response."[39] Gender and sexuality politics, as well as a conflicted relationship to Americanness, all form part of the symbolic field of hip hop music. Home—in the literal, experiential, and imaginative senses—provides the grounds for interpretation, and the home of hip hop is black in melting-pot America.

Hip hop is half black and half Japanese

Digital chips on the shoulders of African

Lips

Hip hop is black Prozac

Hip hop is if you can't beat 'em blunt 'em

Hip hop is black sadomasochism

Where the hurting ends and the feeling begins.

—Greg Tate, "What Is Hip Hop?"

2

My Mic Sound Nice

Art, Community, and Consciousness

Rap music is a mixed medium. As an art form, it combines poetry, prose, song, music, and theater. It may come in the form of narrative, autobiography, science fiction, or debate. The diversity of media poses a challenge for the critic because she or he is called to evaluate the artistic production from a variety of disciplinary perspectives. Moreover, the embodied nature of the art, the slippage that exists between the art and the artist, makes for another set of challenges when it comes to assessment and interpretation on both aesthetic and political levels.

In this chapter, I will put forward a set of arguments about hip hop music as art. I will begin by exposing the central tension between ideology and art that hip hop presents. I will furthermore consider the intertextualites in hip hop, represented musically by the call-response trope, through the lenses of ideology, culture, and art. The rapper or MC is both subject and artist in much hip hop composition; who he or she is, constitutes a direct part of our experience of the music, and often the artist is imagined in the popular realm as doing nothing more than verbally expressing his or her experiences, self, and ideas. The MC usually occupies a self-proclaimed location as representative of his or her community or group—the everyman or everywoman of his or her hood. As a representative, he or she encourages a kind of sociological interpretation of the music, best expressed by the concept of "the real." "This is the documentary story of my world," we are told. There exists in rap music an identity-based teleological stance. The work of the artist is not intended to be apparent so much as the lyricism is supposed to testify to organic brilliance. Often this stance becomes articulated via theological imagery, further obscuring ideas of labor by imagining the subject as divine and divinely inspired. This is not work that makes its seams visible. This stance, while clearly one that is supposed to conjure up the image of a kind of virtuosity and confluence of art and identity, makes it more difficult to understand definitively the location of artistry separate from social scientific claims.

While the music bursts with sociopolitical themes, it is quite dangerous for the critic or listener to interpret it purely as a reflection of social and political conditions, without thought to the presence of artistic choice in every narrative and composition. Purely social scientific interpretations limit analyses and tend toward reductionism. bell hooks writes that "thinking about the history of African-American engagement with performance-as-art, it is useful to distinguish between performance that is used to manipulate in the interests of survival (the notion of wearing a mask), and performance as ritual play (as art). Collapsing the two categories tends to imply that the performative arts in black expressive culture emerge as a response to circumstances of oppression and exploitation."[1] If we heed hooks's warnings and consider hip hop as an art with substantial sociopolitical ramifications and issues attendant to it yet not reducible to them, we avoid reducing the music, or the population it "represents," to a socioeconomic location. We also allow ourselves greater space to critically evaluate the content choices made by the artist. Clarence Lusane argues that "to their legions of fans, the legitimacy of gangsta rappers is conditioned on the real troubles that they find themselves in."[2] Part of the theater of hip hop becomes life and a representation of how life is conducted. As Michael Eric Dyson writes, "The genius of hip-hop is that its adherents convince each other—and judging by the attacks it receives, those outside its ranks—that its devices are meant immediately to disclose the truth of life through report-age. In truth, hip-hoppers construct narrative conventions and develop artistic norms through repeated practice and citation."[3]

Those wishing to support hip hop often feel an impulse toward social scientific explanations in order to defend or justify disturbing messages or practices. Many artists themselves encourage such a stance. Emcees often tell us that they are simply transmitting the "truth" or reality of living in poor urban communities. But realist movements in art of any sort are always decisive periods in which choices of how to represent truth or reality are made. Hip hop realism is filled with metaphors and metonyms of existence that trouble listeners or commentators from a wide range of political, social, and intellectual perspectives.

Let us take an abstract example that is not uncommon. Say there is a song that contains beautiful poetry, delivered in an interesting and compelling way, and backed with well-composed music. Yet it is also a narrative of destruction in which the narrator kills several people, refers to women as whores, and celebrates the excessive use of alcohol and marijuana. That which is artistically excellent in this case also proves politically and morally troubling. The reverse may hold true as well, that music embracing excellent moral values might turn out to be boring. Many people who are supportive of rap, with good intentions, make the mistake, in response to attacks on the music, of arguing that there is good and bad rap, thereby categorizing quality according to politics, such that the positive political message becomes construed as "good" music. However, the correlation of artistic quality and politics does not hold within hip hop any more than it would in another art form. As scholar and jazz musician Saleem Washington stated at the disChord Conference on Popular Music at the University of California, Los Ange-les, in the summer of 1997, oftentimes that which is musically interest-ing or good within hip hop is not that which would be deemed "posi-tive."[4] Or, as Robin Kelley has written, "In my book, the most politically correct rappers will never get my hard-earned ducats if they ain't kickin' some boomin' drum tracks, a fat bass line, a few well-placed JB-style gui-tar riffs, and some stupid, nasty turntable action. If it claims to be hip hop it has to have, as Pete Rock says, 'the breaks . . . the funky breaks . . . the funky breaks.'"[5]

The political Left often cites Public Enemy as one of the greatest rap groups, praising its members for their incisive social critiques. What often gets forgotten is that what made them great artistically was that these incisive critiques and sophisticated arguments came recited in infectious rhythmic style and in front of funky and soulful beats produced by their DJ Terminator X. Their artistry mattered. Lauryn Hill, the first woman to win four Grammy awards in one night, too is a beautiful lyricist as well as an artist who delivers an uplifting, explicitly religious sociopolitical message; she succeeds in her philosophical mission because her artistic strength holds listeners. But there is no inherent correlation between good music and respectability or good music and good politics. Because of the reunion space, discussed in the introduction, the blending of the high and low, the sacred and the profan, and the open discourse encouraged in rap, there is, moreover, no mandate on the artist to be politically uplifting all the time, or even at all. The tension so created for the listener is a tension between ideology and art.

Not only does hip hop manifest a tension between art and ideology but the ideology present in the art frequently responds to the complicated politics of race in America. Observations made by literary figure Charles Johnson about black literature ring true of hip hop as well:

> Black literature abounds with faintly Hegelian variations on the phenomenon of the black body as stained. Once you are so one-sidedly seen by the white Other, you have the option of (A) accepting this being seen from the outside and craftily using the "invisibility" of your interior to deceive and thus to win survival as the folk hero Trickster . . . does. . . . In this case, stain is like the heavy makeup of a clown; it conceals you completely. . . . Or you may (B) seize this situation at its roots by reversing the negative meaning of the black body. "It is beautiful," you might say, "I am a child of the Sun." . . . You applaud your athletic, amorous, and dancing abilities, your street wisdom and savoir faire, your "soul."[6]

The "cultural nationalist" period of hip hop on the one side, and the "gangsta" period on the other perfectly embody Johnson's two responses to white supremacist America. The West Coast gangsta mimicked a stereotype, thus becoming a survivalist hero, whereas the East Coast Afrocentrists with their natural hair and decked out in medallions declared essentialist black beauty and excellence.

As black American music, hip hop, with this tension between ideology and art, presents a serious challenge. Should we indulge our appreciation of the art when its messages prove disturbing? Particularly given the youth of much of hip hop's audience we have to wonder whether this democratic space simply provides a window through which negative values can be transmitted to our children. Some people, from prominent politicians to kitchen critics, have clearly decided that the United States cannot afford the luxury of a music with frequently problematic messages, and have responded by advocating the censorship of certain artists or by proselytizing to convert MCs away from the nastiness or violence in their work.

On the other hand, beyond the tension, there is the possibility, that the disturbing images themselves might in part account for the music's appeal. For a mainstream audience, rap may indulge voyeuristic fantasies of black sociopathy and otherness, while for an oppressed community, these images might engage fantasies of masculine power in people who feel powerless. Hence there are a variety of reasons why a listener might enjoy a song littered with violence and viciousness. While there are many MCs with lyrics that do not express destructive values, we cannot dismiss those that do as illegitimate subjects of artistic analysis, and we cannot dismiss their popularity as media-fueled glamorization of destructiveness.

While fostering progressive political consciousness in young people is of the utmost importance, the ideological reunion of the clean and dirty, of the sacred and profane, is a watershed of the post–civil rights era, one that itself constitutes a kind of black liberation, although one also beleaguered by difficulties. To refuse to concern oneself with proving decency in the face of stereotypes, racism, and white supremacy at least in part provides a psychic liberation. Still, we must develop a cognizance within multiple layers of the black community, and the external community of listeners, both child and adult, of the distinctions between and tensions within art and ideology. That kind of awareness should bring about enlightened decisions about the sort of music one wishes to consume. Recall that we have not expunged all white supremacist or misogynistic texts from English curricula in American high schools and universities, although the most astute of educators attempt to balance an understanding of artistic excellence with ideological critiques that promote contemplation rather than silence. Further, we find in many of those texts sex alongside spirituality, depravity alongside beauty. We should extend the open discourse already extant within hip hop to our conversation about hip hop.

The particular performative space of rap is located at the crossroads of several significant moments. Here one stands at the new grounds of Du Boisian double consciousness, the meeting and conflict of Americanness and blackness, where MCS and DJS are commodified, make commodities, and are both objects and subjects of capitalism as they produce improvisational and oppositional music. In the following two lyrics, the first from De La Soul, the second from A Tribe Called Quest, the MCS express a critical consciousness of that location: "I am Posdonus / I be the new generation of slaves / here to make tapes that my record exec rapes"[7]; and "Industry rule number four thousand and eighty / record company people are shady / so kids watch your back / 'cause they're full of crap / don't doubt it / look at how they act."[8] Jadakiss adds this succinct statement: "Industry is like jail, nigga, double R's runnin' the yard"[9]

This tension-filled dynamic of double consciousness always inflects hip hop discourse. Because it is a spoken art form that cherishes open discourse, we find in hip hop a dialogic space in which artists' voices articulate ideas about existence on a number of registers. The space of hip hop is public and yet interior. It is the music of radios blasting through neighborhoods, parties, and hit lists. Houston Baker has argued that when boom boxes also known as ghetto blasters were popular, the controversy over their use was "more than generational . . . the contest was urbanely propietorial: Who owns the public spaces?"[10] Rap is disseminated through record companies and radio stations far more than it is through local ventures, and yet it maintains a space of intellectual communication existing beyond the institutions of production and transmission. Within that space, the artist and the listener become creatively engaged with a world of ideas and experience. Albert Murray gives the following definition of art:

> Art is the ultimate extension, elaboration, and refinement of the rituals that reenact the primary survival techniques (and hence reinforce the basic orientation toward experience) of a given people in a given time, place and circumstance much the same as holiday commemorations are meant to do. It is the process of extension, elaboration, and refinement that creates the work of art. It is the playful process of extension, elaboration and refinement that gives rise to the options out of which comes the elegance that is the essence of artistic statement. Such playfulness can give an aesthetic dimension to the most pragmatic of actions.[11]

Applying Murray's observation to hip hop, we are asked to assess that extension of ritual and survival, and the kinds of ways in which that extension takes place.

It is thus unsurprising that hip hop figures in many lyrics as a nourishment essential for survival. It feeds the community of listeners. KRS-One announced, "I got the hip hop juice with the hip hop food."[12] Digable Planets rhymed, "Brewin' funk inside my soul kitchen, pull up a chair, here's a bit, have a listen."[13] All the nourishment needed is provided aurally and orally. Butterfly of Digable Planets also rhymed, "It's the children of the concrete / "Livin' off the fruits and the functions of the phat beats / hip hop's all around the members is growin' / Please dig off the sounds 'cause the good vibes they showin'."[14] Lines such as these construct hip hop as life-sustaining, and they also establish a contrast between the coldness of the city, metonymically represented by concrete, and the natural growth of artistic hip hop creation. Butterfly's words also anticipated the mid-1990s flowering of new styles and more sophisticated production in hip hop.

Hip hop nourishes by offering community membership that entails a body of cultural knowledge, yet it also nourishes by offering a counter-hegemonic authority and subjectivity to the force of white supremacy in American culture in the form of the MC. The centrality of the latter's experience and voice often also presents a transcendent or powerful model of survival. As A. L. rhymes in "Lyrics":

> My streets are evil
> minds are feeble
> runnin' illegal
> I'm savage like evil eye
> trainin' my people to a needle
> my mind cerebral
> blesses the mic like a cathedral
> thoughts'll lead you
> verbals feed you
> decede you
> I breed you
> to heed you
> like psychics I came to read you
> hip hop I love you and I need you.[15]

The mind and its creative capacity have transcendent powers in the face of dire streets. A love affair with thought and language offers salvation.

Alternately, some lyrics conflate hip hop with the general chaos of life, rather than a removal from it. And there is an abundance of lyrics describing young rich black folks engaged in consumerist excess. Even those, in their own strange way, do what a survivalist hip hop does better: they open up spaces to challenge the hegemonic structures of understanding and meaning propagated by the dominant culture of white supremacy. As a critic has noted, "The difference between [Wynton] Marsalis (and the tradition of black middle-class respectability he represents) and hip hop is really about who truly deserves to speak for the condition of black souls. Is it our institutionally approved elite, our bohemian bourgeois iconoclasts, or the folk who live on public assistance in the projects and their neighbors, the black working class?"[16]

The enunciative dynamic in hip hop allows for ideological struggle while simultaneously acknowledging identification with Americanism and articulating a creole black American identity. Hence when Foxy Brown or Lil' Kim rhyme about countless highbrow designers and diamonds, they not only express vapid materialistic values but in fact also show their awareness of how, on some level, they transgress notions of racialized space and racialized gender when they—as young, dialect-speaking, ghetto-fabulous black women—enter the Henri Bendel or Bergdorf Goodman department stores. Lil' Kim rhymes in "Get Money": "So you wanna buy me diamonds and Armani suits / Adrienne Vittadini and Chanel Nine boots / Things to make up for all the games and the lies / Oh my God, sayin' I apologize."[17] And Foxy Brown, in "Ain't No Nigga," says: "From Dolce Gabbana to H. Bendel I'm ringing bells / So who the player? I keep you chillin' in the illest gators."[18] Both examples are taken from songs in which the exchange of material goods constitutes a required element of the male-female sexual relationship.

Soon after the two artists came onto the hip hop scene with their rich and vulgar black pinup girl styles, they faced charges of stereotypical pornographic hypersexuality, as well as accusations that they lacked autonomy and self-definition. The furor over the two women's disruptive presence reminded us that no one had quite done what they did before, nor was their image—that of the desiring black sexpot adorned with haute couture and jewels—part of the broad cultural imagination. We might consider the relatively clean-cut Eartha Kitt as the closest forerunner to Lil' Kim and Foxy Brown. Their transgression of class and racial spaces shifted notions about consumerism and gender. Although their work did not explicitly critique class and race politics, their mere presence signaled a shifting concept of how black women were imagined as black wealth and black celebrity multiplied. In addition, the attacks on their presence the two women faced effectively called attention to the fact that transgression does not necessarily entail liberation—the constant operation of white supremacy and sexism almost seamlessly neutralizes many potentially transgressive spaces.

In the song "Slam," Onyx subverts hegemonic discourses by relocating power and goodness in that which is impure and black. Here, Sticky Fingers rhymes:

> I'm a b-boy, standin' in my b-boy stance
>
> Hurry up and give me a microphone before I bust in my pants
>
> The mad author of anguish, my language polluted
>
> Onyx is a heavyweight (and still undisputed)
>
> So take the words right out my mouth or walk a mile in my shoes
>
> I paid so many dues also used and abused and um
>
> So confused, excuse me, for example, I'm an inspiration for a whole generation
>
> And unless you got ten sticky fingers it's an imitation, a figment
>
> Of your imagination, but but but but wait it gets worse
>
> I'm not watered down so I'm dyin' of thirst
>
> Comin' through with the scam
>
> foolproof plan
>
> B-boys make some noise and just, just slam.[19]

This rhyme celebrates "polluted" language as superior and inspirational, a construction that stands in direct opposition to the ways in which things are valued in an imperialist and capitalist society, in which value is accorded in direct proportion to perceived purity in everything from animals to aesthetics. And yet he subverts the Western ideal of purity through the concept of originality by saying, "unless you got ten sticky fingers," that is, are he who uses polluted language, you are an imitation, not as good, false. His impurity is original. He spurns the economy of purity and relocates the economy of originality from high culture and wealth to a young urban black man. Just as the reproduction of the

Mona Lisa will never reach the quality of the original, neither will the reproduction of Sticky Fingers and what he stands for. But what proves even more subversive is that he makes this construction with allusions to Pepsi and Coke. "The inspiration of a generation, the Pepsi generation," was a slogan popular at the time this song came out, as was Coke's motto, "The Real Thing," an accusation of imitation lodged against rival colas. Here, commodity culture and the reproduction that takes place in recorded music are together used to assert originality. The listener witnesses a dance back and forth between the oneness suggested by originality and the multiplicity suggested by commodity. In this song, the abused and disenfranchised are called on to celebrate using the historically white working-class practice of slam dancing. And the critical subjective space is that of the young man and other young men like him. The listener is told to walk in his shoes. He is one of many low-level consumers in a consumer culture, and yet his authority serves to subvert hierarchies of value.

Hip hop music also manifests a commitment to otherness. It centralizes a realm of black existence and yet commits to the otherness of that location with respect to the larger society. On some level, it signals a crisis in black youth politics. It is impossible to isolate, in any coherent fashion, a clear system of political critique with a traceable eschatology or teleology in hip hop. Rather, we find a simultaneous movement of social critique and a celebration of the status quo. For example, while rappers do not espouse racism and imprisonment in the system of criminal law enforcement as positive there is a kind of revelry present in the lyrical treatment of the prisons as a fundamental element to the identity construction of male black youth. What some critics have termed nihilism in hip hop, I would instead describe as a radical commitment to otherness, which confounds those of us whose political standing comes out of either a civil rights or black power tradition.

The historic construction of blackness in opposition to whiteness, in which blackness is demonized, has become part of the art form's consciousness. Whereas previous generations of black Americans utilized various means to establish a self-definition that negated the construction of blackness as demonic or depraved, many members of the hip hop generation have chosen instead to appropriate and exploit those constructions as metaphoric tools for expressing power. Because this gesture is ultimately aggressive (in that it primarily claims power through

the voice of black males, and thus, given the dichotomized racial structure in the United States, takes power away from white America, even if
only by operating through white American fear), the black community
generally does not perceive these acts as those of self-hating traitors, in
the way it might the acts of black people adopting other stereotypical
postures. Rather, these young men may even be seen as champions of
a particular kind of black empowerment.

Of course, such empowerment depends on a larger level of powerlessness. And certainly that larger powerlessness in society is reflected
in the economic politics of the music industry. Hip hop and its products have become a several-billion-dollar industry, but on a number of
levels it maintains an anticapitalist aesthetic, even as it exists as a form
of capitalist production, and even though a number of MCs who lyrically
seem to wholeheartedly embrace conspicuous consumption. The anti-
capitalist vein remains partly because the MCs often accurately understand themselves as exploited workers. In "God Lives Through," Q-Tip
of A Tribe Called Quest rhymes, "Intellect is major / since heads like to
wager / the skills on the hill overlooking dollar bills / Man you're crazy,
thinkin' you can faze / the Ab doesn't study mere nonsense money."[20]
One can, of course, find countless deeply capitalistic lyrics to match
Q-Tip's words decommodifying hip hop. Blackstar, a duo comprised of
Mos Def and Talib Kweli, respond to this dynamic in their CD jacket.
Describing the song "Hater Players," Talib Kweli writes, "We started to
see cats shouting 'player hater' to anyone who had nerve to critique they
wack shit. A lot of rich players are making wack ass music, that's the
bottom line! I remember when the worst thing you could be was a sell
out. Then the sell-outs started running things. We call this song 'Hater
Players' because there are many players who hate the fact that we do this
for love."[21]

The term *player hater,* thrown at those imagined to be envious of one's
wealth or abundant suitors, became a rallying cry for the consumerist
explosion in late 1990s' hip hop, morphing from its original Southern
and Midwestern neo-blaxploitation roots into an unseemly mess. The
critiques of the stance celebrated are necessary and important. But it
is also relevant to understand the way in which hip hop's capitalism is
asserted as a black populist capitalism that exists as a desire for the acquisition of wealth, but also a desire to "stick it" to American economic
and social inequities. And ultimately, hip hop artists, even at their most

wealthy more often than not are at the mercy of and exploited by big-business capitalism for their continued economic success. At any rate, despite a number of notable exceptions, the overwhelming majority of professional hip hop artists are not wealthy, and many find themselves in unfair recording contracts or paid in luxury items and so seduced into debt to the record company. Only a small number of record companies actually owned by artists are not subsidiaries of larger labels that exercise ultimate control. Therefore even the odes to the almighty dollar negotiate an alternative and hybridized (by race and class) notion of capitalism into the popular sphere. The reality is that, by and large, these artists do not experience the black populist wealth they celebrate.

In the record jacket of Meshell Ndegeocello's *Plantation Lullabies*, an album that masterfully combines hip hop, funk, and folk, the artist writes, "Hip Hop is the inverse of capitalism / Hip Hop is the reverse of colonialism / Hip Hop is the world the slaveholder made sent into niggafide future shock."[22] Not *bona fide*, but *niggafide*, a context defined by a legacy of slavery and white supremacy, as well as black subjectivity, language, and culture. The quest for liberation coexists in this art with the desire to be the "baddest Negro" on the plantation, and often the latter aspiration seems more plausible, is pursued most vigorously, and finds expression through cash.

But as Richard Delgado and Jean Stefancic have argued when speaking of the potentials of liberatory speech for colored peoples in a First Amendment context, there is the danger that larger and longer narratives of race might dwarf hip hop speech's potential subversion. They write, "We interpret new stories in light of the old. Ones that deviate too markedly from our pre-existing stock are dismissed as extreme, coercive, political, and wrong. The only stories about race we are prepared to condemn, then, are the old ones giving voice to the racism of an earlier age, ones that society has already begun to reject."[23] I would add stories of past racism which were not explicitly rejected by the civil rights revolution, to the group of stories we fail to understand and address. They go on to say, "We subscribe to a stock of explanatory scripts, plots, narratives and understandings that enable us to make sense of—to construct—our social world. . . . These observations imply that our ability to escape the confines of our own preconceptions is quite limited. The contrary belief—that through speech and remonstrance alone we can endlessly reform ourselves and each other—we call the empathic fallacy."[24] Even the most progressive lyricists are destabilized by what these authors term the empathic fallacy, and certainly the thug narrators, or the player celebrators, are especially vulnerable to being understood in terms of prescribed racial narratives, regardless of the more nuanced levels on which they communicate or aspire to communicate.

Incomprehensibility

One of the communication elements that resists white supremacy and co-optation has been the self-conscious incomprehensibility of hip hop lyricism. Rappers are misunderstood, both intentionally and unintentionally, not only as a side effect of the fact that we rely on figurative pidgins in the United States to cross borders in popular culture; but incomprehensibility is also a protective strategy. The general population often refers to hip hop as music in which "you can't understand what they are saying." By this, they usually mean the words, but even when the words are accessible to a white mainstream or global audience, there remains a frequently inaccessible cultural space—descended from black American history, culture, and language, expanded by the English- and Spanish-speaking Caribbean, which are far more complex than a few slang words and baggy pants. Difficulty is a strategy in hip hop, both in terms of words, which are fast and hard to understand if you are not privy to the hip hop community, and of demands for an authentic personal connection to hip hop and its geography, the hood. Difficulty is a cultural and political strategy, as well as an ideological one. In another context, cultural critic Trinh Minh-ha has rejected calls to clarity in a way apropos for a discussion of hip hop, "To write clearly one must incessantly prune, eliminate, forbid, purge, purify; in other words practice what may be called an ablution of language."[25] The lack of clarity is the structural correlate to the reunion ideal. It represents struggle against the repressiveness of traditional literariness in terms of content censorship, and, more important, in terms of the limitations tradition imposes on structural innovation. It allows for the expansion of black English within the spheres of intellectual exploration. Critical to this activity is the call to engage in the decoding of the messages that hip hop artists make for members of the hip hop nation. One works to understand the cleverness, the allusions, the suggestiveness. And even as hip hop is innovative, such obfuscation is part of black oral tradition. Mel Watkins discusses the lack of clarity as an indicator of cultural exclusivity, and as an intracultural practice, in his book on the history of black comedy, *On the Real Side*, citing Richard Pryor, who once said, "Niggers just have a way of telling you stuff and not telling you stuff, Martians would have a tough time with Niggers. They be translating words, saying a whole lot of things underneath you. All around you. That's our comedy."[26] It is also, more broadly, our language. And hip hop is an iteration of black vernacular, at a nexus or crossroads with our rhythms in—like black folks themselves—the middle of America.

Funk and Soul

> Feelin' somethin' all in your bones. Magically moved by the microphone.
>
> —Three Times Dope, "Greatest Man Alive"

As James Brown demanded of his grooves, hip hop, too, has to be funky to be good. A funky cut makes you want to move and sweat, or perhaps it sends a chill down your spine. It is earthy and erotic, even if not overtly sexy: "Drippin' with the fluid that wets you when you do it, know it like Otis 'cause your style is bogus."[27]

Funkiness might refer to an enticing beat or the smell of sweat-releasing pheromones. Funkiness is of the people, ordinary in an excellent way. It causes hips to sway and backs to curve. It is sensual, stimulating the auditory, visual, tactile, and gustatory senses. It is, as Method Man describes in his lyrics, "Poetry in motion, coast to coastin', rub it in your skin like lotion."[28] Funky sounds inspire both body and mind. The core of funkiness in hip hop is found in the bass: repetitive beats filled with bass that can be felt underneath the feet and inside the chest, bass that makes cars rumble and the floor shake. The percussion engages the listener in a historically learned pattern of response. But it is not just those clear thumping sounds that matter. Syncopation does as well. The senses must be engaged on multiple levels. For a song to "rock" it has to swing, listeners have to be able to move to it on several different rhythms, to feel the different textures of sound. In order for it to "bounce," it cannot be too heavy: even if the song is deep and strong, some lightness must be added to the rhythm in order to keep it coming at the audience, to create a sound arc that will make bodies move slowly up to the apex, which they hit suddenly and distinctly, and then curve down again. Although James Brown, Parliament Funkadelic, and other classic funk and R & B musicians provide much of the foundational musical text for hip hop songs, the funkiness does not simply reflect the use of funk or funky soul music. It is what the MCS, DJS, and producers do to make the song work, the particular combination of rhyming and mixing, along with the musical texts drawn on, that create the funky configuration. As Fife of A Tribe Called Quest rhymed in "Can I Kick It?"

> When it comes to rhythm Quest is your savior
> Follow us for the funky behavior.
> Make a note on the rhythm we gave ya
> Feel free, drop your pants check your hair
> Do you like the garments that we wear?
> I instruct you to be the obeyer
> A rhythm recipe that you'll savor
> Doesn't matter if you're minor or major
> Yes the tribe of the game rhythm player
> and you inhale like a breath of fresh air.[29]

The group's references to a rhythmic sensuality and spirituality that compel motion and self-emancipatory action capture what I said about funkiness in the world of hip hop.

Soul is important to hip hop also. By soul I mean that which has some spiritual depth and deep cultural and historical resonances to be felt through the kind of music and sounds made by the vocalists. Goodie Mob., a group from Atlanta, used their album and song entitled "Soul Food" as a culinary metaphor for the sustenance provided by black cultural traditions rooted in the South. Soulful music is music of joy and pain, unself-consciously wedding melody and moaning, the sound of the dual terror and exultation of being black in America. In 1988, Eric B. and Rakim released *Paid in Full*, which included the cut "I Know You Got Soul." They called on the soulfulness of the listeners with James Brown samples, digitized cymbal crashes, breathing sounds, and a bumping bass line. Rakim told the listeners to use their soulfulness to grasp his words as he ventured back and forth between a discussion of his self-conscious role as an MC in relationship with an audience and metaphysical metaphors about his excellence.

> I got soul
> That's why I came
> To teach those
> Who can't say my name.
> First of all I'm the soloist
> The soul controller
> Rakim gets stronger as I get bolder.[30]

The linguistic references to funkiness or soulfulness sometimes come through the metaphor of addiction in hip hop music. On the one hand, it is used as a reference to the high, that intoxicating pleasure, the music can give the listener. "I don't gang bang / or shoot out bang bang / the relentless lyrics the only dope I slang,"[31] comes from the tongue of Jeru the Damaja. The MC reminds listeners of how good the lyrics can make them feel. He seduces. On the other hand, he also reminds his audience about the yearning for the beats when they are not playing, the longing for renewed stimulation by the poetry. He tempts. On another album, Rakim rhymed about being a "microphone fiend," turning the addiction metaphor on himself. In this song, he talks about jonesing for the satisfaction found only in the high of rhyming.

> I get a craving like a fiend for nicotine
> But I don't need a cigarette, know what I mean?
> I'm ragin', rippin' up the cage 'n don't it sound amazin'
> 'Cause every rhyme is made and thought up
> 'Cause it's sort of an addiction
> Magnetized by the mixin' . . .
> The prescription is a hyper tone that's thorough 'n
> I fiend for a microphone like heroin
> Soon as the bass kicks, I need a fix
> Give me a stage and a mic and a mix[32]

The addiction reference is most dramatically an invocation of the escape provided by art, particularly from the pains of daily life.

The Ancestors

One of the areas in hip hop that offers a very interesting ideological move is attention to the ancestors, to the history behind the music, despite rap's postmodern luster. Hip hop is incredibly nostalgic music. As KRS-One once humorously pointed out, before hip hop was even twenty years old, people were paying homage to the "old school."[33] While the block parties and humble beginnings of the 1970s gave way to late 1980s and early 1990s proclamations about black history and consciousness, which themselves gave way to less political and more decadent trends, the music remained a historical celebration. Popular songs from the 1960s, 1970s, and 1980s have continually surfaced as samples and hooks for hip hop music. Both in the composition of sounds and text, hip hop artists reference each other, in addition to soul, R & B, and funk musicians. In 1986 Rakim rhymed: "I don't bug out or chill / Don't be actin' ill / No tricks in '86 it's time to bill / Eric B. easy on the cut, no mistakes allowed / 'Cause to me MC means move the crowd."[34] Ten years later, Mos Def, rhymed on a De La Soul CD:

> I don't bug out or chill
>
> Don't be actin' ill
>
> No tricks in '96
>
> Native tongues gon' build
>
> But you be easy on the cut no mistakes allowed
>
> 'Cause to me MC means, Make it cream . . .
>
> I'm smooth like gabardine.[35]

While Mos Def riffs on Rakim's language, he also riffs on his tempo, adding pauses and fluctuating intonation, yet loosely maintaining the meter. Heltah Skeltah reference MC Lyte's song "Cappuccino" by rhyming, "Why oh why did I need cappuccino, scar on my face but I'm not Al Pacino." Likewise, Lil' Kim plays on MC Lyte's "10% Dis," the Lyte version being: "Hot damn hot damn ho here we go again / suckers stole a beat but you know they can't win / You stole a beat are you havin' fun / Now me and the Aud' s gonna show you how it's done."[36] Lil' Kim self-consciously cites Lyte's words and name: "Hot damn ho here we go again / Lyte as a Rock bitch / hard as a cock bitch."[37]

Even covers have become part of hip hop with Snoop's remake of the Doug E. Fresh classic "Ladidadi" (with intermittent word changes to suit West Coast slang and styles), and Puffy's remake of Public Enemy's "Public Enemy #1," with word changes reflecting his materialistic "rebellion" and envy-inciting wealth. These references to other artists constitute a signature feature of the hip hop version of the call-response trope's intertextuality. The old school is consistently celebrated in hip hop, even as the music becomes exponentially more sophisticated — particularly among independent artists — more polished, and of a higher sound quality. As the commodification and commercialization that comes along with mainstream appeal threatens notions of community and authenticity in hip hop, nostalgia becomes an authenticating device. Good MCs and DJs not only make the history present but they also enmesh it in the new entity created by the given song, to be enjoyed in a distinct way. Substandard hip hop songs, which have inundated the market, simply consist of rhymes over the music of other artists, but excellent ones take the flavor of an earlier song and add it to the stew, creating something new and special with the old. Hip hop fondly recalls itself as having been, at is origins, something that young blacks and Latinos did for the love of the art form. And the sign of its decline to many hip hop heads is the exploitation of already-cultivated appreciations for a given song or style matched with simplistic rhymes, without any effort to bring the listener somewhere new, to captivate with one's own "flavor."

The nostalgia does not only emerge in response to commercialism, however. It also takes root in the general nostalgia of the post–civil rights and black power movement generation, trying to find symbolisms from those eras that can translate to more elusive contemporary struggles by romanticizing an epoch of political movement and social defiance. The chorus of OutKast's "Southernplayalisticadillacmuzik" goes: "All the players came from far and wide / wearin' Afros and braids kickin' them gangsta rides / now I'm here to tell you there's a better day / when the player's ball is happenin' all day e'ery day."[38]

The nostalgic motif consists of black power and blaxploitation era symbols brought back into the contemporary urban South. Lauryn Hill's music video for "That Thing" features a split screen, one side with Lauryn dreadlocked in late 1990s fashion, the other with Lauryn in a Motown-inspired wig and a 1960s-style minidress. The doo-wop harmonizing at the beginning of the song draws these two eras together in a hip hop composition. This song's theme, which preaches a more conservative sexual morality than most contemporary music does also hearken back to the doo-wop era when mainstream black popular music was clean-cut and wholesome.

The romantic past as it exists in hip hop is not limited to the civil rights movement or the black power era; it might also refer to an Afrocentric pre-enslavement vision of a healthy and essentialized blackness posed in contrast to present dynamics, as in Killah Priest's song "From Then to Now":

> I can't take it
>
> Beauty that was once sacred is now gettin' face lifts,
>
> fake tits and fake lips
>
> Cold embraces, memory erases from the slave ships my princess
>
> I used to spot her from a distance holding my infant, burning incense
>
> The moment intent for her to step into my white tents
>
> Now we step in precincts[39]

The sensual description makes tangible an existence romanticized yet quite emotional and symbolically meaningful. It encourages reengagement with a black holistic sensibility, indicating a kind of celebratory membership in the black community. The concept of membership is important to maintaining the racial and cultural identity of hip hop. And much of the nostalgic reference constitutes a challenge, as if to say, "If you were down, back in the day, you will remember this, or this statement or melody will have some meaning to you." Method Man begins his song "Bring the Pain" with his version of "Ding Dong," a black childhood rhyme. He says, "Yo' mama don't wear no drawers / I saw when she took 'em off / standin' in a welfare line, eatin' swine, tryin' to look fine, with her stank behind."[40] In the same cadence, black children in Chicago in the 1980s sang:

> Leader: Yo' mama don't wear no drawers
>
> Response: Ding Dong
>
> Leader: I saw when she took 'em off
>
> Response: Ding Dong

Leader: She threw them on the table

Response: Ding Dong

Leader: That table was disabled

Response: Ding Dong Dong Dong Dong

DING DONG!

The final couplet changes with each child who takes his or her turn to be the leader. This is an example of the kind of folk speech that predates hip hop, but which is part of the fabric of life and language that shapes and enters the music. Clap games, children's calls, recordings of the voices of great black leaders, mythic Africa, and music of the past all form part of hip hop's nostalgia.

Hip hop constantly references previous black music forms. This stands as testimony to the yearning for grounding in the post–civil rights era, to the nostalgia for the music of youth, but also to the definitive blackness of parents or grandparents generation. Nelson George writes that hip hop is a "postmodern art in that it shamelessly raids older forms of pop culture — kung fu movies, chitlin' circuit comedy, '70s funk, and other equally disparate sources — and reshapes the material to fit the personality of an individual artist and the taste of the times."[41] And he continues, "Some say this is the first generation of black Americans to experience nostalgia."[42] This nostalgia carries through nowhere more publicly than in hip hop. The musical memory for the listener forms part of the new musical experience. But of course listeners who are not members of the black community will not often possess such collective memory and will be less likely to intuitively understand the intertextuality of hip hop.

Another critical question raised by this nostalgia is, how does it coincide with the reunion? Why does the hip hop audience believe that it is OK to embrace the past, to converse with it, without adhering to its ideological divides or rules? It is the speed of late-capitalist production with the theater of freedom in the post–civil rights era that facilitates nostalgic sensibilities without tradition.

Float like a butterfly, sting like a bee, yo! I'm the E of EPMD.

—Erick Sermon of EPMD, "You're a Customer"

You see I floats just like some helium and stings

just like Tabasco, been nice wit my skills ever since I had an Afro!

—Crazy Drayz of Das EFX, "They Want Efx"

I don't fight clean, float like a butterfly,

stings like a scorpion ridin' on the tip of a sick ding a ling.

—Heltah Skeltah, "The Grate Unknown"

3

Stinging Like Tabasco

Structure and Format in Hip Hop Compositions

This chapter begins with lyrical references to Muhammad Ali. Countless such references to Ali exist in hip hop. He was one of the forerunners of hip hop, with his introduction of black oral rhyming culture into the mainstream. Hip hop uses Ali's style—whether referring to his Cassius Clay bragging or his Nation of Islam–inspired conversion into an outspoken black nationalist athlete—as a metaphor for skill and grace. Ali was one of a handful of the first black celebrity figures to bring black language styles and traditions into the public eye with dignity, self-possession, and power. He provided part of the foundation for the explosion of hip hop, an artistic variation of traditional black cultural forms, into the American popular cultural framework.

Boxing may serve as a good metaphor for hip hop anyway. Not only because both foster a diverse group of bragging personalities with aggressive styles but also because they are strategic competitions. Hip hop is poetry that shifts styles of defense and offense, moving between grace and bull-like forward barreling. It dances, it leans back, and then it attacks. It uses the broadest allegory to discuss the individual moment of confrontation. In the so-called "Rumble in the Jungle," the 1974 Muhammad Ali–George Foreman fight, Ali threatened to match Foreman's crushing power with dance. When the actual impact of Foreman's power became apparent, Ali responded with strategy, first surprising Foreman with an insulting right hook, then faking him out for three rounds, using up Foreman's energy, and coming back in the final rounds with new vigor. Analogously, in *8 Mile*, the film loosely based on the early days of Eminem, the climax of the movie occurs when the young rapper prevails in a battle by asserting all of his weaknesses, anticipating his opponents dissing, and thereby subverting power.

Todd Boyd speaks of the relationship between music and sport in African American culture, saying,

> I remember hearing Miles Davis talk about how he structured a trumpet solo after watching a Sugar Ray Robinson boxing match. Sugar Ray was known as a master of style. You know, he would walk into the ring wearing two robes, and he'd take off the outer robe and underneath would be this white silk robe. It was all about presentation and performance. But Miles focused specifically on how Sugar Ray, in the first round of a fight, would set traps for his opponent without springing them. And then he'd come back in the second round and spring one of those traps, and the fight, of course, would be over. And Miles took that idea and applied it to his solo, so at the beginning of the solo there are all these traps set, and in the second half of the solo, he's springing the trap. So you can flow between those two disparate forms and find that sort of inspiration. Art really does lay bare the questions, and the questions can become much more interesting than the answers sometimes.[1]

Likewise, in hip hop tactical shifts occur within the style of metaphor, which is highly variable even within one song, as well as in the distinctive style an artist might have as an individual, or if he or she is part of a group, within the group. Hip hop music is a war of position, and the position one takes manifests itself in the performance or language. One of the most commonly used metaphors in this war is that of murder, one frequently employed in boxing as well. In the film depicting the 1974 Ali-Foreman fight, *When We Were Kings* (dir. Leon Gast, 1996), the people of Zaire, in support of Ali, chant, "Ali bimboye," meaning "Ali, kill him!" Boxers themselves speak metaphorically of murdering opponents. In the lyrics, "Like Ali-Frazier / thriller in Manila / pinpoint, point black microphone killer am I," Chuck D of Public Enemy is the murderer on the microphone, verbally killing competing MCs.[2] The use of murder in hip hop varies. Narratives of gratuitous violence do exist, and they are heavily critiqued by media pundits, yet there are also rhymes in which violence stands in as a symbolic explication of skill, courage, or power, as in the following example: "Picture blood baths in elevator shafts / Like these murderous lyrics tight from genuine craft / Check the print / swear a veteran sparked the letter and / Slow movin' MCs waitin' for the edition."[3]

At times, the MC will directly refer to the symbolism, telling the audience what he or she plans to do lyrically to other MCs; at other times, the reference to skill or power comes obliquely, as in moments of role-play as Asian martial arts experts or mafiosi. The reference to the crafted or powerful violence of another, such as a mafioso, a Bruce Lee, or a boxer, often comes combined with descriptions of the artist's skill. Heltah Skeltah rhyme:

> I control the masses with metaphors that's massive
> Don't ask if the nigga'll . . . bash shit like Cassius
> I'm drastic when it comes to verbs I'll be flippin'
> Cause herbs just be shittin' off the words I be kickin'
> I scold you double-headed swords for the petty
> But I told you bitch niggas that heads ain't ready
> Now I mold you back into the bitch that you are
> Fuckin' with the Ruckus get bruised worse than scars.[4]

Here, the murder metaphor stands alongside proclamations of competitive orality and superiority. It is in fact an ego assassination that takes place through the skillful dis. As in much of hip hop, here we find variations on the game of playing the dozens (an African American folk practice of competitive insult) and its competitive discourse.

Signifying, another element of black language that appears in hip hop, is distinguished in African American culture from the dozens largely for its suggestive and subtextual critique, an expression of cleverness rather than overtness. The folk expression of signifying finds articulation in the stories of the Signifying Monkey, who tells the Lion that the

Elephant has been insulting him. The furious Lion demands an apology from the Elephant, who refuses and roundly stomps him. Only then does the Lion realize his mistake of taking the Monkey's word. So, for example, MC Lyte and Antoinette battled in the late 1990s. MC Lyte, in her song, "10% Dis," rhymed, "Beat biter / dope style taker / tell you to your face you ain't nothing but a faker," a dozens-style confrontation, while Antoinette responded, "Lights out, now the party's over / Home-girl reminds me of my dead dog rover,"[5] using the world *light* as a double entendre, signaling the impending demise of her competitor, and calling her ugly without saying it directly. While the monkey's indirect assault in the folktale comes through false gossip, Antoinette employs the homophone for hers.

Relying on Henry Louis Gates's call for a vernacular-based literary criticism in *The Signifyin(g) Monkey*, Sam Floyd describes the meaning of Signifyin(g) when applied to the black music tradition: "Signifyin(g) is a way of saying one thing and meaning another; it is a reinterpretation, a metaphor for the revision of previous texts and figures; it is tropological thought, repetition with difference, the obscuring of meaning—all to achieve or reverse power, to improve situations, and to achieve pleasing results for the signifier."[6] As Nelson George says, "Recontextualizing someone else's sounds was, after all, how hip hop started."[7] It is a Signifyin(g) form in its origins.

Signifiyin(g) also manifests itself in the previously mentioned multiple registers of hip hop. Access to these registers constitutes a test in familiarity with the artist and, for example, his or her sociopolitical or philosophical location. Sometimes the various registers conflict, so that the first level of text may actually affirm stereotypes of black men, for example, or appear to be misogynistic. Yet a deeper register of the text may then challenge the assumptions, describe feeling locked into the stereotype, reinterprets it to the advantage of the artist, or make fun of the holder of the stereotype.[8] When registers conflict with each other, listeners find themselves in a quandary regarding the music's interpretation. Should it be interpreted according to the deeper registers or the most superficial, more accessible ones? Floyd writes, "Through the energizing and renewing magic of myth and ritual, there emerged from the volatile cauldron of Call-Response a music charged with meanings centuries old—meanings to which the initiated, the knowledgeable, and the culturally sensitive responded in heightened communication."[9] Nelson George has described his surprise at the support for 2 Live Crew, the notoriously misogynistic and exploitative Miami Bass rap group, expressed by black women students during a lecture at Spelman College in Atlanta.[10] What the episode reveals, however, is that the female listeners clearly understood a regional cultural register that told them, "you can escape this misogynistic construction by not behaving in a certain manner" thereby possibly not identifying the misogyny with themselves, even if they perhaps should have been appalled by it.

Beyond the arena of music, the Signifyin(g) call-response trope extends to clothing styles, colloquial speech, spoken word, and the like, all in conversation with rap and rappers. George describes this in video culture: "An exciting interplay—a kind of videographic loop—developed between the consumers and performers. Performers would latch on to a new clothing style in the street. That style would be showcased in a video and the audience would then be turned on to the style, be it Run's hat or Snoop Doggy Dogg's braids. Within a few weeks, an outfit worn in Queens or Compton would suddenly become a national and sometimes international trend. Or the dialogue would go the other way."[11] The call issued from the video to a national audience response is consistently reinterpreted, modified, made local, and then made national again.

The Signifyin(g) that Gates articulated in landmark fashion in his work on the African American literary tradition is abundant in hip hop. Both the cultural tradition of Signifyin(g) that hip hop in many ways descends from, as well as the literary theoretical articulation of signification that Gates conceptualizes form part of the music. Gates quotes linguist Geneva Smitherman's eight features of signification:

1. Indirection, circumlocution
2. Metaphorical-imagistic
3. Humorous, ironic
4. Rhythmic fluence and sound
5. Teachy but not preachy
6. Directed at person or persons usually present in the situational context
7. Punning, play on words
8. Introduction of the semantically or logically unexpected[12]

These elements are present within the universe of the hip hop narrative, but also in the construction of the music, through deejaying, and as part of a musical canon. While the textuality is distinct in hip hop as it is brief, oral, and aural rather than written, and has the appearance of being entirely vernacular (a false appearance, but significant none-theless), it does rely on some of the same tools Gates articulates. The Signifyin(g) on other texts in hip hop occurs both within the world of rap, and across black music, and even across music in general. When Dr. Dre lays lyrics of gangster destruction over mellow soul, his compo-sition signifies on that earlier music's interpretation of black experience and yet uses it as a vernacular for creating the contemporary meaning he articulates. When Biggie Smalls first came out, he was an East Coast signification on West Coast forms of storytelling, language, and celebra-tions of wealth and death. Gates describes Signifyin(g) as it appears in oral tradition:

> Motivated Signifyin(g) is the sort in which the Monkey delights; it func-tions to redress an imbalance of power, to clear a space, rhetorically. To achieve occupancy in the desired space, the Monkey rewrites the re-ceived order by exploiting the Lion's hubris and his inability to read the figurative other other than as the literal. Writers Signify on each other's texts by rewriting the received textual tradition. This sort of Signifyin(g) revision serves, if successful, to create a space for the revising text. It also alters fundamentally the way we read the tradition, by defining the relation of the text at hand to the tradition.[13]

Biggie's genius as an MC was to take heed of the manner in which West Coast rap had eclipsed the East and to adopt and reinterpret the symbols of West Coast hip hop through an East Coast style. In 2003, the Queens-bred 50 Cent, whose album was released at number one, made a similar move integrating Southern and Western hip hop sensibilities into his style. In rap, the figure of the lion as having brute power, as opposed to the intellectual nuance and trickery of the monkey, might be read as white supremacy, but other readings are possible too: it might be read as the power of the trained musician, the power of the civil rights–era establishment for determining black public discourse and concerns, the perceived greater social and economic power of black women as com-pared to black men, all of which might be troped in text. The Signifyin(g) in rap in sophistication far exceeds a simple reference or response—it is engagement with other texts and their traditions in the midst of one's own piece, using the former as part of the ultimate creation of the latter.

In fact, the use of the monkey in the folktale itself reminds us that rap is but a child of earlier forms.

> Of the many colorful figures that appear in black vernacular tales, perhaps only Tar Baby is as enigmatic and compelling as is the oxymoron, the Signifying Monkey. The ironic reversal of a received racist image of the black as simian-like, the Signifying Monkey, he who dwells at the margins of discourse, ever punning, ever troping, ever embodying the ambiguities of language, is our trope for repetition and revision, indeed our trope of chiasmus, repeating and reversing simultaneously as he does in one deft discursive act.[14]

Exploiting the stereotype while simultaneously expressing literary skill is one of the prominent ways of using the black literary tradition.

The complex use of the structures of language and storytelling are critical features that help to describe what hip hop does, and to begin to develop a critical eye toward its evaluation. The basic elements of figurative language abound in the form, particularly metaphor. In hip hop, metaphor allows transcendence. Its frequent use lies at the heart of artistry in hip hop. It plays on the African American male tradition of finding freedom in mobility.[15] Metaphor in hip hop is about motion and transformation; its usage allows the artists to move outside of the boundaries of their communities, and even transcend the limitations of human fallibility.

> Milk: Do you understand the metaphoric phrase "lyte as a rock"? It's explaining how heavy the young lady is, you know what I'm saying, king?
> Gizmo: Yes, my brother, but I would consider "lyte as a rock" a simile because of the usage of the word "as." And now, directly from the planet of Brooklyn, MC Lyte as a rock![16]

This exchange, spoken by MC Lyte's hip hop artist brothers the "Audio Two," a.k.a. Milk and Gizmo, introduces her song "Lyte as a Rock." It explains the simile in the title with the word *heavy* (as a rock), meaning having profound insight and wisdom. This song features a self-conscious use of figurative language, with metaphor and simile functioning as the most important nonliteral elements in the lyrics, a phenomenon found throughout hip hop lyrics.

"I'm like . . ." is probably one of the five most popular phrases to begin hip hop stanzas. Metaphor and simile function in three notable ways in hip hop. First, they fulfill the obvious task of explication. The MC tells the listener about him- or herself, or whatever other subject is up for discussion, through comparison with or use of the characteristics of other objects, creatures, or entities. Second, they serve as great tools for exhortation and proclamation because through the metaphoric naming of great things, the MC proclaims his or her own greatness: "Lyte as a rock / or I should say a boulder rollin' down your neck / poundin' on your shoulders."[17] But perhaps most important, metaphor and simile engage the imagination and expand or transform the universe in which the MC dwells. With them, the author creates a space of possibility.

Emcees often create dramatic contrast within the sphere of the rhyme between life as it exists and life as it might be, and they often juxtapose those two realities. The conclusion of Special Ed's "I Got It Made" is reminiscent of Nikki Giovanni's famous 1970s poem "Ego Trippin'," as he tells his readers through example about his greatness, or rather how he "has it made."[18] Interspersed with tales of part ownership of Tahiti and his personal waiter bringing him potato alligator soufflé, are "My hair was growing too long so I got me a fade / and when my dishes got dirty, I got Cascade / when the weather was hot, I got a spot in the shade."[19] These are distinctly possible and mundane aspects of Special Ed's daily life. The music video to accompany the song was partly shot in front of Erasmus Hall High School in Flatbush, Brooklyn, and in abandoned lots. In the video, the juxtaposition of expansive imaginative possibilities and the daily existence of the teenager in New York proves even more dramatic. During the line "I got a frog, a dog with a solid gold bone," Special Ed smiles and holds up a dirty old bone.

It is important to note, however, that metaphor does not always express great hope or great ability. It can also serve as the expression of despair, stagnation, or destruction. Natural Bee rhymed, "Vermin I terminate verbally / I offend more niggas than the Mark Furman tapes,"[20] manifesting a clever destructive power. The appropriation of the names of the infamous or of weaponry for stage names is a sign of power, but also a glamorization of destruction. Capone, Noreaga (after General Manuel Noriega), Smif-N-Wessun (after the gun manufacturers), and, perhaps most disturbingly, Concentration Camp are names that operate as metaphors of violent destructive capability. So in the midst of the great beauty of expression and emotion that operates through metaphor in hip hop, there exists an ugliness (with cultural antecedents in toasts) that must be acknowledged as well. The tradition of harnassing ugliness to claim power is found in the cultural antecedents of hip hop.

As John Szwed explains, "The most likely candidate for a direct fore-bearer of modern rap is the toast, the rhymed monologue, an African-American poetic form that typically recounts the adventures of a group of heroes who often position themselves against society either as so shrewd and powerful as to be superhuman, or so bad and nasty as to be sub-human."[21] Figurative language is not only used for the self-aggrandizement so popular in hip hop music but also for the sake of making interesting artistic statements. Craig Mack rhymes:

Craig Mack

1000 degrees

You'll be on your knees

You'll be beggin' burning please

Brother freeze man

Undisputed deep-rooted

funk smoke that leaves your brains booted.[22]

Hip hop is high-sensibility music. Even before music videos became popular, the use of visual images was common in the poetry of hip hop. This holistic culture, and participatory performance culture, engages multiple senses anyway, but in addition, the lyrics themselves speak of sensory diversity in describing the effects of the music. Senses are trans-ferred and interchanged. For example, where touch would be, sound has entered, reinforcing the sense of inundation in the musical experience. Heavy D. rhymes: "With moves that sensual / three-dimensional / un-questionable lover's a professional."[23] The multisensory figurative lan-guage makes reference to the fact that the music is simply the most prominent expression of a broader cultural form. In addition to the audi-tory, the visual and the kinetic, the variety of senses and expressions of senses, are experienced as part of hip hop culture. Renowned DJ Kid Capri has said, "I made my tapes sound like a party. No matter what it was. My tapes just made you feel like you were there while the tape was being made."[24]

The aesthetics of the music have demanded that the multisensory experience of live music be incorporated into the recorded compositions, both poetically and in the creation of the sounds of partying. Paul Gilroy, observing such gestures, writes, "The hip hop nation has confined its loudly trumpeted enthusiasm for improvisation within strict limits. Most of the time its favored mode of reality is a virtual one in which only the illusion of spontaneity is created and the balance between rehearsed and improvised elements of the creative event shifts decisively toward the former."[25] Gilroy does not necessarily locate this as a criticism, but rather sees that the process impacts the performance of rap as compared to other black music forms. Certainly, one rarely finds improvisation in performances of popular artists or onstage, where the aesthetic of live performance is marketed rather than the reality. But one does find it at the local venue or party, contexts which continue to provide inspiration for recorded imitations of multisensory improvisation.

Composition

The more common use of the word *composition* is useful as it explains the way in which hip hop meets the African/African American "heterogeneous sound ideal." In *The Power of Black Music*, Sam Floyd cites Olly Wilson in describing this musical ideal "that results from the timbral mosaic created by the interaction between the lead voice, chorus, rattle, metal gong, hand clapping, various wind or strong instruments, and drums which exists in greater or lesser degrees in almost all African ensemble music."[26] By and large, however, hip hop is not the music of singers or instrument players. One of the effects of desegregation in some communities and school cutbacks in others was the loss of a ritualized formal space for instrument learning and practice for many African American children, and this is part of the reason hip hop is not primarily musician's music.

Yet I do not wish to posit rap as a music of deprived resources, suggesting that if only young African Americans had learned to play instruments, they could have made more "valuable" music. One of the genius elements of the creation of hip hop is that it has allowed a reconception of a number of ways to fit the musical ideal, and I say *reconceive* because, as Chuck D told me when I approached him to tell him about this book, "Ain't nothin new under the sun," even without traditional musical tools. Floyd writes about the ideal that "the combination of these sounds creates a contrasting, not a blending conglomerate, resulting in a sound that is ideally suited to the rhythmic, polyphonic and tonal stratifications of African and African American music."[27] In order to do this in hip hop, instead of putting together different kinds of instruments or styles of singers to create a conglomerate, different sorts of repeated sounds and voices—some singing, some talking—are placed together, arranged, manipulated, and transformed with a heavy dependence on technology. Houston Baker described hip hop deejaying as postmodern, saying, "The high technology of advanced sound production was reclaimed by and for human ears and the human body's innovative abilities. A hybrid sound then erupted in seemingly dead urban acoustical spaces. (By *postmodern* I intend the nonauthoritative collaging or archiving of sound and styles that bespeaks a deconstructive hybridity. Linearity and progress yield to a dizzying synchronicity.)"[28] Although he describes the collage effect as postmodern, in fact its reference to the montage of memory creates a deep historical awareness. Artistically what occurs is postmodern construction, but intellectually and emotionally, hip hop makes for a largely compositional form. Construction is at least conceptually the opposite of realism. Theodor W. Adorno posits construction in opposition to composition because while composition is the distinct putting together of elements, construction "tears the elements of reality out of primary context and transforms them to the point they are once again capable of creating a unity."[29] While the constitutive elements of the music of hip hop are almost always clearly distinguishable, maintaining a compositional framework, lyrically there are artists capable within individual songs of blurring the lines of added literary elements—realist, imaginative, metaphoric—to such an extent that the listener is brought into the specific unity of that artist's realm. Rakim has often been regarded as such an artist: "The tempo's a trail / the stage is a cage / the mic is a third rail."[30] We, as the audience, are on his train, riding to the destination of satisfaction having consumed and appreciated his rhyme. Only he, the MC, can get close enough to the site of power and potential execution, the third rail, the microphone, and use its electricity to channel its power into art. We move with him from discrete metaphors into a holistic "Rakim World." In the late 1990s, the Wu-Tang Clan, using themes from Asian martial arts, comic book characters, multiple names and metaphors, and symbolically representing their homes on Staten Island, constructed their own sort of "Wu world," complete with graphics, family trees, and attire. Construction is often the most complex sort of rhyming; it stands next to other sorts of hip hop almost as jazz does to blues. Both are potentially brilliant, but the brilliance of the former comes in part from multitextuality, shape-shifting, and minute interactions put together smoothly and seamlessly. Killah Priest rhymes:

Eat lamb with Abraham and break bread with the Son of Man
So slowly hold these hands and stretch forth from the skies
Like a rubber band begins to pop you above the land out of the
    atmosphere
Don't look back, Why? We're almost there
Just tryin' to prepare and adapt to the air pressure now
We stretchin' for the mental treasure pleasure beyond measure
beyond you can't comprehend the God or the distance
Between stars, pickin' up quasars and signs of radars
We goin' past any astronaut movin' so fast in this aircraft
Everything we pass get hot from the takeoff
The blast turnin' glass into rocks at last!
My supreme task was no longer to walk on green grass till
I become a beam of gas and travel through extreme draft
Unable to be picked up through cable
Out of there each of all manners of sky examiners heaven scanners giant
    antennas and high tech space cameras.
No evidence in any cemetery or obituary
Not found in any library or encyclopedia or media
I'm in star mode![31]

Where is this artist? Beyond ordinary means of research, and also beyond imaginations of celestial realms. He creates through his characterization of physical and intellectual impact a simultaneously attractive and elusive vision of his location. He has constructed a space where we travel with him only through engagement with his artistry.

Deejays and Producers

> I nominated my DJ the president.
> —Rakim, "Eric B is President"

The MC composes the narrative, but the aesthetics of composition are heavily dependent on the DJ or producer, as well as the relationship between the MC and those individuals. The MC, true to the title master of ceremonies, has always been the front man or woman. On stage, the DJ originally spun records standing at a set of turntables behind the MC. As time went on, a number of MCs replaced partnership with a DJ by digital production. Deejays are still not to be forgotten, however, and a number of noted DJs, such as Funkmaster Flex, Kid Capri, DJ Premier, Jazzy Jeff, and Hi-Tek, have released solo albums and all along had informally sold mixed tapes, using a number of different MCs to showcase their skills. On these albums, they seamlessly mix various songs into each other, transitioning between them by matching rhythm time before switching from one record to the next. They may create new rhythms or beats between and within records, pull the record back to the same place again and again to repeat a riff or a set of words, or scratch out rhythms with the needle and play break beats repeatedly, a signature feature of early hip hop. They create what in poetry is called the purple patch, that is, a space where the rhythm is changed for dramatic purpose in order to call particular attention to the words or music at that point. New music is composed using old hip hop songs, funk, soul, ballads, easy listening, rock, and all manner of other music forms. The work of the DJ is the foundation of the particular aesthetic that has emerged within hip hop's specific heterogeneous sound ideal. And even as the DJ becomes less prominent nowadays, in live venues one can see what ferocious, adept, and amazing an artist an excellent DJ actually is, and how easily the DJ can take attention away from the MC if he or she so chooses.

Producers can put the sounds of a door creaking or a television playing in the background, along with various other sounds of home and community, into the musical composition. An excellent producer puts together a multilayered web of sounds using rhythms, beats, and noise. And as live instrumentation becomes more popular in hip hop, as opposed to heavy sampling, producers have to put live music together with other elements in order to satisfy the aesthetic sensibilities cultivated by the auditory tessellations of DJs. For the most part, just playing a song, any song, with rhyming over does not prove satisfying to the hip hop head, even if it's funky. Another digital beat, or sample—or an element from a song or a blend of those elements—have to be included because the heterogeneous aesthetic of hip hop comprises widely divergent elements and the bringing together of disparate sounds.

Within the context of a party, as opposed to a show, a DJ, whose job is not to be a composer but rather to play records, still composes. Although musically the composition is often not as complex as that of a DJ doing a show, it is still complex in terms of community. A good DJ, not just in hip hop but in other musical forms as well, responds to the crowd. Taking in its styles, professions, ages, socioeconomic class, and ethnicities, he or she discerns what will make them dance. A DJ sustains the crowd's interest by playing the correct blend of favorites, unknowns, and the mediocre, putting on records to climax the crowd and then bring it down again gently. Some have signature orders of music styles—reggae, contemporary hip hop, old-school hip hop, R & B—in some combination that allows for smooth transition. By mixing, he (or she, but usually he) teases the crowd with a quiet taste of the next song to be played, a song it might really want to hear. Sometimes he teases the audience even further by making it the song after the next instead of the next song. In transitioning between songs, his beats are put together so they sound good in composition, but still remain recognizable as belonging to separate songs. The DJ at a party might also lead the crowd by calling for different affiliations, identities, or hometowns to be shouted out, asking for particular dances, or creating unexpected silence in order for the people to shout out the missing lines. Each part, and each good party, consists of its own composition led by the DJ and sustained by the energy of the partygoers.

Emcees

> Make the music, make the music, make
> the music, with your mouth.
> —Biz Markie, "Make the Music with Your Mouth Biz"

The MC blends his voice with the DJ and the audience to make the composition complete. Not simply limited to language, the MC in early hip hop was a musician as well. Before expensive drum machines became readily available to the average young person wanting to rhyme, beat boxing was fundamental. Producing the sounds of a drum machine with one's mouth and tongue stands in the tradition of scatting, a style in which vocalists replicate instrument sounds. Rather than instruments, however, beat boxers replicated the sound of late-twentieth-century technology complete with multiple beats, beeps, eeks, motors, and robotlike vocal interruptions. Again, this was hip hop's interpretation of a black music tradition. Floyd cites the "use of wordless sounds for their own value rather than for the communication of verbal meaning" in his charting of the musical continuities of black American music with African music.[32] In the mid-eighties, several prominent MCs were also great beat boxers, such as Buff Love of the Fat Boys, now deceased, Doug E. Fresh, and Biz Markie. In recorded music, beat boxing added another layer of sound to the basic beat and the MC's speaking voice. As increased technology, more sophisticated deejaying, and production became available to the average MC who could easily buy studio time, the art of beat boxing virtually disappeared. This is a shame because beat boxers made some outrageous, funky sounds and, as testified to by a summer 1999 concert featuring old school MC Doug E. Fresh, the artful skill continued to elicit enthusiastic response long after its heyday.

The response elicited by the audience from DJs or MCs forms part of the hip hop composition. Hence Rakim's lyrics: "To me MC means move the crowd."[33] Even as recorded music, rap has a live sensibility, and artists often test songs out on local audiences before recording or deciding on which songs to release. The MC's ability to make the audience participate constitutes an essential measure of his or her success. The music offers a site of collective collaboration, and one of the central methods of collaboration in hip hop is the origin of Floyd's Call-Response trope, the actual call and response, a popularly understood element of black music. Classic calls, repeated again and again over the years, include "Everybody say ho!" then answered by the crowd's "Ho," which is repeated three times, each time slightly differently, and concludes with a variation on "Somebody scream!" causing screams to rise up from the audience. Some call-and-response patterns offer directions for various parts of the crowd to say different things, according to location, gender, place of origin, or some such defining characteristic. Call and response is not limited in hip hop to verbal response but might also manifest itself in body movements. So when the MC says, "throw your hands in the air," "raise the roof," or "give it up," the motion and visual become part of the composite musical experience. To rock it, to set it off, is to create a holistic experience that engages at least three or four of the senses. Even music not intended as dance music should at least make listeners nod their heads, hence songs like the "Nod Your Head to This" or "The Head-Nodder."[34] However, the infectiousness of the grooves might make the audience do a little more: as Mad Skillz says in "The Head-Nodder," "My shit'll have hard niggas in soul train lines, bumpin' with a big black broad named Belinda."[35]

Call-and-response motions include simple arm movements, as well as dances. In "Return of the Boom Bap," one of KRS-One's choruses goes: "Bogle in the dance / Bogle in the dance," referring to a Jamaican dance of pointed fingers, bent elbows, and undulating back and shoulders.[36] In "Ladies Night," Lil' Kim says in the flow of her rhyme, "Let me see you do the bankhead," referring to a Southern dance gone national of rapidly bouncing shoulders as the body rocks back and forth.[37] And who among listeners of hip hop in the mid-eighties could forget the classic dance rap record put out by Joeski Love, "Pee Wee's Dance"? "Listen up party people 'cause the party is burnin' / For a new dance I know you been yearnin' / so for all you people concernin' / the brand new dance called the Pee Wee Herman."[38] Inspired by the awkward gestures of the children's actor who starred on *Pee Wee's Playhouse*, Paul Rubens, the dance and the song had young hip hop heads stepping back and forth with bent knees and trembling fists.

Even outside of parties, open mics, and concerts, the audience and the artist still have a dynamic relationship in freestyle sessions. In the circle of listeners, whether it be one or ten, the listening parties lean in, heads bowed, with their bodies bobbing up and down to provide encouragement for the continuation of the flow. One or two might create a beat (with the mouth) for the freestyler, but in a larger group the majority will become part of the composition with their bodies in motion. The MC of the moment often comes within inches of the listener's face with gestures and movements intended to further communication and keep the flow and rhythm alive. This kind of artist-audience relationship is rooted in the tradition of functional art in that it stresses community and heterogeneity of individuals in the composition. It also stands as an important democratic gesture because it identifies hip hop as a collective everyperson's music. Black American music existed under the threat of co-optation throughout the twentieth century. The black community's presence within the music composition offers protection against co-optation and hierarchical commodification: anyone might emerge from the (theoretical and sometimes literal) crowd and grab the mic if he or she is smart and skilled enough.

The call-and-response theme appears in the interaction between artists as well. Part of what made Run-DMC such great hip hop lyricists was their verbal interaction. They would finish each other's phrases, answer each other's questions, and respond to each other's calls. Their interaction contributed to the heterogeneous sound of the music; DMC's voice was lower and mellower, while Run often hollered himself hoarse.

> Run: Now Peter Piper picked peppers
> DMC: But Run rocked rhymes
> Run: Humpty Dumpty fell down
> DMC: That's his hard times
> Run: Jack B.
> DMC: Nimble
> Run: was
> DMC: Nimble
> Run: and he was quick
> Together: Jam master's much faster, Jack's on Jay's dick.[39]

The fictional Jack B. Nimble "on Jay's dick" is in awe of his lightning-quick DJ stylings, according to the collaborating MCs. The relationship between artists on a cut is generally speaking more about heterogeneity than harmonic sound, with some exceptions as in the group Bone Thugs-N-Harmony, who create rolling sounds with only slightly nuanced vocal differences that do not compete but blend instead.

In "Check the Rhyme," the two MCs of A Tribe Called Quest, Q-Tip and Fife, each have solo sections preceded by a call and response, the response being given by the one who is about to have the solo.

> Fife: You on point Tip?
> Q-Tip: All the time Fife
> Fife: You on point Tip?

Q-Tip: All the time Fife?

Fife: You on point Tip?

Q-Tip: All the time Fife

Fife: Well then play the Resurrection and give the dead some life.

Q-Tip: Okay if knowledge is the key then just show me the lock.[40]

Erick Sermon and Parrish Smith of EPMD (Erick and Parrish Making Dollars) conversed frequently within their rhymes. Sometimes one would personify the individuals that the other encountered in the course of a narrative, and at other times he would play the listener to the narrative, as though a friend were telling him a story, with the appropriate responses and exclamations. In their song "Who Killed Jane?"—concluding the saga of Jane, a transvestite they encounter on each album embroiled in some drama—Erick plays both the police officer and the listening friend.

E (as policeman): Sit up straight, state your name and your birth date
    and your whereabouts last night about eight.

P: Slow down.

E: Slow down?

P: Something's missing, where's my lawyer?

cop grilled me and said

E: Yo there's your lawyer![41] Things'll get rough, so don't act tough and
    try to play games. You headed up north.

P: For what?

E: You know what boy, the death of Jane.

P: You must be insane with no brain sniffin' cocaine, and if I caught a
    body it'd be yours and not Jane's.

E: Oh mister toughie you wish you had a nine to bust me I'm not a child
    I don't play my name ain't Chuckie.

P: Cop got pissed, and stepped back and grabbed his blackjack, swung
    for my dome ducked and caught my damn back.

E (as friend): Ooh.

P: Couldn't feel the pain.

E: Why?

P: Thinkin' 'bout the payback.[42]

Parrish narrates yet also participates in the internal dialogue between him and the cop. This transition between roles is signaled by Erick's personification of the cop. The interaction facilitates temporal shifts between the past and present moments and brings the past moment alive.

Alternately, a number of artists might rhyme on one song without this sort of direct interaction, each separate segment having a different flavor according to the style and voice of the artist. Even then, like a girl warming her body up to the rhythm of the double Dutch ropes before jumping in, we may hear the next MC making rhythmic sounds in preparation for coming forth with his or her own rhymes. Before Lil' Kim's segment in "Benjamins," she grunts "uh uh" on beat and then shouts an aggressive Jamaican patois curse word, with etymological roots in the female reproductive cycle, "What the blood clot!"

In this song, Lil' Kim identifies herself as the only female in her Bad Boy label crew. The crew holds great importance within the performance of hip hop: it is the group of artists who constitute a clique or family within the larger musical community, yet it exceeds the individual act. Within a crew, cameos from other acts are quite common. The Boot Camp Clik, including the Cocoa Brovaz (formerly Smif-N-Wessun, who had to change their name for copyright reasons) Heltah Skeltah, and Black Moon, often make references to each other's names and to the clique, as well as make cameo appearances in each other's songs. Each MC in the group is distinctive, but all of them share an almost harrowing soulful sound and a plethora of metaphoric and personified violent references.

Of course, the consumer appeal of having several popular artists rhyme on one song also serves as a motivation for putting artists from various groups together. A parade of stars can prove a big moneymaker, particularly when it signals the reunion of artists formerly in conflict, like East and West Coast collaborations, or when artists from the former N.W.A. Dr. Dre and Ice Cube, worked together again, or when EPMD reunited with the album *Back in Business* after being broken up for five years.

Given the popularity hip hop has achieved, however, the breadth of recorded sound far exceeds the correlated live interactive space, which is part of Paul Gilroy's observation discussed earlier about limited improvisation in hip hop. The tension created by the limited interactive worlds gives rise to the kind of suspicion and authenticity politics one finds among hip hop audiences in young urban black communities. This community of hip hop listeners—for whom the music defines its generation, who feels it deeply and loves it, and who participates in the culture surrounding hip hop as a whole—sees its role in the composition of the MC as essential. When heads perceive that the intended audience for a cut is not lovers of hip hop, largely those of or connected to the urban black community but rather the general white population, a crossover audience, accusations of selling out come quickly. Some artists have felt this accusation to unwarranted, believing that any time they begin to make a lot of money, they are referred to as sellouts. While there may be some truth to the notion that commercial success in the mainstream puts the artist under greater scrutiny and suspicion, the success of artists like Biggie Smalls, Lauryn Hill, Wyclef Jean, or Wu-Tang, who have had crossover appeal while maintaining a committed following among hip hop heads, demonstrates that the resentment tackles more than the encroachment of capitalism. It also stems from a sense of audience betrayal, as artists who cater to the aesthetics of music, dancing, and styles of those outside the hip hop community disturb the community composition of hip hop culture.

Narrative

In addition to the internal compositional elements, the format of the stories told figure as an important feature of hip hop. These formats largely derive from black folk oral and literary traditions. The narrative is the classic form, often marked as a signature feature of the old school, although all four forms (narrative, exhortation/proclamation, description, battle) I will discuss existed in some form or another in older hip hop songs. The narrative is a yarn, and

> the intention of the narrator of the Yarn is to tell outrageous stories that stretch and shatter credibility, overblown accounts about characters expressed in superlatives: the greatest liar is the hero of the yarn, or the strongest woodman, or the most cunning gambler. We listen incredulously, not believing a single word, our delight based on skepticism and wondering whether the storyteller can top the last, preposterous episode he's spun—by definition the traditional Yarn is always episodic in structure, one outrageous lie after another.[43]

The narrative in hip hop is a kind of storytelling, a late-twentieth century and early-twenty-first-century extension of traditional African American folktales, the MC replacing Dolemite or Brer Rabbit. Within the story, time is traversed, and the topic might be mundane, dramatic, or comic. Oftentimes it contains elements of a morality play. KRS-One's narrative song "Love's Gonna Getcha" explicitly warns the listener against the dangers of drug dealing through a first-person narrative of a poor young black man and his brother who is eventually murdered as a result of his pursuit and "love" for material things.[44] At each stage of the song, the first-person character becomes more deeply entangled in the web of illegal activity, and he repeatedly asks the listener, "Now tell me what the fuck am I supposed to do?" He simultaneously warns others of this kind of life by accurately presenting the dilemmas that might lead a young man to participate in illegal activities and which then might make it extremely difficult to leave them behind. KRS-One here made a meaningful social statement, particularly because it was written in the era of Nancy Reagan's simplistic and ineffective "Just Say No" to drugs campaign. The hip hop piece employed the narrative as a kind of morality play with a political message attached.

Alternately, in a comedic narrative, "Delancey Street," Dana Dane spins a tale about being robbed by three women. They chase him through the streets of Brooklyn until he's cornered in a dead end and must quickly think of a way to get out of the situation. Like Superman he opens up his outer wear and "printed on my shirt just as bold and plain / I'm not the one the rapper Dana Dane / Well the girls caught the message it was plain to see / They might as well have said "Dana Dane you're free."[45] All of the women begin to fawn over him, and the song concludes with them fighting for his attention as he walks away. These two narratives reflect the styles of each of the rappers. KRS-One has been known for years in hip hop as the teacher of social consciousness, and he described the album which featured "Love's Gonna Getcha" as using hip hop as a revolutionary force. Dana Dane was a comedic romantic, the lover winding up in a number of bizarre situations created by female obsession with him. He was "Cinderfella Dana Dane," the male hip hop version of Cinderella, with Bally shoes and a Kangol hat instead of glass slippers and a ball gown. In "Nightmares," he was a young man being chased down high school halls and in a therapist's office by an unattractive woman, Anita the Beast.[46]

A third narrative example may be found in Genius/GZA's dark tales of drug dealing episodes.

> I'm deep down in the back streets in the heart of Medina
> About to set off somethin' more deep than a misdemeanor
> Under the subway waitin' for the train to make noise
> So I blast a nigga and his boys
> For what? He pushed up on the block
> And made the dope sales drop like the crash in the Dow Jones stock
> I had to connect across ceilings to catch more bills than more bitches
>   got birth control pills
> I'm on the part settin' up a deal over blunt smoke
> nigga sleepin' on the bench they had him wired
> Peep my convo, address of my condo
> How I change a nigga name to John Doe
> And while he set up camp
> He got vamped
> But the stake through his heart
> I ripped his fucking lungs apart
> Snake got smoked on the set
> Like Brandon Lee
> Blown out the frame like Pan Am flight 103.[47]

This story line is reminiscent of a gangster flick, complete with territory conflicts and crime setups. Genius/GZA create a harrowing narrative film.

A fourth example of the narrative form can be found in Ice Cube's "It Was a Good Day" from his *Predator* album. In the course of the song, Cube describes his ideal day, which includes a breakfast cooked by his mother without pork, pickup basketball, dominoes, attention from a girl he's been trying to date since the eighth grade, sex with another girl named Kim, and watching a Lakers/Supersonics basketball game which the Lakers win. Equally important are the things absent from this day — police harassment and death in South Central Los Angeles. The music video to accompany this song comes to a dramatic conclusion. After the song ends, Ice Cube enters his home, which is surrounded by police cars and helicopters. The oasis provided by "the good day" is over, and he again falls victim to the surveillance and abuse of the LAPD. Ice Cube rhymes as the everyday black man living in Los Angeles, but a black nationalist consciousness informs his work. It fits that identity or label by insinuating the tragic circumstances of the lives of black men into ritualized pleasurable activities to imply rather than assert a political message (although some of Ice Cube's work is more explicitly political, and other parts of it remain explicitly apolitical). Narratives are used to entertain and educate, but also to explicate the personality and lifestyle the MC projects.

Exhortation/Proclamation

Hip hop has been characterized as bragging music because it is common for entire songs to be dedicated to proclamations about the MC's greatness. Yet this format of proclaiming something, or exhorting an argument, is not limited to the MC alone, although that emerges as the most frequent subject. Many songs serve as advisories or encouragements for the listener to comprehend a given idea. These exhortations and proclamations are composed of sets of short exempla, brief stories, metaphors, or examples to support the general theme. Take, for example, Nas's "It Ain't Hard to Tell":

> It ain't hard to tell
> I excel then prevail
> The mic is contacted I attract clientele
> My mic check is life or death
> Breathin' a sniper's breath
> I exhale the yellow smoke of Buddha through righteous depths
> Deep like the shinin'
> Sparkle like a diamond sneak an Uzi on the Island in my army jacket
>   linin'
> Hit the earth like a comet invasion
> Nas is like the Afrocentric Asian
> half man half amazin'
> 'cause in my physical I can express through song

Delete stress like Motrin
then extend strong.[48]

He shifts between metaphors of elemental greatness to street hardness, exemplified by smuggling weapons into the prison on Rikers Island.

LL Cool J's song "I'm Bad," from the *Bigger and Deffer* album, offers the following set of example:

I'm like Tyson
Icin' I'm a sole jaguar
Makin' sure you don't try to battle me no more
Got concrete rhymes been rappin' for ten years
And even when I'm braggin' I'm bein' sincere
MCs can't win I'll make 'em rust like tin
They call me jaws my hat is like a sharks fin.[49]

This set tells the listener that the artist has the skills of boxer Mike Tyson, then heavyweight champion and a metaphor for strength, that he rhymes alone with the predatory instincts of a wildcat, that he is established and experienced, and that despite his metaphoric bragging, he's serious about his abilities. LL has always worn a hat, it is his signature, and he likens it to the symbol of danger that the fin was in the movie *Jaws*. Each exemplum supports his contention that he is bad in the black English sense of the word meaning "good."

While "I'm Bad" is a self-exhortation song, the next song on the CD, "Kanday," is an exhortation about another person, a girl with whom LL is fictively involved. Here, he rhymes:

Her body's bad
The girl's built
Skin like silk
Wet steamy warm just like a hot cup of milk
She's all the way live
Keeps me satisfied
I don't go outside
I like to stay inside her
Ways are like an angel with bright white wings

And I'm crazy bout the way Kanday shakes her thing.

Wouldn't leave her for nothing only a crazy man would

That's why I had to tell you that I Feel Good, Whoo!

about Kanday![50]

Kanday's sexy attributes and her effect on the MC here become the focus of the proclamation. The subject of an exhortation might range from either positive or negative assessments of the opposite sex to the superiority of one's neighborhood or region. Examples for the latter can be found in "Deja Vu (Uptown Baby)" by Lord Tariq and Peter Gunz, "California Love" by Tupac Shakur, "Southside: Houston, Texas" by Scarface, or the classic "South Bronx" by Boogie Down Productions, rhymed by KRS-One. The song might even focus on the brand of sneakers one favors. Many people will be familiar with Run-DMC's "My Adidas" in this vein, but there was also "Nike" by Heavy D. and the Boyz, and several MCs who made songs or references to Filas in the early to mid-1980s.[51]

Some exhortations/proclamations constitute theories about some sort of practice, for example, a discourse about how an MC should rhyme, or an idea about how one should operate within the world. Run-DMC combined a theory about artistic excellence with self-proclamation in the song "Perfection" from the *Raising Hell* album.

> Run: Perfection to D is quite essential, he has to live up to his potential.
> DMC: I work real hard all day and night I get to it and do it 'cause I want it right. I got Bass
> Run: Tone
> DMC: A new
> Run: Cologne
> DMC: And then I rock a funky
> Run: Rhyme
> DMC: On the micro-
> Run: Phone[52]

The components of DMC's aspiration toward perfection include not only labor but the right sound elements, including the bass, an attention to sound quality, and funky rhymes. Among the list of accusations against hip hop as a viable art form is the criticism that the music is not "about" anything. When people voice this accusation, they are usually talking about the exhortation/proclamation form, which only loosely centers around a general theme and allows the author, through the use of exempla, to spiral into a wide diversity of formulations, metaphors, and analogies to make the point. The creative space is so expansive that the logic of the moment can be lost to the casual listener, whether that logic be an exhortation of the MC's greatness, an expression of his or her lyrical dexterity, or some other engaged idea.

Description

Similar to narratives, descriptive rhymes often outline a particular situation, dynamic, or thing, but they lack the linear time frame the narrative form possesses. It is difficult to find descriptive rhymes that are not also somehow exhortations on wax, but freestyling, improvisational rhyming, is more often predominantly descriptive. An excellent freestyler can comment on his or her environs, what clothes people have on, the dynamics in the room, much like an excellent comedian who can make jokes about the crowd on the spot. Or the freestyler might engage in a stream of consciousness in which coherence is less important than the quality and cleverness of individual ideas (as opposed to the entire piece) and the flow of the rhyming. Take this example from Greg Nice of the duo Nice 'N Smooth: "Greg Nice / My life's like a fairy tale / Orca was a great big whale / I knew a fat girl who broke the scale / You won't tell / I won't tell."[53] Greg Nice's narrative is comprised of a string of non sequiturs, and so it sounds like the spontaneous flow of a freestyler, rather than a written song. The disjointedness has its own idiosyncratic appeal, like the bizarreness of a Lewis Carroll poem.

Battle

Rap's competitive origins have received much discussion. In the genre's early days, MCS and DJS went up against each other in talent shows or battles, and the best was decided on by the crowd. What was earlier called breaking and boogaloo was redesignated in the 1990s as "battle dancing." This phenomenon moved from the live party to wax and the dis or battle records of the mid- to late 1980s, sometimes to become pyramids of rhymes all in conversation with one another. The 1984 "Roxanne Roxanne," by U.T.F.O. (the Untouchable Force Organization), was a song dissing a stuck-up girl. Roxanne Shante responded with "Roxanne's Revenge," as did another woman, who called herself the Real Roxanne, with her self-titled "Real Roxanne." Sparky D also had some words for Roxanne, such as "Roxanne you're through / girl Ima walk all over you," and then came another song by U.T.F.O, "Roxanne's a Man."[54] Boogie Down Productions and the Juice Crew had a historic conflict, which began with Boogie Down Productions challenging MC Shan's song "The Bridge" about the early days of hip hop in Queens. In response KRS-One rhymed, in "The Bridge Is Over," "Bronx created hip hop / Queens will only get dropped you still tellin' lies to me / Everybody's talkin' 'bout the Juice Crew funny but you still tellin' lies to me."[55] His cadence mimicked the Billy Joel song "It's Still Rock 'n' Roll to Me," another song hailing musical authenticity.

The conflict in battle records supports the discursive space in hip hop, which allows the listener to make evaluations about the relative merits of songs or artists. Today one is much more likely to hear "The Bridge Is Over" than "The Bridge" because "The Bridge Is Over" was ultimately determined to be the better song and because KRS-One's career has had much greater longevity and national prominence than MC Shan's, although Shan, too, was a great MC.

Conflicts manufactured by corporate entities knowing that a good fight will improve sales have somewhat compromised the competitive thrust of hip hop. Nonetheless, competition is sustained to some extent, even though the competition now witnessed by audiences of recorded music often is no longer intimate to a culturally specific hip hop community as it once was. Battle records between the East and West Coasts in the mid 1990s signaled an end to battling as a demonstration and sharpening of skills, because in those days, the critical measure for the audience had more to do with one's origins than with who was the better MC. In the postcoastal feuding world, battling records not motivated by regional affiliation or corporate manipulation have continued to appear, though in smaller numbers: 1998 witnessed a surprise attack on LL Cool J by a relative newcomer, Canibus, which the old-school rapper responded to in kind. Canibus's song was called "2nd Round K.O.," in reference to LL's use of boxing metaphors and imagery. Even this example proved more personal than battle records once were. Canibus's attack did not just focus on rhyming skills or clothes or general wackness; it attacked actions, and it made accusations of hypocrisy. "Battle songs" in the post-battle era that have maintained an attention to artistic or stylistic weaknesses are usually songs aimed at a prospective or imagined competitor, rather than a specific one. The Poor Righteous Teachers' "Da Rill Shit" may serve as an example:

> MCs try to do me
> I'm not livin' like that
> Speak that wack behind my back
> 'Cause in my face you'll get waxed
> I'm the best 'cause I'm convinced
> 'Cause I ain't been stopped yet
> I'm straight from Trenton out the projects
> In the Wild Wild West
> If you want me come and find me
> You, your posse, and your friends
> Your family, your dog Toto, neighbors, lovers, and kids
> Line 'em up and watch 'em fall
> Faster than you'd believe . . .[56]

Wise Intelligent owes a debt here to Rakim for his classic phrasing of collecting a mass of competitors who might be swept away in a single blow: "I take seven MCs put 'em in a line / I take seven more brothers that think they can rhyme / Well it'll take seven more before I go for mine / That's 21 MCs ate up at the same time."[57]

Exhortations of power seduce listeners as much as the cleverness with which the MCs imagine the configuration of competitors. In general, the formats of the songs provide a basic framework, although the formats are intertwined and combined regularly. One might find a distinct format in each stanza, or songs in which within each sentence there is a combination of formats.

Allegory

Allegorical tales have tradition in African American culture. In the context of telling "big lies" the idiosyncrasy, greatness, strength, or skill of a folk hero or of oneself might find expression. Within the context of narrative songs, or as exempla in exhortatory songs, allegorical tales are used to entertain and inform. In one of MC Lyte's songs from her first album, "Kickin' 4 Brooklyn," she tells a story that sounds rather like an old Southern tale of the frightful power of a High John de Conqueror or some such character. She rhymes:

> I was chillin' in Flatbush mindin' my own
> When a girl walked up with a chrome microphone
> She said Hey MC Lyte, I heard about you
> So here's the microphone let's see what you can do
> So I took the microphone and threw it to the ground
> 'Cause I needs no assist when it come to gettin' down
> When I started to rap, she started shake
> She knew to confront me was truly a mistake
> So she took the microphone off the great concrete
> And before I turned around she was down the street.[58]

This fictional episode alerts us to Lyte's courage and ability to compete, as well as to incite fear. The rhyme stands as an assertion of her artistic ability. The presentation does the same work as she crafts an entertaining story to make this assertion. The allegorical tale provides a format that supplements the arguments made in the song as a whole, and also supplements the metaphor or simile of an individual line.

Realism

> What you think now, I think I love you, what you feel now,
> I feel I need you. What you know, to be real, it's got to be real!
> —Cheryl Lynn, "To Be Real"

Following a discussion of the constructive elements and composition of hip hop, as well as the formats of hip hop storytelling, a discussion of genre is appropriate. While several genres analogous to literary genres exist in hip hop, I would like to focus on hip hop's form of realism because it tells us something about the political, artistic, and philosophical ethos of the music. In the 1990s, the call to "keep it real" became a rallying cry in hip hop. The 1970s classic song, "To Be Real" is about genuine love, emotional authenticity, and depth, a loyalty that superficial or material matters cannot bastardize. Calls to keep it real in hip hop, however, have included celebrations of the social effects of urban decay and poverty, for example, assertions of a paranoid vigilance in protecting one's dignity, which leads to violent action or ruthless individualism à la "fuck the world / don't ask me for shit / cause anything you do you got to work hard for it / honeys shake they hips / you don't stop / and niggas pack the clip / keep on."[59] The "real" is also an authenticating device responding to the removal of rap music from the organic relationship with the communities creating it. It demands that artists maintain or use symbols asserting their allegiance to black youth populations, or subgroups within that community. The real for hip hoppers means setting the terms for allegiance. It does not disallow fiction, imaginative constructions, or hip hop's traditional journey into myth. Rather, it is an explicitly ideological stand against selling one's soul to the devils of capitalism or assimilation as one sells the art form and lives life. The frequent calls in the hip hop community to keep it real not only require the maintenance of an authentic black urban identity; they also constitute a theoretical space that functions as a living testimony to African American experience. As Nas says in "Represent," "Straight up, shit is real and any day could be your last in the jungle."[60] Being "real" is a call to authenticity that becomes a political act. Such symbols of authenticity in hip hop are not only found in cinema verité representation of ghetto existence but also in honest portrayals that may be abstract insofar as their truths are emotional, rather than completely factual. In the spring of 1996, a comedian on an episode of the HBO comedy series *Russell Simmons Def Comedy Jam* noted that if rappers killed as many people as they claimed to, they would all be in jail, concluding with the words, "That ain't real." Hence, the "Real" with a capital *R*, constitutes a political rather than purely sociological stance that gives testimony to the emotional state resulting from the experience of poverty, blackness, and the crises of urbanity. Mobb Deep rhymes,

> I keep it real
> Pack steel
> Like my man YG
> When a fool try to play me
> Wet him up
> And I'm Swayze.[61]

In another song, the group asserts, "We livin' this 'til the day that we die / Survival of the Fittest / Only the strong survive."[62] Both lyrics express the artists' commitment to realness. While an assertion of social Darwinist aggression forms part of the Real in hip hop, it is by no means the sum total. The Real is the location where an individual remains committed to his or her community, professes that allegiance, and remains honestly and organically rooted in his or her position in the world:

> My mentality is money-orientated
>
> I'm destined to live the dream for all my peeps who never made it
>
> 'Cause yeah we were beginners in the hood as Five Percenters
>
> But somethin' musta got in us 'cause all of us turned to sinners
>
> Some rest in peace, some sittin' in San Quentin
>
> And others such as myself we tryin' to carry on tradition[63]

Taking its name from a literary genre, realism in hip hop is an artistic format inextricably linked to the material conditions of black American urban communities.

Witnessing proves incredibly important in hip hop. Being present for the ills of the ghetto and watching someone go through the transformations of drug abuse, murder, poverty, and mental illness can be as traumatic as experiencing those things. Hip hop at once witnesses and then testifies to certain events, whether or not the speaker participates in them, and acts as a witness to realism in the religious sense, as someone or something bears witness to life's hardship and difficulty. Michael Eric Dyson asks, "Did Tupac draw from his own experiences or did he raid the experiences of others to spin his haunting tales of urban woe and social neglect? If he did would he be different from any other artist whose primary obligation is to make art out of imagination, fiction, and fantasy? Stories don't have to be real to be true. Wouldn't Tupac have been artistically authentic in borrowing the lives, experiences, and stories of others as the grist for his powerful rap narratives?"[64]

Hip hop music concerns itself with both the self and the we. Its consciousness is both of the ego and of the collective. While explorations and expressions of the self abound as descendents of big lies, toasts, and folk ballads from the African American oral tradition, they are not ultimately individualistic, even when referring primarily to the individual. The stories of Dolemite and Stagolee were narratives about heroic figures repeated in communities across the country. The repetition made them collective, as did their articulation of the community's sentiments. The heroes' ability to traverse the boundaries of society tightly bound by white supremacy and religious convention made them popular figures. In hip hop, the community sustains that tradition of self-expression, and the artistically depicted self is overwhelmingly a self the listener can identify with, either through the depictions of life it offers, through the aspirations and hopes it articulates, or through the language, clothing, and body politics of the artists, who operate as cultural signifiers. The community as an identifying and authenticating force holds huge significance, especially as artists validate themselves against claims of artifice. I have often thought that hip hop offers the first popular cultural space in the African American community that celebrates, rather than rejects as an embarrassment, one's origins in the projects (that is, not when the projects were new and considered a step up from tenements, but the projects as they are today, the dwelling place of the underclass). References to the projects in part give testament to a certain hardness or edge, and they also assert a class-based proud identification with poor black people.

Hip hop music celebrates Me and We, as opposed to You. At various moments in hip hop, the Other is the competing MC or DJ, the challenger in a fight, or white people. The Other might also emerge as a sympathetic opposite, such as the audience being seduced by the rhymes. But either way, the Other occupies a position of relative powerlessness vis-à-vis the I. The frequent exception to this rule would come in the form past-tense narratives about being dissed or hurt by a lover or a friend, but in the present confrontation of Me and You, the Me is always at an advantage, either due to knowledge, ability, or power. As the producers and DJs produce the show, the MC emerges as an actor on the stage, not a supplicating performer, but a captivating one. In the composition, he or she engages the audience and gets its feedback and participation, but the MC still remains the leader, the distinguished Self among the collective heads. This is obvious to the listener of hip hop, but relevant to point out in comparison with other music forms. The importance of the Self at once stands as the perfect expression of American politico-religious identification and individualism and yet also becomes translatable into a communitarian consciousness, locating hip hop voices as metonymic black expression.

In the wake of hip hop's meteoric rise to the top of American popular music, mass-produced hip hop maintains its "authenticity" in part by encouraging artists to live out the artistic narratives they portray. Motown was notorious for its efforts to groom and socialize its artists, and hip hop business apparently provides its own kind of grooming —to hardness, sensationalism, and scandal, all of which sell records. This "real deal" is apparently what the consumer wants. In the United States, that means the grittier, edgier, more fantastically urban. This authenticity is double-voiced, at once constituting an exploitation of racist imagery and an expression of the problems of the ghetto.

In "Village Ghetto Land," Stevie Wonder asks, "Now some folks say we should be glad for what we have. Tell me would you be happy, livin' in this ghetto land?"[65] His question concerns how one would feel, and implicitly and perhaps even more profoundly, who one would be in the ghetto? What does this space create? Of course the answer is diverse— endlessly diverse—as is the collection of human beings living in poor communities of color in the United States. And yet the space art provides differs from the geography and complexity of a community. In comparison to "reality," art suffers limitations, but it can also do things that life cannot. It can provide coherence of structure and form, it can separate out particular elements and emotions, and it can choose certain images and metaphors about the world, be they horrific or beautiful. And those choices, which operate as signs within the artistic space, define the thing or place or person signified.

At the turn of the century, American literary realists concerned themselves with depicting what was real and true about daily life. Even as they did this, artists and audiences understood that the depictions were ideologically charged and artistically crafted. Simply put, both readers and critics knew they were making choices. However, it proves comparatively difficult for listeners and critics to understand the realism in hip hop as something crafted, ideological, and resulting from artistic choices. Why? One frequent answer claims that the music's audience is too young and unsophisticated to distinguish between entertainment and reality; another finds that critics scapegoat hip hop as opposed to other music styles because of racism or a generation gap. And both hold some truth. Yet the difficulty results from a far more convoluted dynamic than these answers can account for.

In part, the difficulty of realism in hip hop comes from the autobiographical nature of the music, and of African American folk literary culture, which entails the telling of one's story in epic or comic terms. Artists tell about their lives, and it is the task of the critic to avoid making one-to-one correlations between the music and the artists, to avoid a venture into some strange brand of artistic determinism, even as he or she trusts the artist to tell the audience something. This task has become more difficult with the 1990s, which witnessed many hip hop artists actively requesting that their words be taken as authentic, asking their listeners to ferret out "fakes" and reject them. Nevertheless, the epic terms of the tales distinguish them as artistic productions. As Killah Priest succinctly puts it in "Fake MCs": "Too many MCs in the East wanna be gangsters / Too many gangsters in the West wanna be rappers / Buncha actors / I oughta smack ya."[66]

The Real, or realism in hip hop as a movement, takes on two perspectives, "telling" narratives and "being" narratives, which, in terms of understanding hip hop as the production of a community and of individual artists, are mutually dependent. In "Cell Therapy," by Goodie MOb., we hear a "telling" narrative.

> My family moved in our apartment complex
> The gate with a serial code was put up next
> They claim that this community is so drug-free
> But it don't look that way to me
> Cause I can see the young bloods hanging out at the store
> 24-7 junkies looking for a hit of the blow
> It's powerful
> Oh you know what else they tryin' to do
> Make a curfew especially for me and you
> The traces of the new world order
> Time is gettin' shorter
> If we don't get prepared people it's gon be a slaughter
> My mind won't allow me to not be curious
> My folks don't understand so they don't take it serious
> But every now and then
> I wonder if that gate was put up to keep crime out or keep our ass in[67]

Even in a narrative context, the speaker provides an internal critique of sociological conditions and the prospects of social control through planned communities. The function of the rhyme, then, is to inform and enlighten, rather than simply depict. Contrast this with a "being" narrative from Nas:

> Yo! They call me Nas I'm not your legal type of fella
> Moët drinkin' marijuana smokin' street dweller
> Whose always on the corner rollin' up bless
> When I dress it's never nothin' less than Guess
> Cold be walkin' with a bop and my hat turned back
> Love committin' sin and my friends sell crack
> This nigga raps with a razor, keep it under my tongue
> The school dropout, never liked that shit from day one
> 'Cause life ain't shit but stress, fake niggas and crabs guts
> So I guzzle my Hennessey while pullin' on mad blunts
> The brutalizer crew de-sizer accelerator
> The type of nigga who be pissin' in your elevator[68]

Nas personifies a self-celebrating nihilist living a life of drugs, depression, and aggression. The difference between a being and a telling narrative is that between personification and third-person didactics. Songs about the lives of gangsters, for example, come in two varieties, the first-person story of a gangster, and the third-person story about gangsterism. When the audience listens to the third-person telling story, its comprehension depends on either knowing the character from the inside—through first-person narrative, the archetypes present in "being" tales—or knowing the actual lives in black urban communities.

Various character types are consistently personified in hip hop. Some we might believe as "real," while others clearly come across as "fictional." Listeners more readily find the drug dealer authentic than an urban guerrilla or prison escapee, to use some of the roles Ice Cube has played. This is in part attributable to the fact that hustlers and dealers commonly form integral parts of the underground economy of US cities. They are characters people can point to in communities, just like preachers, grandmothers, store owners, and crackheads. And it is frequently unclear in hip hop where art ends and life begins. The personification of the life of a thug, hustler, or dealer might become complicated by some artists' personal involvement, past or present, with those activities.

Furthermore, the tendency to accept the Real as real has to do with the democratic nature of the art form. Hip hop is supposed to be an everyperson's music, so when the artist takes on a familiar role, the people should be able to believe it if it is good. Keeping it real emerged as a shared community ethos and any debate over its meaning was minimal. Unfortunately, criticisms of the Real primarily challenged it with the positive-negative of music, messages, and images. The more interesting challenge, however, would concern the choices made in depictions of everyday realities and the contingent ideology that the artists promote with those choices. If violence or drug dealing constitute signature features of life in black communities, expunging these things from the music will not provide an ideal solution to the problems people have with the Real. The question is: Why is the violence of the illegal underground economy, for example, more compelling than other features of community life?

There are several answers to that question. US culture socializes the country's residents to yearn for a particular brand of excitement and glamour in entertainment. Sensational conflict exists on television shows from the "real" Jerry Springer and *Cops* to crime dramas, and in countless action films with sequence after sequence of gratuitous violence. The only comparable titillation to be found in the daily life of black and poor communities exists in the intrigues of illegal activity. Furthermore, the consistent depictions of black Americans as murderers, robbers, and rapists in entertainment and news media not only incites yearnings for images of *Cosby Show*–like professionals and *227*-like lower middle-class working people but also creates the desire to breathe life into empty stereotypes. Hip hop provides the most provocative, humane, and insightful images of the black underworld in the popular media.

> Hear shots and sirens
> When I fiend first they yo' rings
> Now they my rings
> So give it up punk then I just
> Put another jack in progress
> It's the American way
> 'Cause I'm the G.A.N.G.S.T.A.

In the shadow of Hollywood dynastic wealth and on what was the Western frontier, jacking or robbery of various sorts do seem to be the American way, as does conspicuous consumption, which motivates the illegal acquisition of jewelry and other "things." How, one asks, does this gang-ster pursuit qualitatively differ from that of the white gangster families who so glamorously made money off of liquor during Prohibition? Is it the ferocious black body that gives the gangster his bite?

The personifications and realist depictions in hip hop reflect this vivid concern. Such reflection occurs through (1) the exploitation of the fear of these figures extant in the black community (the artist personifies the greatest threat in the hood); or (2) the provision of a narrative that truly shows the source of those concerns; or (3) the provision of an ex-ample for listeners of what not to become. The criticisms the gangster image in hip hop faces resemble those directed at celebrated black nov-elist Richard Wright. Charles Johnson writes that Wright's writing con-tained "a realism that gained its visceral power at the expense of portray-ing positive cultural features in black life—in other words, much that is affirmative and joyful in black culture is lost in the literary Lifeworld of Richard Wright."[69] Another critic, in describing *The Outsider*, writes, "Wright creates an almost superhuman (clearly Nietzschean) black hero whose alienation and dread place him both outside of and yet very much inside modern American, that is to say Western, civilization. In contrast to (but recalling) Du Bois' representation of double consciousness as a horrifying burden in *The Souls of Black Folk*, Wright's complex image of blackness as double vision is a source of strategic power, freedom and knowledge."[70]

Added to the complex of factors is the dynamic that results from hip hop becoming commercially successful in the mainstream. In the late 1980s and early 1990s, artists began appearing who personified gang-sters without ever having experienced that lifestyle: record companies manufactured gangsters for their sensational appeal. The co-optation of hip hop by the mainstream therefore became associated with "fake gang-sterism." Gangsterism turned into a commercial tool, sold for its gore like an action flick. Hip hop heads made efforts to weed out the com-mercial gangsters from the "real" ones, and so rumors of the suburban birthplaces and respectable middle-class childhoods of certain MCs sur-faced as evidence of their inauthenticity, even though hip hop had been a cross-class art form for years. In order to retain a sense of authen-ticity and connectedness to black communities, and also for the glamour provided by celebrity, various artists began to live out the narratives of gangster lives. The list of hip hop artists arrested or imprisoned *since* becoming celebrities is extremely long and includes Snoop Doggy Dogg, Marion "Suge" Knight, Slick Rick, Biggie Smalls, Tupac Shakur, Queen Latifah, Mystikal, Busta Rhymes, Shyne, and numerous others. Further, it is no accident that as Public Enemy, a group pronouncing revolutionary ideology, became widely popular, the mainstream media began its attacks on rap, criticizing anything from 2 Live Crew's explicit sexuality to violence and gangsterism. Virtually every hip hop artist mentioned in the mainstream news suffered transmogrification into a gangster rapper, even if he or she came from a place that didn't have gangs per se. And, according to the news, "gangster rap" was bad. If that label did not work for particular artists, they were togged as misogynists or sex fiends, regardless of the context of the sexuality in the music. Black voices untempered by institutions of white acceptability, and having the potential to inspire protest or at least epistemological transformation, frightened and disturbed, and were therefore demonized. And so in the 1990s, when realism became self-conscious enough as to support the phrase *keeping it real*, the practice of ghetto realism or thug realism facilitated the scapegoating of rap by both conservative and liberal voices.

But keeping it real encompasses more than knowing the seamier side of life in the ghetto firsthand, even as violence and thuggishness have become symbolic elements of the hood. Andrew Ross writes about the art's authenticity, " 'representing' involves a demonstrated loyalty to the storytelling genre itself. Genre justice, earned at the mic, determines how respect is distributed, even to the non-gangsta hardcore. The rapper's aim is to convince an audience that his 'shit is real,' but this is a much more complex task than simply proving that the events he described actually happened to him."[71] Like any term describing a genre or ideology, the phrase *keeping it real* has a range of interpretations. For some, it mainly means the rejection of sanitized Hollywood depictions of life and of conscious efforts to cross over and become accepted by white audiences. In this case, the phrase may or may not have anything to do with the content of the rhyme itself, but it will definitely concern itself with the artist's perspective and the culturally based styles of composition. For others, the phrase refers to the retention of the artistry, craft, and sense of community that hip hop has at its best, and the rejection of the production of simplistic pop rhymes. For still others, it means telling a story of how life in the hood is, in any number of ways, for good and bad. And for others again, it means, disappointingly a glo-

rification of gunplay and the ills of the ghetto. I say disappointingly because regardless of the artistic merit of the work of a number of artists
who believe to keep it real by celebrating destruction, there is a cost that
results from the ideological force hip hop has with young people.

That does not mean to say that hip hop causes violence. Of the complex web of elements in play in the lives of adolescents, it seems that
music would be rather low on the list of critical factors determining their
behavior or values. Yet regardless of where it stands on the list, the idea
that the music could cause a single act of violence or illegal activity is
far from compelling. The issue is not that hip hop causes violence or
whether hip hop causes violence. The United States has a violent culture
compounded by devastating health and wealth disparities. The issue is
that hip hop carries an ideological message about merit, human worth,
and excellence, and if that message glorifies that which ails the community without any internal critique, doesn't it then become a politically objectionable ideology to be challenged by those seeking justice
and equity for black Americans? Clearly, many within the hip hop community believe the answer to that question to be yes, as many with a
preference for something more complex and profound, another kind
of real, attack the current notion of the Real as a jubilant and reckless
gangsterism.

Attention to the exegeses of realist tales reveals textual and subtextual
interpretations that may differ from straightforward gangster or hustler
realism. The literal exegesis of hip hop realism elucidates and interprets
the life personified or discussed in the given city or community. This
literal exegesis is centered around a specific space or identity and might
include regional references, as well as economic, cultural, institutional,
and social elements. The subtext often offers an allegorical explanation
that speaks to more universal crises, allegories either of black existence
in America as caught in the tension between being Othered and marginalized and having aspirations toward the American dream or, more
universal still, of a consciousness caught between selfishness and gen-
erosity, individualism and humanism. In Master P's "Is There a Heaven
for a Gangster?" the literal exegesis is the moral crisis facing a gangster
who has wounded, killed, used, and abused others. The allegorical exegesis comprises the description of guilt, the quest for salvation despite
sin, and the individual supplication to God for forgiveness.

Scarface, a Texas MC, specializes in a sort of descriptive realism. Descriptive realism creates a world for the listener which includes the cars, conflicts, and love of life in a given neighborhood, a veritable cinema verité. Scarface often punctuates his descriptive realism with some argument about the conditions of the ghetto, or with musings about how one should live within that context. Take this example from the song "Don't Testify":

> We got some niggas we been feudin' with
>
> Caught one of his homies with cheese and startin' sangin'
>
> Told the guy from interstate traffic and stuff
>
> Offered him five of his k's and it's crackin' him up
>
> Now we dealin' with this nigga who been talkin' this shit
>
> Worst thing is his real man runnin' the brick
>
> And all the workers on the block is kinda scared
>
> To come workin' cause 5-0 been here five times and not searchin'.[72]

The ultimate lesson of the song is that the ethics of illegal activity demand silence about operations at risk of death: "You know the rules / don't get high on your own supply and don't testify / You know the rules / don't testify / if you don't you live if you do you die."[73]

Argumentative realism has as its purpose a critique of social conditions through description. Most MCs engage in some sort of combination of descriptive and argumentative realism, being neither overwhelmingly concerned with argument nor neglecting it. Within the context of argumentative realism, one finds warnings about the dangers of illegal activity or mistreatment of others or oneself, or warnings to those entering the community without experience there. One also finds arguments in support of movements for social justice, and, on the other hand, justifications for illegal activity based on the limited options available to residents of industry-deprived urban centers.

Naturalism as a variation on realism appears when the allegorical exegesis provided by the MC makes conflict universal and essential. Mobb Deep, who I would call a naturalist group, refrain on one of their songs, "We livin' this till the day that we die / survival of the fittest, only the strong survive."[74] And on another song, listeners hear, "As time goes by / an eye for an eye / we in this together son / your beef is mine / as long as the sunshine will light up the sky / we in this together son / your beef is mine."[75] The essential terms are taken from social Darwinism and Old Testament justice, respectively. The allegorical exegesis offers a grim interpretation of life's elements, but the literal exegesis proves even grimmer: "There's a war going on outside no one is safe from / you could run but you can't hide forever / from these streets that we done took / you walkin' with your head down scared to look / . . . / My part of the town is similar to Vietnam."[76] The group describes a war zone in its community, and furthermore asserts itself as being "real" in terms of having been involved in violent conflict and the criminal justice system—as opposed to those who rhyme about it but do not really have the experience to back it up. Another Mobb Deep rhyme revealing the artists' authenticity runs:

> Sometimes I wish I had three different faces
> I'm going to court in three places for three cases
> One in Queens, Manhattan, one in Brooklyn
> They way things is lookin' Imma see Central bookings
> 'Cause facin' three three-to-nines is mad time
> After in concurrence for assault and two nines
> I gotta maintain cause stress on the brain
> Could lead to a motherfuckin' suicide thing
> Plus my probation, the ill violation
> How the fuck did I get in this tight situation?[77]

The language of the criminal law enforcement system interspersed with the anguished thoughts of a young man facing years in prison constitutes realism par excellence. The song provides a moving and captivating narrative and, according to the artists, a truthful one. It is notable that what has been chosen as the subject of the realist account is the very real problem of black male involvement with the criminal justice system. The speaker seeks to express his concerns and elicit a response and identification with the seemingly deterministic conditions of the lives of young black men. In an interlude between songs, one of the members of Mobb Deep talks about his authentic experience in the streets and critiques fake thugs, after which he has the following to say about yet another brand of MC: "And oh yeah, to all them rap-ass niggas with your half-ass rhymes / talkin' 'bout how much you get high, how much weed you smoke and that crazy space shit that don't even make no sense / don't ever speak to me when you see me / You know what I'm sayin? / Word! Imma have to get on some ol' high school shit and start punchin' niggas for livin / Yo, I'm finished what I had to say, y'all can continue on."[78]

By disparaging "that crazy space shit that don't even make no sense," he offers a naturalist critique of the exploration of esoteric, romantic, and otherworldly elements present in hip hop as something irrelevant, something not responsive to material concerns of black neighborhoods. But the kind of esoteric magical realism in hip hop is in fact a rather authentic reflection of an Afrocentrist, mysticist subculture in black urban centers. A brand of magical realism exists in hip hop in which the realities of daily life become interspersed with magical elements that, similar to metaphors, allow for the expression of depth or a sort of artistic and spiritual power, and also enrich the texts with an alternative aesthetic. Digable Planets, a group that appeared in the early 1990s as a sort of black alternative/Afrocentric Brooklyn trio, used insect identities and stratospheric references as symbolism for their spiritualist politics:

> Voodoo Eshu Benin
>
> Gangster lean
>
> Where I'm from
>
> It's interplanetary
>
> My insects movements vary . . .
>
> It's hip
>
> What's hip
>
> When hip is just the norm
>
> When planets pledge allegiance to the funk in all its forms
>
> The braids, the fades, the prints on all the shirts
>
> My grandmother told my mother "it's Africa at work."[79]

The first two lines tie African spiritual practices to the politics of the body: the gangster lean, black coolness seen in daily life in Brooklyn (voodoo being both a Haitian and Louisianian syncretic religion, Eshu being an orisha deity symbolic of the crossroads in the Yoruba pantheon, which is syncretized with Christianity, other African religions, and Native American religions). The populace represented as planets gives a sense of infinite and grand possibility, since space is infinite, yet the reference to oneself as an insect marks a stance of great humility as an individual in the world.

Magic realism was not limited to the heyday of short Nubian locks and mellow "conscious" MCs of the early 1990s; it has taken on a variety of forms. For example, Ice Cube's rhymes, "Gangstas Fairytale" and "Gangstas Fairytale Too" both frame real-life interactions with fantastic fairy tale characters in magic realist fashion. Although LL Cool J's "My Rhyme Ain't Done" is similar in that it blends a fictional world with the "real," it is different in that instead of placing fictional characters in a real world context as Ice Cube does, LL places his real self in a fictional world. And it becomes fantasy in the sense that fantasy, as Adorno says in *Aesthetic Theory*, presents the nonempirical as if it were empirical.[80] LL rhymes about his encounter with the 1950s sitcom characters from the Honeymooners:

> Ralph wanted me to bust a couple of rhymes
> But I had my eyes on Alice's behind
> Norton came down right about that time
> Lookin' in the fridge so we could wine and dine
> I said to myself I should give 'em a taste
> So I pulled the microphone out my black briefcase
> Said it ain't Bob Hope or Barry Manilow
> Then I borrowed Norton's hat 'cause I forgot my Kangol
> Ralph said I got a scheme, let me get to it, Norton my pal
> I said yo don't even do it, they were all Honeymooners and I met
> everyone, that story is over but my rhyme ain't done.[81]

LL metaphorically jumps into the television screen. He uses Ed Norton's signature cap as a replacement for his own signature terry-cloth Kangol, and he anticipates the disastrous consequences of Ralph's scheme, as all of Ralph's schemes would fall apart, consistently providing the audience with cringing amusement. This literary moment, then, is at once magical realist and comedic. Comedy, like magic realism takes, on a variety of manifestations in hip hop. Realism in hip hop, while fraught with difficulties and contradictions, is important for its introduction of contemporary social issues into American popular music with unprecedented consistency and for shifting attention from the love story to more difficult questions of culture and identity.

One of the things hip hop criticism should do, in addition to providing interesting and informative analyses of the art form, is to use the creativity and ideology contained within the music to enrich the ways we think about society and the ways we create contemporary theory. The knowledge such criticism provides should not merely influence our understanding of the art itself but also our intellectual processes in general. Realism encourages a critique of the media and reflects the significant realities of social inequality.

When the society in which you live scorns you,

you become the glorious outlaw.

—Brother Blue

4

The Glorious Outlaw

Hip Hop Narratives, American Law, and

the Court of Public Opinion

Brother Blue, a beloved elder in the greater Boston area, is a brilliant septuagenarian storyteller and poet. He wears blue and images of rainbows all over his body. Talking about hip hop, he provided me with the foregoing epigram, and I requested his permission to cite it because it so succinctly addresses the contentious relationship hip hop articulates between the urban poor and the rules of the society that has relegated them thusly.

Hip hop embraces the outlaw. Outlaw status is conferred only metaphorically through lawbreaking, but on a deeper, more symbolic level, it is achieved through a position of resistance to the confines of status quo existence.

> "Outlaw" means outside the purview of mainstream law, that is, outside of the law's regard and protection. The state of being on the out-

side is both a matter of fact—imposed by dominant legal discourse that silences, marginalizes and constructs black life as dangerous and deviant—and a matter of choice, in the sense that black communities often place themselves in deliberate opposition to mainstream cultural and legal norms when those norms ill serve such communities. "Outlaw culture" refers to a network of shared institutions, values and practices through which subordinated groups, elaborate an autonomous, oppositional consciousness.[1]

The outlawry present in hip hop is multifaceted. At times, it is literal, appearing in the personification of the outlaw or through outlaw values, but it is also present in the sense of opposition to norms that unfairly punish black communities or discount the complexity of choices faced by those black and poor in the United States, and it presents itself in the creation of alternative values, norms, and ideals in contrast to those embraced in American society. Moreover, outlawry may manifest itself as an individual assertion or as a collective sensibility, either in the form of an archetype (the "bad nigga," the thug, the roughneck, the convict) or in a celebration of outlaw community.

The outlaw, when personified in hip hop, often fits into what Cornel West has called the marginalist tradition of response to the conditions of African American life. He writes that "The Afro-American marginalist tradition promotes a self-image of both confinement and creativity, restriction and revolt. It encompasses a highly individualistic rebellion of Afro-Americans who are marginal to, or exist on the edges of, Afro-American culture and see little use in assimilating into the American mainstream. It expresses a critical disposition toward Afro-American culture and American society."[2] Similar musical stances in hip hop proffer not simply a disregard for the mainstream but a radical individualism. In his work, West goes on to assert that, "the marginalist response is important because it grapples with a personal torment endemic to modernity. This torment is an inevitable alienation and sense of revolt from one's racial group, society, and world, if felt only for a few moments."[3] The outlaw is a heroic figure even when he or she is marginalist, although it is rare for an outlaw to present a figure for emulation per se. In the African American folk tradition, the "bad nigga" emerged as heroic for flouting authority but was also considered a dangerous figure, both for and within the community. His or her sense of risk and aggression posed one form of danger, and the kind of desperation and depression found in other iterations of the marginalist tradition provide yet another. The considerations of giving up, of sinking into the mire rather than finding a higher ground, have always proven dangerous to African American consciousness. Writing about Biggie Small's first album, a critic argues, "Like Slick Rick, Big's form was a storytelling style replete with costars, characters created from his own alter ego. He contextualized the intergenerational schism created by the drug trade with songs like 'Things Done Changed.' Suicide was the album's metaphor for the widespread depression, despair, and hopelessness facing the kamikaze capitalists that New Yorkers simply dubbed hustlers."[4] On the one hand, the consciousness of the hustler or thug, the outlaw, provides insight into the psyches of a community rarely humanized in our society. But in a different fashion, the role of the drug dealer or hustler as an outlaw has also been used as a metaphor for a larger ethic of outlawry within hip hop. Robin Kelley writes of gangsta rap,

> Gang-bangin' itself has never even been a central theme in the music. Many of the violence lyrics are not intended literally. Rather they are boasting raps in which the imagery of gang bangin' is used metaphorically to challenge competitors on the mic. . . . When the imagery of crime and violence is not used metaphorically, exaggerated and invented boasts of criminal acts should be regarded as part of a larger set of signifying practices. . . . Growing out of a much older set of cultural practices, these masculinist narratives are essentially verbal duels over who is the baddest motherfucker around.[5]

The metaphor of the drug dealer both reflects an actual category of human existence and provides a symbolic means of articulating a kind of power within the hood, an overwhelmingly powerless context, and an exploitation of the power created by fear of the hood experienced by outsiders.[6]

The drug-dealing outlaw also has corollaries in mainstream American culture and media. The glamour of an international spy, a wealthy mobster, a double agent, finds its ghettoized face in the drug lord. But hip hop does not simply provide a mimicking space; it often carries a subversive message with it. The glamour of the high-rolling drug dealer is exploited for the sake of a counter-hegemonic space, an alternative power in the face of white supremacy and the panoptic surveillance of black bodies in ghettos.

The use of drugs, as well as drug dealing, are an outlaw practice frequently affirmed in hip hop: "Befitting the outlaw character of the hardcore rapper, ingesting huge amounts of legal and illegal substances amounts to a ghetto pass and a union card. Getting high is at once pleasurable and political: It heightens the joys to be found in thug life while blowing smoke rings around the constraints of the state."[7] In addition to metaphors of drug addiction, there is a plethora of references to drug use within hip hop, particularly used by the artists when it comes to drinking liquor (e.g., forty ounces of beer, Moët, Cristal, Alizé, and whatever the newest popular drink might be) and smoking marijuana. Tha Alkaholiks define themselves in their name, by addiction; however alcohol references generally describe recreation or set the mood of a piece. In contrast, marijuana—weed, izm, buddha, chronic, cess, joints, blunts, ls, js, and the numerous other names for it and the sort of cigarettes used to smoke it—has a wider range of contextual meanings. Lyrics about the act of smoking abound, even inspiring whole songs such as "Mad Izm" by Channel Live, or "How High" by Redman and Method Man.[8] In part, this attention reflects the notion that achieving a physical high allows one to attain a higher state of consciousness or spirituality, and also allows one to transcend the details of the mundane world that might otherwise burden the creative process. Channel Live rhymed: "Wake up in the morning got the yearnin' for herb / Which loosens up the nouns metaphors and verbs / And adjectives / Ain't it magic kid what I'm kickin' / multiflavored bags of cess for the pickin'."[9] The idea that drugs free up the creative process has been part of American artistic culture for a number of generations. Because marijuana does not cause a physiological addiction (although it can create a psychological one), it is seen as a relatively innocuous means of achieving that transcendent state. It is a drug that maintains a romantic air. Rick James's, "Mary Jane," which sounds like a love song for those ignorant of drug parlance, had his hip hop–soul match from balladeer D'Angelo, who sang to marijuana with the words of a lover, "Brown sugar baby, I gets high off your love, don't know how to behave."[10]

Within hip hop culture, smoking weed is often seen as a bonding activity. In "How High," Method Man says, as a sign of friendship, "If Red rolls the blunt I'm the second one to hit it."[11] Another marijuana reference that appears in hip hop is to the community created out of its use. KRS-One's humorous song "I'm Dreamin'" is a narrative fantasy about the personification of a blunt (marijuana rolled up in cigar paper), the hip hop drug of choice. KRS-One writes an extended metonymic metaphor in which he is the blunt, called "I Can't Wake Up." In it he raps, "I'm dreamin' / about bein' a blunt / I'm runnin' around and I just can't wake up."[12] As the process of rolling the blunt—slicing open the cigar, dumping out the tobacco—is described, the narrator, KRS-One, portrays himself as a comedic victim of violence: "I'm thinking this is major / I gotta bunch of people chasin' me with a razor."[13] The song becomes a long explanation of how, as a blunt, he is passed around a large group of rappers and DJs. He tailors his rhythmic personifications of them to their individual personalities and idiosyncrasies. It is comedic and yet it becomes a description of a sort of secular consubstantiation, where his sacrificial existence as a blunt nourishes the hip hop community.

The other compelling aspect of mild drug use as it is discussed in hip hop music is the cocky spurning of legality in the pursuit of relaxation and recreation. This sort of use takes place in the context of some other activities. For Snoop in "Gin and Juice," it is partying with his homey and some women they plan to have sex with. He rhymes the following about his first few hits: "Later on that day / My homey Dr. Dre came through with a gang 'a Tanqueray / And a fat ass J of some bubonic chronic that made me choke / Shit this ain't no joke / I had to back up off of it and sit my ass down / Tanqueray and chronic yeah I'm fucked up now."[14] But the concurrent recreation might be freestyling (Mother Superia refrains in "Most of All": "Most of all I like to freestyle every day / most of all I like the cess around my way")[15] and playing cards, dominoes, or computer games like Sega or Nintendo. These activities might seem like mundane relaxed trifles, but they also require faculties and skills. The ability to sustain computational strategic and motor dexterity despite intoxication presents a classic element of African American recreational practice (for those familiar with African American communities, recall the old folks playing bid whist and drinking in the kitchen at night). One might get loose, but one should also remain able to think well in that state. That stance of a somewhat arrogant brilliance forms part of the aesthetic and part of weed smoking in hip hop. A friend once told me that the key to understanding Bone Thugs-N-Harmony's incredibly fast, tongue-rolling lyrics was to get high; then everything would become clear because it was "high" music. The high is imagined as a physiological analog to the emotion of getting into the funky stuff in all of these diverse manners. The illegal activity, outside of social norms, actually is a space within, an alternative space behind the Du Boisian veil, and outside African American modes of social respectability as well.

The outlaw image appears in very obvious symbols and metaphors in the music, but it also exists on a more esoteric level in the intellectual world of hip hop. The name of the rap duo OutKast is brilliant for its concise articulation and celebration of life behind the Du Boisian veil. The ease with which African Americans can accept conspiracy theories as truth lends evidence to this distinct outcast epistemological framework. Given the inconsistency between the constitutional and symbolic meanings of Americanness and the experiences of African Americans, we are left with a healthy suspicion and curiosity. OutKast centralizes the position of Otherness as a site of privileged knowledge and potential. Similarly, the Fugees took their name from the word *refugee*, another take on outcast identity. The group, comprising two Haitian Americans and one African American, affirmed the position of the Other coming into the American nation impoverished and powerless in the way OutKast affirms the historical outcast position of African Americans. The Fugees subverted the image and position of the refugee as a powerless drain on resources into the source of brilliant insight and creativity, inspiring through diverse and hybrid musical productions. Both designations suggest the multiple borders of race, nation, and normative acculturations outside of which a rich black world exists and pose an alternative space, ethos, and set of rules with different norms.

Hip hop lyricists often refer to "the cipher," a conceptual space in which heightened consciousness exists. The cipher is a privileged outlaw space. Those inside the cipher are central, so it claims an insider rather than outsider consciousness. The best way to describe the term, one popularized by the Five Percent Nation, is that it indicates a mystical and transcendent yet human state, that it creates a vibe amid a community, as well as a spirit of artistic production or intellectual/spiritual discursive moments. A classic example would be the cipher created in a group of freestylers at the moment of their shared rhyming. Access to the cipher is denied to the ignorant or unenlightened. And the negative energy of one person might mess up the cipher. The etymological origin of the term—which as a noun is a sort of symbol and as a verb describes the ability to decode and encode—provides a good way of understanding the hip hop cipher, inside which one becomes part of a temporally bound and exclusive language. The assertion of an alternative ethos and subjectivity outside of mainstream norms often serves to provide a vastly different analysis of literal outlawry. In his book, *Negrophobia*, legal scholar Jody Armour describes the manner in which narrative determines ideas of consent or blame, arguing that the frame of the narrative, the length of the story told, might radically shift the way we analyze its elements.[16] I would argue that Armour's argument is quite applicable to hip hop. The narratives of gangsterism, drug dealing, and other violence often explain these practices with poverty, desperation, lack of educational opportunity, or a conflicted relationship to a father. This expands the narrative, shifting the interpretive paradigm of outlaw activity to a sociological analysis. Nelson George asserts that "gangsta rap (or reality rap or whatever descriptive phrase you like) is the direct by-product of the crack explosion. Unless you grasp that connection nothing else that happened in hip hop's journey to national scapegoat will make sense. This is not a chicken-or-the-egg riddle—first came crack rocks, then gangsta rap."[17] He goes on to argue, "There is an elemental nihilism in the most controversial crack-era hip hop that wasn't concocted by the rappers but reflects the mentality and fears of young Americans of every color and class living an exhausting, edgy existence, in and out of big cities."[18]

Armour discusses the extension of the time frame beyond the act in the law. In these cases, the time frame and state of mind are extensions of representations in court and on television news media. They often tell the story of their illegal activity as resulting from limited options, and they depict the slide into criminality. It is the very narrative that conservatives frequently resist being presented in court, and moreover it is the narrative that cannot appear in court. For laypersons court language and discourse is exclusive, and for all it prohibits free and nuanced verbal exchange. Courtroom language, even framed by defense attorneys, is not on the terms of the defendant. Black male rappers personify, or witness-personify, the narrative of the black male engaged in criminal activity who increasingly populates North American prisons, and that narrative is one of social marginalization and its concomitant psychological and emotional issues. Marginalization proves more complex, however, due to the exploitation and tricksterlike subversions so integral to black popular culture traditions. It would be simple if hip hop simply provided sociological analyses of black urbanity. However, numerous hip hop artists instead exploit the white fear of the black as-sailant as a source of power. In so doing, they mimic and adopt the very American construction of the black monster.

In *Location of Culture*, postcolonial theorist Homi Bhabha describes colonial mimicry of the colonizer by the colonized as a disruption of the conception of the colonizer's essential superiority.[19] It is not, Bhabha tells us, a Fanonian mask, but rather a complete becoming of that which is constructed as white. Individuals engaging in this form of mimicry in black America today would generally be considered sellouts. Yet hip hop engages in another form of mimicry, one which offers a social critique and a disruption of white supremacist authority. That would be "thug mimicry," a becoming of, a turning into, black American stereotypes. The figures of the brute, the thief, the drug dealer, the sloth, the pimp, and the prostitute are all present in hip hop music. Unlike Bhabha's mimicry, thug mimicry does not subvert notions of essentialist superi-ority by becoming indistinguishable from the oppressor; rather, it dis-locates the authority for defining the black underworld and manipulat-ing the negative images of black America in order to serve the interests of white America. The artist might mirror the stereotype of the black assailant or criminal effectively and subvert not in terms of critiquing the stereotype itself, but in terms of giving a voice to the stereotypical figure. This embodiment becomes an indictment of white supremacy when listeners hear, in the context of his or her narrative, a critique of the sociological conditions — poverty, police brutality, and joblessness — that contributed to his or her becoming this person. Here, thugs them-selves, rather than mainstream analysts, have the authority to explain their actions, and they generally do not attribute them to a deficient cul-ture or inherited racial flaws, but to hunger and lousy schools and tragic formative experiences.

Herman Gray has argued that "Dr. Dre, Too Short, Ice-T, Ice Cube, Tupac Shakur, Snoop Doggy Dogg, O Dog . . . and other rappers have used cinema and music video to appropriate this surveyed and policed space . . . to construct or reconstruct the image of black masculinity into one of hyper-blackness based on fear and dread."[20] Living in the strange location of recognizing stereotypes as a function of oppression and yet being socialized to identify oneself, or at least being unable to escape being identified by others, with such metaphors of blackness necessi-tates the creation of a space to decode them in order to find an identity that centered around oppression and Otherness. One potential way to decode lies in the conscious mimicry of stereotypes in such a way as to reveal them as false or at least not metonymically sound. Ice Cube repeatedly uses mimicry—both of black stereotypes and white supremacist voices—to challenge the authority of negative images of blackness. In his song "Guerrillas in tha Mist," he portrays himself and his then crew, the Lench Mob, as a sort of violent and brutal militia of which the world should beware.[21] By using *guerrilla* instead of *gorilla* in his title, he at once posits a subversion of the stereotyping of black people as simian and uses the notion of an animalistic black threat to support the theme of violent revolution. The gorillas are really guerrillas, and while white America fears the "gorillas" it created, they will be acting as guerrillas. This stance resembles Tupac Shakur's during his public brushes with the law that led to imprisonment, when he stated that America ate its babies, saying, to paraphrase, "whatever I am, you created me!" As Robin Kelley noted, "Officers who were part of the Gang Related Active Trafficker Suppression program were told to interrogate anyone who they suspect is a gang member, basing their assumptions on their dress or their use of gang hand signals." Opposition to this kind of marking, which in effect is a battle for the right to free expression and unfettered mobility in public spaces, has been a central subtheme in gangsta rap's discursive war of position against police repression."[22]

I do not want to suggest that thug-personifying realism originated more in the subversive mimicry of white supremacist images of black men than in the concerns of the black community itself. The crises of urbanity, most graphically depicted in crime, but also including health, work, education, and a host of other issues, weighs heavily on the minds of most African Americans; hence a fascination with the danger in our communities and its specific revelations. Critics often charge that hip hop glamorizes violence and other criminal activity. While it is true that some hip hop romanticizes violence or crime, far more of it explains it and makes a case for listeners to evaluate. Even the paranoid meanderings of a gang member expressed through a rapper often present a realistic expression of the psychological impact of being caught in an underworld web. Mimicry of Italian mafiosi, martial arts villains, and the like also challenge the discrepancy between how these figures are received, interpreted, and glorified in American culture and how black gangsterism is reviled.

In fact, narratives about the law, and narrative critiques of the law, within hip hop go hand in hand with the work of critical race, law, and literature scholars who appeal to narrative to critique legal institutions. Both scholars and hip hop artists employ and interpret discourses about being framed, about linguistic differences reflecting worldview differences, critiques of legal procedures, observations about the devaluation of black life in the criminal justice system. Sometimes a black rapper's voice will occupy that of a police officer or judge, thereby subverting the usual courtroom situation in which a white person's voice represents the black. The formalism of those vocal representations stands in sharp contrast to the nuances of the artists' voices and experiences, making for a powerful critique of the justice system's application to black life. Thug mimicry as I assert it through various means mitigates the image of the outlaw. Although it has some appeal to numerous advocates of the law and literature and critical studies movements, the argument that narrative might prove mitigating, or constitutes a powerful explanatory tool, also implicitly necessitates a victimized status.[23] To mitigate harms, one must have been the victim of harms, and sympathy must be elicited. Hip hop resists victimhood, preferring, much like the arm of the women's movement that engages in activism around sexual assault, the concept of the survivor.[24] Survivors do not define themselves by their victimization, instead fighting against it and examining the social practices that lead to such violence. What, then, does a hip hop voice have to offer to understandings of the criminal law if it replaces the victimized excuse of poverty and abuse to mitigate criminal acts with a survivor explanation?

I believe it provides an insightful and direct social critique, rather than individualized evaluation. It basically charges that as long as the United States allows children to be reared in poverty, with gross economic and social disparities, it will have individuals like these personifications to contend with. Society, hip hop proclaims, needs to wake up. American society's resistance to hearing that message signals its selfishness and/or laziness. Hip hop's claims challenge the ease with which pundits talk about freedom of choice, or offer up as examples all those poor people who do not become criminals (as though there ever existed a situation in which everyone in a given group responded in the same manner, and as though differences of response refuted societal pressure itself). Rap music provides not an evaluation of blame, but a sophisticated interpretive framework from which to consider racism on both socioeconomic and ideological levels.

Post-Moynihan Blues

> At the heart of the deterioration of the fabric of the Negro
> society is the deterioration of the Negro family. It is the funda-
> mental cause of the weakness of the Negro community. . . .
> In essence, the Negro community has been forced into a
> matriarchal structure, which, because it is so out of line with
> the rest of the American society, seriously retards
> the progress of the group as a whole.
> —Bill Moynihan

One dimension of hip hop outlawry is what I would term post-Moynihan blues. The social scientific evaluations of black people in the post–civil rights era, encased in liberal discourse, heralded an era that saw deficit models as progressive, inundating black people with images and arguments of our own pathological victimization—black women as welfare queens and black men as violent offenders. On some level, hip hop constitutes an extended engagement with these representations, their internalization in the self-conception of black communities, and the efforts to locate a humanistic, non–social scientific self in the midst of all that social science. It is alarming how many black people from various walks of life have accepted "culture-of-poverty" theories of the demise of the black family and notions of black sociopathy. Engagement with that identity takes place in hip hop, and it also fuels some of the critique of hip hop. Both sides of the fence are impacted by Moynihan constructs of debilitating black matriarchy and cultures of poverty, either using them as justifications that explain thug mimicry or using them to critique the community context out of which it emerges. All too often, neither perspective questions whether Moynihan provided a full or accurate depiction of the lives and culture of the black poor.

Of course, because hip hop is an art form complex to analyze, the real difficulty comes with what I would term the court of public opinion and the ethical evaluation of the art by said court. A number of prominent black figures such as Calvin Butts and neighborhood pundits either condemn or strongly critique the presence of violence, criminal activity, and the like in hip hop. There is, they say, the problem of representation. What does this art choose to say, they ask, and why does it translate to a life-performance art that gets rappers in trouble with the law? Why, they also ask, does an artist insist on living a ghetto thug narrative once he or she has money and access?

Most often, the given answer is that these artists are attempting to maintain street credibility or authenticity. While that may certainly hold true, I think there is more: The artist, in the effort to personify and testify, is in some sense trapped by that testimony. He or she becomes a target followed by police and put under scrutiny. To buckle into strait-laced respectability under such scrutiny might in fact seem like selling out the testimony. A parallel surveillance takes place here: the surveillance of the black superstar who speaks the emotion of the panoptic victim is analogous to the surveillance of communities. Yet even so, the question returns—why do many rappers do illegal things and/or rap about them?

The answer probably differs for each person, but certainly drug use and other kinds of illegal behavior (trashing hotels, beating women, etc.) are normalized in American fantasies and realities of rock star existence. The reason hip hop is more vulnerable to these accusations is not simple racism, although it is that too. (True to the old story of double standards, hip hop artists are not only not supposed to act like other rock stars; they are also under greater scrutiny because they are black artists performing black music.) In addition, however, the United States resists certain kinds of black wealth. Black wealth is supposed to have a respectable face. For black people to make it, they are supposed to fit into a white American comfort zone—charismatic entertainers to be paid for, or Bill Cosby–style professionals, or, even better, actually meretricious Colin Powell–style achievers. If successful black people fit none of these categories, much speculation arises as to how this "bad nigga" was "let in."

In hip hop, then, outlaw art finds appreciation. This occurs even in the realm of its definition as music. Rap breaks the rules as hip hop in general breaks rules in other forms of expressive culture (dress, dance, and visual arts). It has challenged the features that define musical composition and language, adhering to others. It claims neither instrumentality, nor harmony, nor complete originality; rather, it celebrates Call-Response and collage composition. It is not simply music in which outlawry is discussed; it is outlaw music. Whether one defines hip hop as art or not has a number of consequences, both in terms of cultural politics and of legal protection. When hip hop is not seen as an art form, it becomes deprived of the kind of First Amendment protection and consideration ascribed to art. Tricia Rose once described an encounter with a music professor who, unable to hear the musicality in rap, stated that there was none there. Yet she argues that musical forebears from whom rappers sample should be compensated by those who use their work, although she does not locate the primary blame for the theft with rappers, but rather with the record companies who exploited the original artists. I think the two observations are related. If the sample sincerely forms part of a new artistic formation, why should the copyright hold? Sampling lies at the heart of whether or not hip hop constitutes art because it implies a conversation about what makes for artistic creation. As a legal academic, I assert that the legal standard for copyright violation of music has been too rigid when it comes to hip hop. In those cases in which the rap is simply placed over another song's instrumental, a copyright violation has obviously taken place; the music of another has been used for rapper's profit. But in the case of a smaller splice, which acquires distinct meaning in the context of three or four or ten other samples, the outcome constitutes a new composition. As Rose herself argues, "Redefining the constitution of narrative originality, composition, and collective memory, rap artists challenge institutional apparatuses that define property, technological innovation, and authorship."[25]

The question of whether hip hop should be categorized as art in the long term will, of course, prove relevant for First Amendment claims and critiques. The status of art protects colloquial vulgarities against obscenity claims. To the extent that we know that what becomes classified as obscene and what as art remains quite subjective, race, or racially identified artistic forms, as suspect categories should form part of the analysis. The charges of obscenity and copyright violation are philosophically connected because the underlying question remains whether hip hop is allowed to occupy the cultural territory of art, and thereby of freedom of expression and of original production. Nelson George writes, "It was only when progressive groups such as PE and De La Soul began expanding beyond black music for samples that the form truly

attracted negative attention."[26] The response to law and to the legal definition of protected music has been to avoid the law.

As a critic has noted, "By 1992 legal precedents had changed the playing field to such a point that classics like *3 Feet High and Rising*, *Paul's
Boutique*, and *It Takes a Nation of Millions to Hold Us Back* would have
been impossibly expensive to make if every sample were paid for. On the
West Coast, Dr. Dre found a way around the legal restrictions by recording his own version of a song—called an 'interpolation'—thus paying
royalties to the composer but not the record label that released the original version."[27] She continues, "Today's sharpest producers—Premier,
RZA, Timbaland, Organized Noize—have avoided both excessive royalty
payments and the monotony of overused samples by building tracks out
of minute, unrecognizable bits of recorded music."[28] The musical pieces
used have shifted without disfigurement of the compositional aesthetic,
again challenging the conceptions of ownership and originality. From
the outlaw to the obscene, the location of hip hop with respect to ideas
of legality are often reducible, on some level, to notions of respectability
and MCs' refusal to appeal to it. Critique of hip hop has often come about
in the context of a moral panic. By this I do not simply mean the panic
created by news broadcasts of murderers who claim to have been motivated by Tupac, but the dispersed panic of citizens confronted by hip
hop's texts and arguments. This moral panic has been used to justify the
failures of the legal and economic order to protect black men in particular. Tricia Rose writes,

> Rev. Calvin Butts' bulldozing of hundreds of rap CDs to protest violence
> and misogyny in rap and an endless stream of hearings in the House
> and Senate are not taking place in a political vacuum. They are orbit-
> ing around the frenzy of crime legislation intent on accelerating the
> construction of more prisons, longer sentences for juveniles, and per-
> manent incarceration after three so-called 'strikes.' . . . Hip-hop cul-
> ture and rap music have become cultural emblems for America's young
> black city kids, only a small percentage of whom participate in street
> crimes. The more public opinion, political leaders, and policymakers
> criminalize hip-hop as the cultural example of a criminal way of think-
> ing, the more imaginary black monsters will surface.[29]

An entrenched black leadership has also employed the moral panic as
a means of challenging the authority of hip hop as a voice of black

America. In the process of panicked discussion, these "leaders" offer themselves up as alternatives and as agents of power, roles they believe result from their monitoring and condemnation of the music from within the black community. This proves particularly important in the context of black young people's lack of civic involvement in institutions outside of the church because black political leadership is destabilizing its own role among a population that largely fails to vote. Black critics of hip hop engage in self-authenticating rituals, establishing themselves as knowers ready to challenge the authority of hip hop's voice. But the black political establishment, as respected and recognized by the mainstream, generally fails to possess the kind of outlaw consciousness that appears to appeal to many young black audiences with counter-hegemonic ideas, if only as a critique of narrative middle-class white ethics, economic inequalities, and legal disparities. The black social and political leadership would do well to be imaginative with the ideas of outlawry expressed in hip hop and to explore them on a philosophical level in order to understand how to engage young black people in civic institutions.

5

B-Boys, Players, and Preachers

Reading Masculinity

It was the summer of 1999, on a subway platform in New York City. I cannot remember how the conversation began, but it seemed innocent enough at first. He was young, dreadlocked, in a baggy, charcoal gray jean suit. He spoke in the blended language of hip hop and the Five Percent Nation. He said something disparaging about gay people and God. I told him I disagreed with his heterosexism. The friendly conversation momentarily turned sour as he accused me first of lesbianism, and then of being a devil. He called me filthy in a particularly misogynistic way. He told me I was a failure as a black woman and that the fact that my friend was African (she arrived in the middle of the conversation) did not grant me any authenticity. He then told me that I, being a devil, failed to see him. He spoke assertively, artistically, and hurtfully, weaving language to terrible conclusions. It was a bizarre moment, and yet I understood so many of the signifiers—"you can't see me," and "devil," and the preaching cadence with which he addressed me, and his rage at my disagreement. It was a strange moment because I thought, even as he spewed venom at me, that he was strangely working out a gender identity, and doing so in the cultural landscape I inhabited as well—the language and style of hip hop. This young man was part of hip hop as much as the hip hop artist, a feminist man, who shared his plate of food with me and discussed the literariness of the lyrics he composed during a conference, as much as the hip hop artist who invited me backstage after a show and introduced me to the women MCs in his crew when I told him I was interested in writing about gender and hip hop, and as much as the young men with whom I used to roam around the city reciting lyrics, sometimes freestyling, being the woman in the crew. After all the times I had seen hip hop provide the occasion for bonding and expression among the young men in my world, and after all the times I had received an invitation to enter into that world, in the horrible moment on the subway platform I also witnessed an ugly side of hip hop masculinity, in which a young man dictated, interpreted, and condemned me in an instant, with oratorical incisiveness.

Gender in hip hop proves complicated terrain, filled with the pitfalls of what Michael Eric Dyson has termed "femiphobia."[1] And yet it also constitutes a powerful location for asserting the particularity of black male identity. Hip hop is masculine music. In this chapter, I discuss masculinity in hip hop as a version of black urban masculinity, complicated by the American exploitation of black male identity and fraught with sexist troping. I argue that masculinity in hip hop reflects the desire to assert black male subjectivity, and that it sometimes does so at the expense of black female subjectivity and by subjugating women's bodies, while at other times it simply reveals the complexity of black male identity.

In recent years, various scholars have noted that gender, race, and class are not autonomous or even merely intersecting categories. Instead, these identities continually and mutually construct each other, becoming interdependently defined. In Evelyn Brooks Higginbotham's article "African American Women's History and the Metalanguage of Race,"[2] she argues that the overdetermination of race in the United States makes gender itself a racial construct. Historically, black emotiveness was translated into a description of the black "race" as a "female" among races, and the ritualized humiliation of black bodies during the enslavement and Jim Crow eras sexualized racial politics in the United

States irrevocably. Throughout the history of African American art and politics, the creation of a gendered space, free from the manipulation of whites, has always proven central to the project of pursuing black liberation. That gendered space, regardless of its at times internally troubled history, has often functioned as a resistant narrative to white supremacy.

As the term *patriarchy* has been adopted for the discussion of sexual politics in the black community, it has become glaringly apparent that it neglects many historical and current realities about class, social power, economic market places, the prison industrial complex, and trauma. I want to excise the assumption of patriarchy from this discussion of black masculinity. The *white male patriarch* describes a powerful and resonant social role. The black male patriarch, where he exists, lives a fragile existence, mediated by his own encounters with white male patriarchy. I want to clarify here that I am not making an argument for or on behalf of a matriarchal black culture. Nor am I making assertions about family structure and intersectionality, or participating in the always fruitless competition about who suffers more oppression, black men or women. Rather, I am looking at black male identity in a given genre, born of particular gender experiences intersecting but not in union with those of white men. In so doing, I attempt to free myself from a term that I believe adds more confusion than clarity. Darrell Dawsey writes the following about the image of black men in *Living to Tell about It: Young Black Men in America Speak Their Piece*: "To be sure we have been the topic of intense debate and discussion in America, by both Blacks and whites. Our humanity has been stripped, restored, attacked, defended, impugned and explained in literature more often than we'd like to recall. We have been hyped and stereotyped, valorized and demonized."[3] Black men as gendered and racial beings occupy a specific, constructed and oppressed role in society, one from which they must be liberated with a sophisticated political understanding of the grounds of their oppression.

Recognizing that black men experience gendered oppression does not render sexist practice on the part of black men irrelevant or forgivable. Black women's experiences, and analysis of our experiences, conducted through profound feminist/womanist scholarship has more than revealed the importance of interrogating black male sexism. Rather, recognizing the gendered/racial oppression of black men demands that we consider black male gender politics in relation to their gender oppression alongside traditional conceptions of masculine privilege. This marks a call for greater intellectual and political complexity in the spirit of Patricia Hill Collins's notion of the matrices of domination that can make us simultaneously oppressed and oppressor, given the various layers of our identities and of the positions we hold in society.[4]

The consumption of black male bodies has proven a popular feature of North American culture. If one thinks of the athlete, the thug, the kinetic entertainer, the idea of inherent physical ability and intellectual inability, and the hypersexual threat, there emerges an obsession with and the observation, parody, and mutilation of black male bodies. Contemporary pornographic obsessions with the size of black male genitalia show us that an earlier era's paranoid fixation on black male sexuality and the fear of black humanity—which manifested itself in, among other things, the lynch victim's castration and the stuffing of his genitals into his mouth—lie only a bit beneath the surface at the beginning of the twenty-first century (and let us not forget the murder of James Byrd here). The consumption of black male bodies constitutes a gender-based oppression because representations come as two-dimensional images, on the basis of which society at large is encouraged to evaluate all black men. Objectified, catalogued, and exploited, their full humanity is masked. Discussions of black male patriarchy or sexism should therefore always first consider the intersectionality of blackness and masculinity, as these discussions may otherwise easily fall into determinative pejoratives building on the gendered oppression of black men.

In the late twentieth century, the poster boys for sexism, sexual depravity, and misogyny in American popular culture were disproportionately black and male (think Mike Tyson, O. J. Simpson, Michael Jackson, and Clarence Thomas). This was the case even though the mainstream feminist movement is overwhelmingly comprised of white women sexually partnered with white men. Displacement of the average white male perpetrator with the black male symbol allows for the effort to dismantle one form of oppression to be manipulated to fuel another. As President Clinton's sexual scandal emerged in the media, he underwent a "blackening"; suddenly black support for and identification with Clinton became a media fascination in ways it never had before, despite the fact that over the course of his presidency he had already nominated more African Americans to office than any other president. Hence, his relationship with black individuals was nothing new. On the other hand, the disservices to the black poor wreaked by his domestic policies call into serious question any ideological identification between him and the black community. His blackening at this moment was telling for its implication of some contagious black-sanctioned immorality.

From the fear of black male sexuality—highlighted by the sensational appeal of talk shows depicting white women abused at the hands of black male lovers after the Simpson trial—to the commodification of the black male athlete's body ("If I could be like Mike") to the beating death of a black man and the depiction of black male sexuality as depraved— casually inserted into the racist 1995 film *Kids* (dir. Larry Clark)—this history of black male objectification is reinscribed into American con- sciousness daily. Cultural critic bell hooks has written: "The black body has always received attention within the framework of white supremacy, as racist/sexist iconography has been deployed to perpetuate notions of innate biological inferiority. Against this cultural backdrop, every move- ment for black liberation in this society, whether reformist or radical, has had to formulate a counter-hegemonic discourse of the body to effec- tively resist white supremacy."[5] She further recalls that "when I first began to study feminist theory, I was always puzzled by the scholarship around, 'women and nature,' which would talk in universalizing gener- alizations about patriarchy equating the female being with the body and the male with the mind, because I was so acutely conscious of the way in which black males have always been seen as more body than mind."[6] Hooks talks about how black men are subject to patriarchal objectifica- tion through white male gaze, and thereby become feminized. She ar- gues that black men have fought back by embracing hypermasculinity. Ed Guerrero notes that American society receives two images of black masculinity through the media: "One the one hand, we are treated to the grand celebrity spectacle of black male athletes, movie stars, and pop entertainers doing what all celebrities are promoted as doing best, that is, conspicuously enjoying the wealth and privilege that fuel the ordinary citizen's material fantasies."[7] By contrast, as the alternative image, "we are also subjected to the real-time devastation, slaughter, and body count of a steady stream of faceless black males on the 6 and 11 o'clock news."[8]

Hip hop marries these two images into one unified picture of the black male superstar and thug. It does not choose to reject the negative and embrace the positive, but attempts to engage both in all their difficulty through the performative process. Hooks has written that the performative space for African Americans has been "a place where we have claimed subjugated knowledge and historical memory. Along with this, it has also been a space of transgression where new identities and radicalized black subjectivities emerge, illuminating our place in history in ways that challenge and interrogate, that highlight the shifting nature of black experience. African American performance has been a site for the imagination of future possibilities."[9] In hip hop, we see the political, imaginary, and historical reckoning that hooks asserts as part of the African American performative tradition, and thus masculinity in hip hop is both about political possibility and a reality tempered by social conditioning. The black male rapper teases out the contradictions and complexities of his existence in the public conversation that is the music. Definitive conclusions are few, but stimulating observations and responses are many. Yet this does not constitute a new engagement with complex race and gender politics for black men, as Herman Gray has noted:

> Self-representations of black masculinity in the United States are historically constructed by and against dominant (and dominating) discourses of masculinity and race, specifically (whiteness). For example, the black jazz men of the 1950s and 1960s, notably Miles Davis and Coltrane, are particularly emblematic of the complex social relations (race, class, sexual) and cultural politics surrounding the self-construction and representation of the black masculine in the public sphere. As modern innovators in musical aesthetics, cultural vision, and personal style, these men challenged dominant cultural assumptions about masculinity and whiteness.[10]

The movement from objectification to subject status happens on various levels in hip hop. The already discussed self-assertion that occurs in the vocal text is primary, but the visual symbolism of dress and body decoration is another, and the objectification of women's bodies yet another. Hypermasculinity in this moment marks one way of challenging a sense of race and gender powerlessness.

The Visual

Unlike other celebrities who generally adorn themselves with haute couture or other forms of ostentation to signify their fame, rappers have often worn what other young black young wear: Timberland boots, baggy jeans, Tommy Hilfiger shirts and coats, hockey jerseys, athletic attire, and the like. They are unconstricting and colorful clothes that fit into an aesthetic of comfort and brilliance. The black male body that finds itself under constant public scrutiny, from police searches to the professional basketball court, is hidden by the broad and vibrant shapes created by loose clothing. Lyrics that invoke an empowering invisibility constitute verbal corollaries of these body politics. Channel Live rhymes: "Just rotating lyrical rhythms / . . . You can't see we're intellectuals / Your shallow mentality you just starvin' / I'm rollin' in on 'em like Calvin Butts up in Harlem."[11] And Keith Murray rhymes, "I channel my anger from the double-edged banger / And turn into the microphone strangler / Stop tryin' to see what your eyes can't follow / Say goodnight to the world and goodbye to tomorrow."[12] Lines about invisibility are prevalent in hip hop. They assert the power of the unknown, the mystic forces of the Invisible Man, as well as an intellectual depth that eludes challengers in the tradition of the Platonian shadow gazers, or, in the understanding of the Five Percent Nation, of those 85 percent of the population that is "deaf, dumb, and blind." But perhaps most important in terms of aesthetics, you can't get with what you can't see; you can't become a part of this or that MC's style, he tells the challenger, because he's just too fly.

When MCs and DJs dress in the way brothers in the hood dress, they participate in African American youth conceptions of beauty, an accessible and collective beauty. When I walk down the street and see groups of young black men and women, with uniforms of jeans, boots, down jackets, and patterned color variations, I am reminded of photographs of African fabric design, of groups of people garbed in what we have been socialized to see as wearable art. Hip hop dress is both art and politics because it constitutes an antiestablishment aesthetics of the casual, an antiobjectified aesthetic of the abstract, as opposed to the revealed body. In writing of Tupac's body as a representative body as well as a martyred, Michael Eric Dyson uses these words: "I will narrate your lives through my chaotic, desperate, self-destructive public life. And when I die, it will be to immortalize the similar deaths of anonymous black males whose names will never scar the tissue of public attention."[13]

Method Man creeps from behind a brick wall with half of his braided hair undone and sticking in various directions, his eyes crossed and his mouth open. Ol' Dirty Bastard brings his mouth crowded with gold teeth inches from the camera for a disturbing close-up in his videos. Coolio penetratingly stares with his signature hair standing on end and his lined black eyes unmoving. Whether comedic or horrific, the MC who makes efforts at looking bizarre or less than attractive constitutes an interesting feature of hip hop body politics. When MCs make themselves ugly instead of pursuing the more democratic beauty I referred to earlier, they identify with the collective yet call attention to their differentiation with ugliness. In the 1980s, rappers such as Flava Flav from Public Enemy and Biz Markie used ugliness for comedic purposes, but for later MCs, ugliness is neither limited to comedy nor to horror. It also proves defiant. The MC who makes himself ugly may be accomplished despite Hollywood standards of prettiness.

In contrast to the textual adornment of Tupac's body, MCs such as Ja Rule and LL have occasionally used upper body nudity in shows and music videos. This trend is growing and it appears that the nudity is often a marketing device for constructing the artist as a sex symbol. To the extent tht such images could be seen as objectifying, that potential is undercut by the MCs imagined sexual control of women's bodies on stage, in lyrics, and in music videos.

White Men

The assertion of black male subjectivity achieves its most problematic manifestation over the bodies of women. In order to understand this phenomenon, we must first think about black masculinity in relation to white masculinity. It is, in fact, a sense of powerlessness in the face of white masculinity, and the fear of being pimped at the hands of wealthy white recording moguls, that guides the hypermasculinist moment, and the heterosexist moment as racial anxiety is articulated through a patriarchal cultural lens when the fear of being "bitched" finds artistic expression.

Donald Trump, Bill Gates, and Bill Clinton, white men who have played the game successfully, are often appreciated in depoliticized form as role models for street players in hip hop. Envy of white males prevails, even alongside assertions of white male sexual or social inferiority. Thus a tension exists in the relationship to white masculinity.

And then of course there is the issue of the white male consumer. Ellis Cashmore argues that the consumer of hip hop has codified this most popular music as the music that best plays into racist white fantasies:

Rap may sound like liberal whites' worst nightmare: stories of violent, misogynist black men willing to resist the forces of law and order even if it means their own physical annihilation. But it was also a dream. And the commercial success tells us more about the larger reality in which rap was received than about the people who produced it.

Think of the representation of black males in rap: aggressive and minatory; exactly the qualities imputed to brute niggers in colonial days.[14]

In the article "Gangsta Rap in the '90s," the author writes, "Bored suburban white kids fiending for a taste of the fast life are constantly fed the idea that non-white youth lead far more exciting lives due to their high-risk social status as 'endangered species.'"[15]

It is certainly true that a part of rap's appeal derives from it playing into racist fantasies of black existence, and that the market supports the kind of music that easily fits into notions of black experience. Yet it is not the case that this necessarily neutralizes the importance of the black male hip hop artist's subjective self-rendering. Nelson George makes an analogy between hip hop and the battle royal, but the fundamental difference lies in that the battles only engage the body, not the intellect or vocabulary, both of which are necessarily present in hip hop.[16] The self-defined articulation of existence differs from the plantation brute or the "bad nigga" of plantation lore. There is a difference between hip hop and the nightly news, and that is that hip hop is written by black men instead of white. One might respond that Bert Williams, although a brilliant comedian, played into white stereotypes, not unlike hip hop artists. Yet here is the difference: Violent rage is an understandable although generally not wise reaction to the conditions of the ghetto. Its articulation by black agents, even though playing into racist fantasies, is instructive. Social marginalization often leads to an insensitivity to the concerns of other groups and even other members of one's own group. Understanding this, our witness of black violence and misogyny should provoke analysis and alarm more than offense.

Moreover, the prevalence of black male violence should not be constructed as a sign of black men's brutishness, but of the brutality of American racism and class inequality. My critique therefore rejects a politics of respectability with regard to hip hop that implicitly says, "look at how white people are seeing us," or, "look at how this facilitates racism," because there is no need to facilitate it. Even when the vast majority of our public representation showed the clean-cut, straitlaced

African American, the image of the black brute did not disappear. Also, in hip hop, the double voice resides in the fact that this character who is so easily cast into white night terror fantasies, also says something complex about his psychology, emotions, and life. One wonders if a white male listener hears it. Perhaps some do and others do not, but certainly the fact that the music taps into suburban teenagers feelings' of frustration, rage, social isolation—an individualized and modest parallel to the feelings of black men created by the social conditions in which African Americans live—indicates that the conversation with young white men is more complicated than cynics generally think. And as George argues, "The romance of the outlaw mystique of drugs and dealing is not foreign to young people—another reason why gangsta records, supposedly so distant from the white teen experience, are in fact quite familiar. Even the urban context of the records is not as mysterious or exotic, as commentators assert, since many suburban dealers and addicts use urban 'hoods as drive through windows."[17] The question is whether the use of hip hop will remain purely selfish or will translate to a generation of whites who as adults will have a politics that addresses the frustration of broader social marginalization experienced by African Americans. It is possible that the music will simply be responsive to self-reflexive concerns, for it is clear that the attraction to hip hop is in part a response to the desire for culture which motivates white suburban consumers who believe they lack culture due to the normativity of whiteness in the United States. They long for rituals, rules, and codes, which they hope to purchase at the local mall in the rap section.

But the white male consumer and record company producer retains a position of power over black male subjectivity that has a complicated sexual politics. George Cunningham talks about significant events of the civil rights movement and of the eighties, referring to the Charles Stuart case, Tawana Brawley, and others, developing an analysis of a "triangle of desire between black men, white men and women." He writes,

> The triangle positions black men and white men as adversaries in a contest over the body of women. This triangular structuring of relationships is similar, often behaves like, and can often be read as Sigmund Freud's oedipal triangle, René Girard's triangle of mimetic desire, and Eve Sedgwick's triangle of homosocial desire. . . . Focusing on a triangulation as a configurative site of the relationship of racial and gendered bodies to each other provides a way of thinking and talking about the

simultaneity of race and gender that traditional binary logics do not afford.[18]

He continues, "In Oedipus . . . inappropriate desires (for the mother or father) are located in the child who must enter into the family and society by sacrificing those desires to the law of the father. In a similar movement, the oedipalized vision of contemporary triangles of desire locates aberrant desires in the white male others, white and black women and black men. The white male becomes the innocent and offers the only possibility of reconstituting social order."[19] White male "fathering" continues to take place in the economic landscape of hip hop, a reality of which artists are painfully aware and which, I would argue, animates and fuels a hypermasculinist gender identity in response. The white male consumer, who accounts for the greatest consumption of hip hop today, not only exploits, fuels, and exemplifies the social conditions leading to hypermasculinity in hip hop in the sense that record companies encourage images from artists that are appealing to consumers, but he also exists as a voyeur to the sexual politics between black men and women as they are presented in hip hop. Black male hip hop artists do not simply assert power over women's bodies in a kind of effort to create imaginative patriarchy; they also use black women as a kind of commodity expression of wealth and sexual power in the face of racialized economic powerlessness.

Black Women

Tension exists within the black community about black feminist discourse, not only because of the sensitive and profound gender issues it considers and challenges but also because of black male and female anxiety that black female critics will indirectly support black men's unnamed gender oppression. Hip hop has been called misogynistic music yet for the aforementioned reasons, many lovers of hip hop resist this. At times, it is difficult to distinguish between those accusations of sexism in hip hop that are meaningful and insightful and those that simply emerge to engage the gender/racial oppression of black men. Michael Eric Dyson has developed a compelling analysis of the gender politics in hip hop, coining the term *femiphobia*. He writes: "Femiphobia has become a crucial aspect of the culture of signification in rap that influences the lyrics of hip-hop artists, measures authentic rap—and hence, male—identity, specifies a pervasive machismo, and forges masculine bonds within the culture."[20] It is a terrible quandary to feel that in order to liberate one gender in the community, the other has to suffer further oppression, a quandary presented both for those primarily concerned with black women and those primarily concerned with black men. For a number of years, I hesitated to discuss the problematic images of women present within hip hop because of my own resentment of the ways in which hip hop was scapegoated by an entire national culture that supports exploitative and destructive images of women, and also because of my protective inclinations toward black men and black music. I figured enough had already been written and spoken about misogyny in hip hop. I have come to understand that in order to discuss masculinity in hip hop thoroughly, one must acknowledge the problematic nature of the "bitches and hoes" phenomenon, and yet avoid reducing the music's masculinity to that, or to a kind of depravity of which such misogyny is one example. In fact hip hop presents us with a complex masculinity.

Hip hop as a genre has received a great deal of criticism for misogynist lyrics and sexist representations of women, particularly in music videos. Too often, hip hop portrays women as gold diggers seeking only to take advantage of men, as disease carriers and self-hating, hypersexualized animals who shake their stuff for the camera, and as symbols of capitalist acquisition. Biggie Smalls rhymes, "Bitches I like 'em brainless / guns I like 'em stainless steel / I'm worth a fuckin' fortune like the wheel,"[21] locating the completely objectified "brainless" female body as one of the possessions symbolic of his identity as a "badman." Snoop Doggy Dogg's infamous "We don't love them hoes" suggests a disdainful objectification of the female body. The roles of the mack, pimp, or player with regard to the female body all emerge out of the African American badman tradition. The badman is an outlaw, challenging a societal order antithetical to the expression of African American humanity. He is a rebel to society, living on the margins of a black community that at once regards him as a hero and a threat. Jack Johnson, the great black boxer who frightened white America into a search for a great white hope, was perhaps the first media-established black American badman, notorious for gross expenditures of money, (white) womanizing, and general irreverence. In this way, he was a forerunner to contemporary hip hop images.

The tradition of the badman, taken from the folktales of Stagolee and Shine, and transposed onto popular media forms, continued into the blaxploitation-era films and their protagonists Superfly, the Mack, and Dolomite (who was an oral culture hero before he was a media culture hero) and further. These films, in addition to white mafia epic gangster films, shape the badman image of today's hip hop celebrities, who borrow from and identify with the badman tradition. West Coast MCS draw particularly strongly on 1970s badman figures. The badman uses the female body as an object of his sexual prowess, as a geography on which to graft the territory of his badness. The construction of the badman is related to the historical white male authority's hypersexualization of the African American man as an excuse for abusing him and as a means of attempting to destroy an alternative human masculinity in society. Nelson George writes: "In a warped and unhealthy way the pimp's ability to control his environment (i.e., his stable of women) has always been viewed as an example of black male authority over his domain. Despite decades of moral censure from church leaders and those incensed by his exploitation of women, the pimp endures as an antihero among young black males."[22] The badman plays on all of white America's fears about the "big black dick" and, most frighteningly (for the mainstream), is imagined as individually triumphant in the battle with white America rather than as falling victim to lynching or castration. The badman does not remain within the realms of acceptable black behavior established through community norms, but he is heroic by virtue of his very lawlessness in a society where law has often proven the definitive sign of African American inequity, either by means of legal or judicial injustice.

To speak about gender relationships in hip hop is to speak about identity formation in the hip hop narrative. As I said before, hip hop as an art form is gendered male, despite the presence of some excellent female artists. And because, like race, gender is a category shaped through opposition, women prove fundamental to constructions of masculinity in hip hop. Regardless of its location within a folk tradition, the sexism in hip hop has been roundly critiqued, and yet the very existence of this critique constitutes a central feature of the badman tradition since his is a social role construed as antithetical to being a "credit to his race" in any way.

In addition to misogynist and heterosexist discourses employed for the sake of asserting a kind of hypermasculinity contradicting the sense of powerlessness experienced by black men in relation to white men, one finds other kinds of hypermasculinist symbolisms.

Metonyms of Manhood

The chorus of the Lost Boys' first single goes,

To the Jeeps
The Lex, coupés the Beamers and the Benz
To all of my ladies and my mens
And all of my people in the pens
Keep your head up
And to the hood
East Coast, West Coast worldwide
Ain't nothin wrong with puffin' on lai
And if you wit me let me hear you say right.[23]

The cars, the penitentiary, the blunt, and the struggle, all stand in as metonyms for hip hop heads that appear in these lines. They represent signature features of the community. In "Nappy Heads" by the Fugees, hair is metonymic, as are street origins and/or gang affiliations in Cypress Hill's "Throw Your Set in the Air," which riffs on the old-school chant, "Just throw your hands in the air / and wave 'em like you just don't care / and if you're ready to rock with us tonight / somebody say oh yeah."[24] The metonym created by the individual MC represents the collective and signifies identity. As Marcellus Blount and George Cunningham write in the introduction to *Representing Black Men*, "The stabilizing of the gendered male self and the reconstruction of the true black man are among the defining obsessions of contemporary racial discourse."[25] Metonyms that stand in for the experiences of black men, such as the penitentiary or the "set," and the political positioning of the MC in response to the larger social order, through signs of "ugliness" or the blunt, for example, as an illegal and hence counterauthoritarian symbol, constitute gestures of black masculinity under construction and in definition in US society. The conflict of Americanness as the site of both possibility and despair, divided along white/black racial lines, always courses through this defining and constructing process. In "Where Ya At Y'all," the Million Man March song one of the MCS rhymes,

> Damn, that's how you know the world about to end
> Rain, hail snow earthquakes and a million black men
> Up under God indivisible, with liberty and justice for all
> Cause y'all the mate is miserable
> With this American Nightmare
> That's why October 16 we gon be right there
> Like yeah
> The same Niggas that you want gone
> Gon be about a million deep
> On your front lawn.[26]

He invests the historically hypocritical pledge of allegiance with his faith and demands the execution of its promises. He teases American society for its construction of the frightening black man and sees the march as a subversion of that stereotype, intended to oppress, making it into a construct that gives power to a political and social demand for justice with the power of numbers and intimidation.

Emcees also play out a number of archetypal roles, and although certainly not all MCS take on one, they present an interesting variety of black male self-construction. There is, of course, the gangster, an identity perfected on the West Coast and drawn from the real-life gang battles over economic control of drug markets in communities from Los Angeles to Seattle. His ruthless survivalism and violence make him at once a powerful and tragic figure. The more polished role-playing of gangsterism is found in hip hop appropriations of mob styles seen in Hollywood movies such as the *Godfather* trilogy (dir. Francis Ford Coppola) or *Scarface* (dir. Brian De Palma). In "Friend or Foe," Jay-Z takes on a mafia role with the following lines: "Friend or foe / yo state your biz / Ya tend to dough, ah there it is / Me? I run the show / and these kids don't like nobody comin' around here fuckin' with the dough and shit."[27] He acts out the suave intimidation of the mobster, as well as his business control: "Let me guess they said it was money around here / and the rest is me stoppin' you from gettin' it, correct? / Sorry to hear that / My guess is you got work at the hotel / I take care of that."[28] That cornering power, and the polite threat so often glamorized by Hollywood, are invoked as well: "You're twitchin' / don't do that, you're makin' me nervous / My crew well they do pack, them niggas is murderous / So please will you put your hand back in sight / They don't like to see me nervous / You can understand that right?"[29] Intensely macho codes of membership and silk suits together add a kind of rugged sophistication to impulses similar to those given in more realistic depictions of gangsterism. The dealer surfaces as the gangster's humbler brother, often involved in criminal activities simply as a means of getting by, and often caught in a moral crisis or articulating pedagogic tales about the urban wasteland.

Besides members of the mob, the Asian martial artist appears as the other film-inspired character fixation in hip hop. His combination of discipline, dexterity, excellence, mysterious tradition, and improvisational fighting ability seduces MCs and listeners because of hip hop culture's love of improvisation, difficulty, and the kind of expertise that makes the difficult appear smooth and easy.

While the East Coast has few self-proclaimed gangsters, it does have hustlers (as does the Southeast). The hustler distinguishes himself from the gangster in large part because he fights no war based on affiliation, but also because he maintains the trickster mentality of overcoming, albeit illegally, the limitations set by social class. He embraces the ethos of an underdog getting over. Texas MC Scarface refrains, "All I ever wanted to do in my life was be a hustler."[30]

Related to the hustler is the player or pimp, whose power lies in both the acquisition of wealth and female bodies. His power is based on an interactive dynamic in which the player holds control through both his will and manipulation of the bodies and resources of others. As a student of mine once astutely pointed out, many critics of hip hop fail to distinguish between the sexism of a pimp identity and that of the lover. The lover is a seductive male MC who uses his skills to become a Casanova, rather than to commodify or exploit women's bodies. He is smooth rather than manipulative, although the distinction is fine.

And then there is the scholar/intellectual. Emcees with this persona cherish vocabulary and sophisticated rhyming, and they tout the life of the mind. They are not limited to the college-educated among the MCs, but they all (sometimes arrogantly) pursue a higher knowledge that will enable them to educate their listeners. Notable MCs who fit into this category include Common, the members of De La Soul, Mos Def,

Talib Kweli, A Tribe Called Quest, and Guru, in whose work the political power of hip hop is imagined to be exercised through intellectual social change. All of these archetypes mentioned represent images of manhood, and they achieve meaning through how they model certain relationships to the world. For example, the following lyrics from Mos Def:

> The body of my text possess extra strength
> Power-liftin' powerless up, out of this towerin' inferno
> My ink so hot it burn through the journal
> I'm blacker than midnight on Broadway and Myrtle
> Hip hop passed all your tall social hurdles.[31]

Relationships between men in hip hop, both hostile and warm, have often been seen as manifestations of hypermasculinity. That loving relationships between peers overwhelmingly appear between men and not across gender lines is frequently described as an expression of sexism. While I agree that much of hip hop composition discourages the softness of romantic sensitivity, I also understand the accentuation of friendship between men in hip hop as a liberatory move that increases assertions of black male humanity, complexity, and subjectivity, particularly in a social context in which black men are consistently depicted as in violent conflict or competition with one another in virtually every other public context. Critics like Nelson George have argued for the existence of a kind of homoeroticism in hip hop, which he connects to imprisonment and femiphobia. While his arguments prove compelling I fear they may encourage us to reduce black male intimacy to misogyny, criminality, or pathology, and do so in a manner that entails a latent homophobia. Discourses on the importance black male friendship have been present through much of African American history and in black language. When I was coming of age, the terminology used was *my man* or *my main man*. More recently, in the world of hip hop, it has been *partner*, *boy*, or *homey*, to name a few examples. Black male loving friendship constitutes a profound feature of hip hop. KRS-One continues to pay tribute to the memory of his partner in early days, Scott La Rock, years after his murder, describing their relationship as one of shared breath and spirit. Heavy D. dedicated his album *Peaceful Journey* to one of his dancers who died in a tragic accident.[32] Puffy's mourning of Biggie's death was visceral. A ride through black communities throughout the United States will reveal numerous murals, often tributes to slain friends. In death, but in life as well, one's boys, one's crew, are celebrated. In "The Warning," Biggie Smalls's friend warns him about an impending robbery of his house. In the course of the lyrics, during which he finds out about the plan, he demonstrates the idea of the love that his "nigga" has for him.

> Who the fuck is this
> Pagin' me at five forty-six in the mornin'
> Crack of dawnin'
> Yawnin'
> Wipe the cold out my eye
> Who's this pagin me and why . . .
> It's My Nigga Pop from the barber shop
> Told me he was in the gamblin' spot
> Heard the intricate plot . . .
>
> Pop: You know them Niggas up in Brownsville that you rolled dice with,
>   smoked blunts and got nice with?
>
> Biggie: Yeah my Nigga Fame up in Prospect
> Naw them my Niggas nah
> Love wouldn't disrespect
>
> Pop: I didn't say them
> They schooled me to some Niggas that you knew from back when
> When you was clockin' minor figures.[33]

Even as the song develops into vengeful violence, the strength of friendship emerges powerfully. In the midst of the violence and decadence often present in hip hop, love still surfaces. In fact, it is usually the crew that protects one from absolute vulnerability and isolation. There is a great deal of discussion about the violent forces in hip hop, but what about the countervailing forces of love?

The ultimate in black male friendship in hip hop has to a large extent been the person who is willing to die for his boy. In the years of the drug-related violence that penetrated black communities across the United States, the image of someone who could be trusted, and who would be on one's side regardless, of course emerged as a powerful one. There-fore the relationship between friendship and violence, while perhaps disturbing, is also rational given the economic landscape of the commu-nities out of which hip hop grew. Friendship in hip hop presents one of the features of the celebration of the everyman in the culture. To be per-ceived at once as an exceptional talent, a celebrity, and the black every-man emerging from the hood where countless similar brothers dwell, is the goal of the "real" or "true" hip hop artist. I put these terms in quotes here because they indicate a linguistic and ideological distinction be-tween artists who derive their authenticity from an organic attachment to and approval from young black American hip hop heads and those created by stylists, packaged to appeal to the mainstream, and motivated purely by profit.

In "Whutcha Want," Nine tells of his life's desires: professional excel-lence, an overflowing quantity of ammunition for protection and style, a community, and fame.

> What you want Nine?
> Phat beats for my rhymes
> What you want Nine?
> Mad clips for my nines
> What you want Nine
> An ill posse
> And my name up in lights
> N.I.N.E.[34]

As he rhymes in the video—hair dreadlocked, jeans cut fully, and sitting in a Jeep—he represents every black American male, dreaming the black American dream. This is not the collective dream of liberation and jus-tice, but the individual dream that one's life situation (relative financial stability and physical mobility) might allow one to transcend the most brutal aspects of American racism while maintaining a holistic black identity, a dream that in popular culture often seems limited to those celebrities who simultaneously use their blackness as a commodity and as an in-your-face defiance in the tradition of the black popular culture historical giant Richard Pryor, or the less illustrious turn-of-the-century celebrities Charles Barkley or Dennis Rodman. This figure depends on but is not of capitalist America. Biggie Smalls rhymes,

Remember rappin' Duke

Da ha Da ha

You never thought that hip hop would take it this far

Now I'm in the limelight 'cause I rhyme tight

Time to get paid

Blow up like the World Trade

Born sinner

The opposite of a winner

'Member when I used to eat sardines for dinner.[35]

Biggie Smalls, in a seize-the-day gesture, acknowledges his surprise at the development of a broad appeal for hip hop, while at the same time he comfortably asserts his place at the center of the action. He analogizes his own transformation from what in the American social order constitutes a "loser" to a celebrity with the transformation of hip hop from parody (like the song of the rappin' Duke) to its current stature. And yet his frequent use of rhymes depicting his life before he "blew up," indicate that his success remained fundamentally tied to maintaining that former identity. In a similar spirit, Lord Finesse rhymes, "a Top Cat that rocks rap from the part of the Boogie Down Bronx where the cabs don't stop at."[36] Emcees in the African American tradition understand success as tied to a self-awareness and honesty about identity and position—in this case as a person emerging from a poor black context.

Part of the seduction of rap for mainstream America, particularly white young people, lies in its iconoclasm in relation to white American cultural norms. It is Other, it is hard, and it is deviant. On the other hand, black listeners of hip hop, in a gesture revealing an anxiety about the increased commercialism of rap and a strong identification with the art form as their own, demand that hip hop music be "Real" and remain true to the experiences of black America. In "How High," Redman rhymes, "Fuck the Billboard / I'm a bullet on my block."[37] These complex factors create the black everyman in the rap celebrity. Using individual fame as a vehicle, the duality of the black everyman and fame contests the general American objectification of black male representation by generating a broad black male subjectivity through the voice of the MC.

In "Get Down," Craig Mack rhymes,

Imma reign

Reign forever

Rain like bad weather

Reign like whoever never

A brand new sheriff that's in town

Gettin' down

Leavin' bodies buried in the ground.[38]

Using the homophone *reign/rain*, he puts a multiplicity of meanings in the oral space of his self-identification. His "royalty" indicates wealth and inherited importance. Yet he also proves elemental and powerful like rain from the heavens. Rain as an image is both ordinary and holy because it defies human control, gives life, and yet forms an integral part of everyday existence. Craig Mack, in the concluding triplet, comes into the music community from a position of authority, as a sheriff, and through the strength of his groove, defeating all challengers. Physical politics again prove important to understanding this song's dualities: Craig Mack is a plain man, dressed smartly but unexceptionally, with an afro and sneakers. His gesture of power that enthuses audiences with his prowess is a lifting of the arms and the growled exclamation "Ahh." He is average and amazing at once.

The duality of the black everyman/rap star is, of course, in large part born of the reality that many MCs morph from being regular brothers in the hood into celebrities. Through excellence and personal narrative, they wish to represent for the people and environment they call home, but they also want to provide a more general story of black urban youth in the United States. Moreover, they recognize that regardless of their growing fame and fortunes, they still cannot escape the vicissitudes of American racism.

In his song "Illegal Search," LL Cool J rhymes about the police harassment of young black men who have any sort of material luxury: "What the hell are you searching for / can't a young brother make money anymore?"[39] He does not distinguish himself as a celebrity, but he uses his celebrity status, by making the song, to depict the experience of "brothers," including himself, assumed to be criminals for being black, young, and materially advantaged. This particular example highlights the counterintuitive social interpretation of black American existence prevalent throughout US history. Just as nineteenth-century black women who stayed at home instead of working elsewhere were seen as loafers, whereas white women were expected to stay at home as an expression of their femininity, black people with material advantages are constructed as criminal or undeserving (drug dealers or bene-ficiaries of affirmative action, take your pick), while white folks and immigrants who achieve financial success are hailed as heroes of the American dream. Media depictions of the black poor focus on laziness, hypersexuality, and a manipulative nature, while the white poor are pri-marily depicted as stupid and the Asian immigrant poor as suffering noble victims. These differences may serve as another example of the way in which American systemic rules fundamentally dislocate black folks from identification with larger social mythologies about financial success and morality.

In Bone Thugs-N-Harmony's hit, "First of Tha Month," they rhyme about high drug sales on the day that welfare checks come out, the first of each month. The refrain goes, "Wake up wake up wake up wake up wake up / It's the first of the month / So get up get up get up get up / So cash your checks and get up."[40] They then rhyme,

> Double up nigga, what you need?
>
> We got weed
>
> To get P.O.D.ed
>
> Fiend for the green leaves
>
> It's the first for sure better lay low
>
> Cause the po-po creep when they roll so
>
> If you can't get away
>
> Better toss that llello
>
> Keep your bankroll
>
> Yeah, we havin' a celebration
>
> Lov' to stay high
>
> And you better believe when it's time to grind
>
> I'm down for mine
>
> Crime after crime
>
> Finda creep to the pad 'cause mom's got the grub on the grill
>
> If we act a fool ooh
>
> You know it's the first of the month and—
>
> My nigga we chills for real.[41]

There is a tragic mundanity in the way the group describes the great profits to be reaped from welfare recipients called to wake up only to fulfill drug yearnings. Similar tragedy adheres to the ironically gentle community image of young men gathering to the back of a mother's yard to excitedly eat barbecue—only a phrase after referring to the obligation to retaliate for a beloved's murder. We can see the crushing arms of capitalism and poverty intruding into the loving space of community as the voiceless, drug-abusing zombies are lured into becoming profit potential for a group of young men. The black male MC who identifies with the hood, the dealer, or the gang member in part recognizes the futility of identification with any mainstream constructions of success unless he is willing to risk "exceptional Negro syndrome," whereby he becomes deracialized until his next misstep, and so he embraces a sort of black market code of success within the capitalist framework.

Identification with the black everyman by discussing the underground ghetto economy as capitalist activity proves subversive, but it still remains trapped within the problematic framework of the destruction that capitalism produces in black communities. In a supremely anticapitalist gesture, however, rappers also identify with the black everyman through historical reflection. Such reflection appears in both the discussion of racial/national history and of personal history. KRS-One raps,

> Overseer, Overseer, Ove'see Ov'se' Office Officer
> Yeah Officer from Overseer
> You need a little clarity
> Check the similarity
> The overseer rolls around the plantation
> The officer is out patrollin' all the nation
> The overseer has the right to get ill
> And if you fought back the overseer had the right to kill
> The officer has the right to arrest
> And if you fight back he'll put a hole in your chest
> They both ride horses
> After four hundred years I got no choices
> The police them 'ave a lickle gun[42]
> So when I'm on the street I walk around with a bigger one.[43]

When he says, "After four hundred years I got no choices," the artist identifies himself as a representative figure of all black people from enslavement to the present who have suffered policing by a corrupt white authority. He becomes, in effect, black history through collective memory and demonstrates desperation and anger at remaining oppressed across centuries through the metaphor of his big gun.

In "Where Ya At Y'all," the hip hop anthem for the Million Man March comprised of a medley of different rappers' voices, DA Smart's rhyme begins:

> Somebody stole me
>
> You took me from Kunta to Toby
>
> And mold me
>
> In a way that you free me
>
> But still hold me
>
> What you tryin' to pull eatin' us like cannibals?
>
> Whatever happened to that forty acres and that animal?
>
> Now you tryin' to use integration just to fool us
>
> Like Malcolm said we been hoodwinked and bamboozled
>
> Mama cryin'
>
> And I ain't lyin'
>
> I'm goin' to Washington for justice and get it
>
> Or die tryin'.[44]

The rapper describes himself as Kunta Kinte, the popular primordial African American since the production of Alex Haley's *Roots* as a television series in the 1970s. Kunta is tortured into claiming the European name Toby that will be a signature of his transformation from free African to enslaved African American. DA Smart obviously recognizes the historical gap between enslavement and the present, but he asserts the continuation of an abusive conditioning that enslaves African Americans. The body of the MC becomes the space for other bodies to manifest, much in the way African American women's fiction has given voice to the grandmothers who had no public voice.

Personal histories allow for the emergence of the black everyman as well. Narratives of growing up are common in hip hop, and they often use aspects of popular culture, food, games, and mother talk as signifiers for a black American childhood experience. When the MC recalls a youthful existence, the listener will feel part of that existence filled with sounds, clothes, and culture *if* he or she is a full member of the hip hop nation. So the collective of performers and audience grows back together, undifferentiated, marking a blurring between the performer/audience relationship in which the performer merely evokes emotion and represents the audience. Biggie Smalls gives a personal history through the sounds of his environs, parents, and streets and mixes them with songs: Curtis Mayfield's "Superfly" at his birth, The Audio Two's "Top Billin'" (a hip hop classic) at adolescence, and Snoop Doggy Dogg's rhyming voice as he emerges from prison about to make his watershed move to becoming an MC. Many West Coast rappers, like Snoop Doggy Dogg, participate in a perpetual historical reflection by sampling heavily from 1970s funk music which represents the consciousness and rhythms of the formative years of many MCs and DJs. Biggie Smalls also raps the following about his childhood: "It was all a dream / I used to read Word Up! magazine / Salt-N-Pepa and Heavy D. up in the limousine / Hangin' pictures on the wall / Every Saturday "Rap Attack" / Mr. Magic, Marley Marl."[45] And Crazy Drayz of Das EFX rhymes, "I still be gettin' chills when Niggas play 'The Bridge Is Over.' "[46] The memory Crazy Drayz recalls is not of the battle but of the energy of hip hop as a young, emergent art form. And the community of listeners he is addressing, the hip hop nation, remembers the song with a collective emotion. When that song comes on at parties full of black Generation Xers, heads start to nod, hands go in the air, and mouths recite lyrics.

In "Can You BE BLACK and Look at This? Reading the Rodney King Videos," Elizabeth Alexander writes,

> In these anti-essentialist, post-identity discursive times, I nonetheless believe there is a place for a bottom line, and the bottom line here argues that different groups possess sometimes subconscious collective memories which are frequently forged and maintained through a storytelling tradition, however difficult that may be to pin down, as well as through individual experience. When a black man can be set on fire amidst racial epithets in the street because he inhabits a black body, as recently occurred in Florida, there must be a place for theorizing black bodily experiences into the larger discourse of identity politics.[47]

The historical everyman in hip hop exists in such a theoretical space, a space that recognizes collective memory, as well as the power of racial body politics, by occupying the space of a range of black bodies, a shared yet individualized expression of consciousness. The everyman in hip hop is most dramatically signified on a literary level by the use of the word *nigga*. It centralizes black masculinity as the face of humanity.

Nigga and Niggerettes?

> Like a palimpsest, the word is a tissue of interpretations,
> but many of them male-chauvinist and bigoted. Language is the
> experience, the sight (broad or blind) of others formed into word.
> If blue can embody royalty, cold, sadness, infinity, the celestial, black
> music, tranquility, and a score of other meanings simultaneously,
> it is because blue in its fullness is a common property, like an old
> Baptist church, layer upon layer of sense that opens onto the
> antithetical vision and perspectives of our predecessors.
> —Albert Murray, *The Blue Devils of Nada*

The word *nigga* is in some ways an extension of the idea of the black everyman, and it has become a public word in hip hop. While it is still racialized, it is now used interchangeably with *man*, therefore operating to centralize the black male experience. However, *nigga* is not synonymous with *black* because the former signifies a racial category *combined with* white supremacy, poverty, and social marginalization. As Robin D. G. Kelley writes, "Nigga is not merely another word for black. Products of the postindustrial ghetto, the characters in gangsta rap constantly remind listeners that they are still second-class citizens—'niggaz'— whose collective lived experiences suggest that nothing has changed for them as opposed to the black middle class."[48] It is a masculinist word. Niggas are men, and even though the word sometimes describes people generally, is the referent remains a masculine subject. It is also a word around which friendship and intimacy become constructed. As Nelson George asserts, the phrase "'you my nigga' becomes a way of bonding around a term that was historically used by whites to degrade blacks. Thus it deprives racist whites of the prerogative of naming blacks in harmful ways, since blacks have adapted it to their culture in playful or at least signifying fashion."[49]

There is nothing new about the use of the word *nigga* in this way *within* the black community. What is new is that as hip hop has become very public music, the word is constantly uttered in the presence of white people. There is no private space to distinguish between the nigga in the black linguistic world and the nigga in the white. Black adults and/or pundits who critique hip hop often talk about how the use of the word belies a historical ignorance, and signals a failure to understand its power to hurt. And they do not understand why rap artists use it, but the real question they are asking is why rappers use it in the public space of recorded music. It would be disingenuous to act as though young people were not learning the use of the word from older generations. The alarmed response is reasonable because as the word becomes public, it crosses a frightening boundary. First, it becomes ubiquitous, "It's downright infectious. Like olives, nigger leaves a sour taste in your mouth, but once you acquire a tolerance, it has a distinctive saltiness you begin to crave."[50] And then it validates the term in the imagination of nonblack audiences, "By exploiting the fear and freedom associated with this word, rappers Eazy-E, Ice Cube, Dr. Dre, MC Ren, and DJ Yella realized they could capitalize on America's secret fascination with its own pathology."[51] *Nigga*, in its loud articulation, has presented a large space of social discomfort, a line in the sand which the artists continually ask their listeners to cross, enticing and challenging. It marks a provocative irreverence with potentially large but unknowable consequences. It is tricksterism par excellence.

When women actually do enter loving or collegial spaces within hip hop, that is, women other than mothers and grandmothers, who are traditionally venerated in African American culture (Eminem provides a noteworthy exception to this general rule),[52] it is as they enter the space of black male friendship, or becoming niggas. In "All I Need," Method Man shares his space in a profound romantic and friendship-based love. He rhymes,

> I realize you didn't have to fuck with me
> But you did
> Now I'm goin' all out kid
> And I got mad love to give
> You my Nigga.
> You're all I need.[53]

"You my nigga" or "my nigga" are phrases indicating black male-male loving friendship. As Dawsey writes, "To call a friend "ya nigga" is a sure sign of respect and love."[54] In an untrustworthy world, where black-on-black violence has created anxious interactions between black men, the phrase means trust and a profound expression of intimacy. By calling his woman "my nigga," Method Man opens a space for her in his heart where gendered conflicts and abusive constructions of women do not exist. He removes the gender politics by momentarily positioning her in this male space, and yet she is not masculinized. She is explained as, described as, and considered a woman. Through the song, he assumes the traditional male role of providing financial security, "I'ma walk these dogs so we can live / in a phat ass crib with thousands of kids"; however, given the popular characterization of black men as absent from the home and as irresponsible, and the reality of many black families as single female–headed households, his assertion of this position does not serve as an example of sexist construction, but rather as one of committed responsibility.

But Method Man also rhymes:

> Instead of having hoes suck my dick up
> I used to do stickups
> 'Cause hoes is irritatin' like the hiccups
> Excuse me
> Blood just flows through me
> Like trees to branches
> Cliffs to avalanches
> It's the preying mantis
> Deep like the mind of Farrakhan
> A motherfuckin' rap phenomenon.[55]

While here he makes his rejection of women due to an objectifying annoyance in the context of a fluid naturalism, in another song he asserts one of the most gender-liberated positions in hip hop history. Method Man is locked in a hybrid discourse about gender that debates ideology and praxis through the transformative process of coming to a "position." However, because hip hop is so concerned with the nuances of debate, settled positions on issues are not so normalized for there to exist any urgency for MCs to reach them. The community merely requires some engagement with the primary issues.

Returning to Method Man's "All I Need," a duet with R & B vocalist Mary J. Blige and a riff on the Marvin Gaye/Tammi Terrell hit, he rhymes, "Shorty I'm there for you any time you need me / Me and you girl in our world, believe me."[56] The relevance of these lines is that the world is construed as a shared space in which the man is imagined as the woman's emotional support. Both of these assertions offer transformative moves. The precedents to this song can be found in other hip hop male/female duets, two of which were made by Ice Cube and Yo Yo. In their first duet, "It's a Man's World," Yo Yo responds to Ice Cube's invocation of James Brown's classic "This is a Man's World thank you very much" with "But it wouldn't be a damn thing without a woman's touch."[57] The woman enters the sphere of relevance by adding a touch to the male space. Although it may be an essential one, it still remains only a touch. "It's a Man's World" begins as a verbal joust between a man and woman over whose verbal skills are better, and it concludes with mutual affirmation and admiration. While many of the duets are "love narratives" all the way through, the space for that love to emerge has been, and often continues to be, an explicitly sexual space, or a (completely) traditionally male space, as we see in the "bad couples" situation. Mobb Deep's CD jacket for *The Infamous* includes shout-outs to their "Niggas and Niggerettes," and coed groups like the Fugees and the Digable Planets, or crews like Junior M.A.F.I.A. or the Ruff Ryders, each of which have one female member, demonstrate that contexts do exist in which women share the same subjective spaces as men. This shared subjectivity to some degree deflects the Othering of a generalized female body through which much of the misogyny in hip hop lyrics emerges. When the Lady of Rage rhymes, "I rocks rough and stuff with my Afro puffs," a male voice responds, "Rock on with your bad self." She then says, "I am the roughest, roughest, roughest / I am the toughest, toughest, toughest,"[58] and the response to her call is male affirmation: "Yeah." This supportive testimony to her ferocity puts her "down" with the "fellas" as a subjective, powerful personality.

Such opening up of gendered space to create camaraderie is related to and perhaps constitutes a progression from the partners in crime or bad couple songs. As Greg Tate writes, "In modern music, only hip hop portrays the combative nature of male-female psychodrama with as much cruelty, clarity and hilarity as classic blues."[59] Such hilarity and discourse of cruelty extend to the relationships partners in crime take to the world. In Ice Cube and Yo Yo's second duet, "The Bonnie and Clyde Theme," in which they emerge as cohustlers, the refrain goes, "Got me a down girl on my team / the Bonnie and Clyde Theme / Yeah Got me a down ass Nigga on my team / the Bonnie and Clyde theme."[60] Biggie Smalls rhymes in "Me and My Bitch," a song dedicated to his former hustling partner and lover, that he prefers a partner who can run like a badman such as himself: "I want a bitch that like to play cilo and crack / Packin' gats in a coach bag / Scheming dime bags." He describes the intimacy between himself and the woman on whom the narrative focuses, "We lie together / cry together / I swear I hope we fuckin' die together," as well as her role in his criminal activities, "She help me plan out my robberies on my enemies." Finally, he describes the heartbreak he feels when she dies, letting her occupy the space in hood narratives generally reserved for one's boy or (male) nigga (à la Ricky in the movie *Boyz 'N the Hood* or O-Dawg in the movie *Menace II Society*, and countless young black men in nonfictionalized communities across the United States): "It didn't take long before the tears start / I saw my bitch dead with the gunshot to the heart / And I know it was meant for me / I guess them Niggas felt they had to kill the closest one to me / And when I find them their life is to an end / They killed my best friend."[61]

Apache, several years previous to this song, also expressed a rarely described intimacy with a female lover and partner in his song "Gangsta Bitch," at the end of which he admits, "When my bitch died I lost my best friend."[62] However, even when such intimacy exists, it simultaneously moves toward codifying gender stereotypes in partner songs. An example can be found in the duet "Ain't No Nigga," a riff on the soul classic "Ain't no Woman."

> Foxy Brown: Ain't no nigga like the one I got
>
> Jay-Z: No one can fuck you better
>
> Foxy Brown: He sleeps around but he gives me a lot
>
> Jay-Z: Keep you in diamonds and leather
>
> Jay-Z: Ain't no stoppin' this, no lie. Promise to stay monogamous, I try. But love you know these hoes be makin' me weak. Y'all know how it goes so I stay deep.
>
> Foxy Brown: What up boo, just keep me laced in the illest snakes
>
> Bankrolls and shit
>
> Back rubs in the French tub

Mackinest bitch, wifey Nigga

So when you flip that coke

'Member them days you was dead broke

But now you stylin' I raised you

Basically made you

Into a don flippin' weight, hero'n and shit.[63]

In this song, ruthless materialism and a polygamous union's "first-wife" consciousness forgive infidelity, attributed to lascivious "hoes" rather than to a less-than-ideal partner. The classic soul song "Ain't No Woman" has been referenced, the construction of relationships now reconfigured from heartfelt and antimaterialistic, albeit vaguely sexist (in that the man is the center of the relationship), romance to a relationship based on the erotics of capital, bartering, and bargaining.

And yet, there are also hip hop pieces in the tradition of soul or R & B love songs. "I Need Love" by LL Cool J signaled a landmark moment of tenderness, as did "One Love" by Whodini, both released in the mid-1980s.[64] The Poor Righteous Teachers' "Shakiyla" sounded like a Five Percenter version of a 1950s doo-wop song, dedicated to a particular woman's appeal and grace. The Lyrics of "Brown Skin Lady" by Black Star, affirmed the beauty of a brown-skinned black woman, as opposed to the music video prioritization of straight hair and light complexions.

I don't get many compliments but I am confident

Used to have a complex about getting too complex

You got me willin' to try

Look me in the eye

My head is still in the sky since you walked on by

I'm feelin' high

Got my imagination flickerin' like hot flames is how it seems

You make me want to ride a Coltrane to a love supreme

My brown lady creates environments for happy brown babies

I know it sounds it crazy but your skin's an inspiration for cocoa butter

You provoke a brother we should get to know one other

I discover when I bring you through my people say true

All I can say is all praise due, I thank God for a beauty like you.[65]

And so despite the viciousness of "crabs and bitches" talk, there are also tender and loving moments in hip hop. Likewise, despite the hyper-masculinity often used as a form of subjectification for black men in hip hop, there also exists another important masculinist moment in the music which provides dramatic descriptions of the psychic-artistic space of black manhood, one that does not do so over the bodies of others. This space of masculinist articulation is present in the use of religious imagery.

Religious Imagery

In a patriarchal society, God is imagined as male. But the complexity of Christ stems from his dual roles: he is sacrificial lamb and vulnerable martyr and yet also an all-powerful being; he takes on the role of the re-viled, threatened, and murdered, and yet he also comes as a savior. The use of Christian, Islamic, and other religious imagery in hip hop offers a nuanced exploration of the vulnerability of black masculinity. In particular, the presence of the Five Percent Nation in hip hop and in hip hop lyrics, a religion in which black masculinity is regarded as divine and even godly, signals the spiritual fixation on masculine identity. In the words of William Eric Perkins, "Islamic rappers bring to hip hop a powerful sense of recovering and reinventing history, packaging it as 'science' for the visual generation. Invoking much of the eclectic and popular science of the Nation of Islam, its various factions, and the re-surgence led by Minister Louis Farrakhan, they represent a submerged voice of the black rap underground."[66] To the extent that hip hop is both art and culture, the ideology proves significant enough in the creation of hip hop music to compel an inquiry into the question of spirituality as it is tied to ideology.

The Nation of Islam, and particularly the Five Percent Nation, holds the most apparent influence in explicitly religio-political lyrics, particularly from groups like Brand Nubian or the Poor Righteous Teachers. The Five Percent Nation splintered off from the Nation of Islam under the teachings of Clarence X, believing that 10 percent of the population are evil, 85 percent are the "deaf, dumb, and blind" (meaning unaware), and that the remaining 5 percent have true enlightenment. Numerology and mysticism shape the specific face of the religion. The Five Percenters also believe in the divinity of each man, referring to men as gods, and women as earths (to symbolize their fertility). Their positions are rhetorically stylized, and the appeal for hip hop artists and audiences probably in the populist identification of divinity with the everyman, thus adding a spiritual dimension to the democratic ethos of hip hop and tapping into the importance of symbolic language for hip hop heads. Also, the religion's self-identification as a black form of spirituality resonates with hip hop. The following lyrics may serve as an example of the way in which the language of the Five Percent Nation has become integrated into rhymes:

> You wanna be me but can't see with a telescope
> You seek and search but still you can't find
> You're weak and it hurts to be deaf dumb and blind
> A supreme mind will take you out of your paralysis
> I grip the mic so tight I get calluses
> And your analysis is that the Lord whips rhymes into shape with
>   a mic cord
> I do it good 'cause I'm a positive black man
> Eatin' up suckers as if I was Pacman
> Not a dapper dan fan I stay casual
> To rock like the J it comes gradual
> You gotta know the rest are lies and dumb
> And understand the culture of freedom
> Power equally with the Gods
> So you can build and form your cipher
> All your life you must teach truth
> of the true and living God not a mystery spook
> And when you do that pursue that goal which makes student enroll
> and only then you'll prosper.[67]

Through lyrics, Five Percenters hope to enlighten their listeners with the truth of their message, and to encourage self-knowledge. The sentence "You can't see me" is put forth in Five Percent terms as an assertion of the listener's ignorance or "blindness," but it also transforms the black "invisible man" into a powerful personage in society. And it also articulates yet another dimension of the self-conscious incomprehensibility or difficulty within hip hop; multiple tiers of understanding and subtextual discourse hide in some of the music, and they only reveal themselves to those who know where and how to look.

Although the political dimension of Christianity in hip hop is less apparent, the impact of Christianity on some MCs proves interesting. In 1999, Mase proclaimed that he was giving up hip hop because of his Christianity. And scandal ensued over a Nas video in which he and Puffy both appeared crucified. Apparently Puffy's minister counseled him that this image was an immoral self-depiction, so that the artist requested his participation in the crucifixion scene to be removed, although the original version aired accidentally, much to Puffy's chagrin. The rest of the story has degenerated into gossip, but the relevant point here is that one can point to two examples of church ideology coming into conflict with the performance choices of entertainers. So-called Christian rap maintains the morality and messages of black Protestant church communities. Its success has proven slow, although Kirk Franklin, a modern gospel singer, has incorporated a number of popular music elements, including hip hop, into gospel music in exciting ways. However, the reverse, putting gospel into hip hop, has been very difficult, perhaps because of the idea of reunion I discussed in the introduction. Yet this does not mean to suggest that Christianity fails to have a presence in hip hop. It does, in fact, have a sophisticated and complex face, as it would, given that the majority of African Americans adhere to Christianity and that the faith constitutes a central site of black musical development. The Christian church courses through most African American cultural spaces. References to Christian imagery, to salvation, resurrection, transfiguration, and apocalypse all appear within hip hop. Emcees have at numerous times represented themselves as Christ-like figures. This is art as politics, because it locates the status of savior in the minds and bodies of young black people. Like Five Percenter theology, this stance celebrates the divinity of the individual and revitalizes the notion of people as part of the body of Christ, while at the same time using the power of the image for self-aggrandizement and mysticism.

> You better believe Khrist is nice
> Kill devils with holy water
> MCs I slaughter just a thought

Survival a sport and your idols

Enable you strength to see

Quotes from the Bible they're psychotic

Half man and half demon

Been around the world 666 years and still fiendin'

And I have the name Khrist 'cause I was chosen to given strength.[68]

Here, the MC who has taken the name Khrist, uses the power of the holy over the evil as the symbol for his own ability to smite competitors. In "Manifesto," Talib Kweli moves between appropriating the omniscience of the divine to the blessed, to becoming one possessed by religious ecstasy and ministering: "My style just is all that's seen and all that's heard / God gave us music so we pray with our words / So Hi-Tek be in constant meditation like Monk / While Kweli speaks in tongues to get your intellect drunk."[69] The DJ meditates while the MC reveals truth through the language of his possession. The artists often present themselves as ministers, speaking of hip hop as a calling and of the mic as the tool allowing the MC to spiritually feed the audience.

However, as the episodes with Puffy and Mase mentioned earlier indicate, the open discourse in which even individual songs conjoin the sacred and profane still does not appease the remaining abundant anxiety about inconsistencies between the messages that some hip hop artists put forth and their religious principles. Gangster narratives in particular have included entreaties to a higher power for salvation from the life of a "G." Master P's "Is There Heaven for a Gangster?" or Tupac's "Is There Heaven for a G?" speak to the moral quandaries of gangster-ism. Such songs describe desperation and contemplation.

Alternately, there are songs reviling religious imagery and appropriating either demonic power or claiming a blues-style sinnerman identity. Biggie Smalls, for example, rhymed about not wanting to go to heaven with all the goody-goodies, which would mean "no sleepin' all day / no gettin' my dick licked."[70] In this alternatively humorous and depressive, but ultimately deeply tragicomic song, he prefers to spend eternity with the hustlers and ne'er-do-wells. Run-DMC's "Raising Hell" imagined rhymes that created a burning inferno around the listener:

It's highly appraised when the hell is raised

So demanding and commanding that you all stand dazed

The unbelieving receiving prophesy so true

I cut the head off the devil and I throw it at you

The mighty mic control already bought his soul

The rap king is so bold when I rock and roll

Black hat is my crown symbolizing the sound

Signifying we won't stay around, Bust it![71]

The soul is captured within the music.

That hip hop is at once political, spiritual, and intellectual guarantees an ideological conflict in its midst. The Nation of Islam and the Five Percent Nation, which are both critical of Christianity and very present within hip hop, may be partially responsible for the delay in the development of explicitly Christian messages in hip hop. The counter-mainstream positioning of these groups appeals to the oppositional and counter-hegemonic sensibilities within the culture. Mainstream religion has a more difficult time fitting into this orientation, even among a population that generally adheres to mainstream forms of faith. Rappers Common and Cee-Lo, however, in their song "G.O.D.," make powerful arguments against the messages of the two Islamic organizations, although they do appreciate their nationalism and insights. In the process of their rhyming, the two artists also explain the ambivalence some members of the hip hop community have with Christianity and Christian institutions, even as hip hop widely employs Christian symbolism. Cee-Lo rhymes: "Let me voice my concerns / So many of my fellow brothers have given themselves a title that they actions didn't earn / But innocence is in the same breath as ignorance / Self-consciously seeming to find an impressionable mind to convince."[72] He describes the mental vulnerability that allows individuals to be seduced into considering themselves "gods." Then he explains that even though he too was drawn by the insights of the leaders of this ideology, he would eventually maintain the Christian belief in the sinful nature of human beings. He also ultimately challenges the Nation of Islam's correlation of black political consciousness with the notion of a white devil: "Some leaders are granted with insight / and its all in plan / but it took me some time to overstand / you still created with imperfections of man / so with followin' I disagree / By no means have I forgotten or forgiven what's been done to me / But I do know the devil ain't no white man / the devil is a spiritual mind is color blind."[73] Finally, Cee-Lo questions the spiritual rhetoric of MCs who also celebrate behavior and materialism inconsistent with an identity of individual divinity: "How can you call yourself god when you let a world of possessions become an obsession? / And the way you write your rhymes and can't follow your lesson / If a seed's sown you make sure it's known / You make sure it's grown / If you god then save your own don't mentally enslave your own."[74]

In Common's portion of the rhyme, he preaches religious openmindedness and freedom, and yet he also articulates the source of much disenchantment with the Christian church and its refusal to engage spiritual questions and challenges. He makes clear the same danger exists in the teachings of the Nation of Islam as well:

> As a child given religion with no answer as to why
>
> Just told believe in Jesus 'cause for me he did die
>
> Curiosity killed the catechism understandin' and wisdom
>
> Became the rhythm that I played to and became a slave to master self
>
> A rich man is one with knowledge, happiness and his health
>
> My mind has dealt with the books of Zen, Tao? The lesson
>
> Koran and the Bible to me they are vital . . .
>
> People of the venom try to trim on and use religion as an emblem
>
> When it should be a natural way of life, who are they or I to say to who
>
> you pray ain't right.[75]

Common's celebration of religious tolerance and its use as a shield instead of a sword is of course a toast to Americanism and American democratic ideology, at least the country's professed ideology. It is lyrical pedagogy, encouraging reflection and inquiry. The debate the song engages in remains, importantly, within the context of a hip hop community, and therefore must be distinguished from mainstream assaults on the Nation of Islam, which object less to its religious philosophy than to its assertive black nationalism. The discursive space is internal to the community and demonstrates how hip hop is at once self-protective and self-challenging.

The ministerial function all this religious symbolism and argumentation adheres to of course constitutes yet another masculinist space in African American culture. The MC sees himself as a kind of preacher, a traditional space of authority for black men, and assumes the kind of intellectualism, exposition, and arrogance accorded that role. Masculinity in hip hop emerges, as we have seen, as a complex landscape, born of the absurdity of American race and gender constructs, as well as of the particular creation of commodity and identity in this culture. Despite its problematic manifestations, in the spaces of friendship and in articulations of vulnerability and spirituality, hip hop's representation of masculinity demonstrates the complex yet beautiful face of black manhood. Dominant stereotypes of black masculinity are present in hip hop, and yet a critical reading of the texts demands both an understanding of the stereotypes and of their subversion, as well as of the range of narrative and artistic argumentation taking place within the music as it depicts black manhood.

6

The Venus Hip Hop and the Pink Ghetto

Negotiating Spaces for Women

The first critical work I ever read about hip hop was about a woman. It was a *New York Times* article about the 1986 song by MC Lyte, "I Cram to Understand You," a plaintive appeal by and narrative about a young woman dealing with her boyfriend's drug addiction. Lyte soon became a respected MC, although one plagued by accusations of being "masculine," a raspy-voiced young woman in sweats and gold chains, bilevel golden brown hair, and a makeup free face. She was skilled, however, and offered an alternative to the "pink ghetto" that the equally skilled yet very femme Salt-N-Pepa seemed to inhabit, at least in the psychic world of hip hop.

In 2003, it proved difficult to find a woman who did not exploit her sexuality among the most popular female MCs. While Lyte in her heyday made occasional sexual references, thus coding herself as a sexual being, the role of desired object did not figure prominently in her music. Such an aversion to being defined as a "sexy" MC was nothing rare among women artists popular in the late 1980s through the early 1990s. After the turn of the twentieth century, however, it became clear that sexuality, sexual objectification, and beautification constituted fundamental parts of the marketing of the female MC, thus collapsing distinctions between the video "hoe" and the female artist. Even the anti–sex object role model, Missy Elliot, adhered to a kind of glam beauty with heavy makeup, false eyelashes, and a successful weight loss campaign that brought her down to a slender silhouette, a dramatic departure from her former "thickness." Hers was just one of a series of visual transformations that seemed to bring women hip hop artists in line with mainstream conceptions of beauty. Others included Eve, Lauryn Hill (although she reverted back), Erykah Badu, and Queen Latifah. The visual landscape of women hip hop artists represents the contested terrain of the black female body in the music, and made clear how fraught with sexism and objectification hip hop is, even for the feminists or self-articulating women in the culture.

This chapter considers the difficult role women have played in hip hop, the conflicted assertions of gender identity on the part of women, their efforts to carve out a space as a form of feminism, the abundant sexism in the music, and the possibilities for greater gender liberation in hip hop's future.

Women hip hop artists and producers have faced a difficult path in the male-dominated musical form, but from the early years on, they have emerged as a force, trying to make a place for themselves. One of the first ways women entered the music, and were able to receive respect as artists, was by occupying styles of presentation and archetypal roles coded as male in the world of hip hop or in the larger world of black popular culture. As a masculinist form with masculinist aesthetics, hip hop, and the art form's masculinist ideals of excellence and competitiveness, have often forced women to occupy roles gendered male. The role of the badman in black folk culture, a role descended from slavery, has been widely embraced in hip hop identity. So, understandably, we find a host of female "badmen" in hip hop who use the language of violence, power, and subversive tricksterism to articulate their artistic prowess. Boss, a woman MC, when accused of lacking femininity, responded to such comments with the following statement: "There's a lot of pressure on female rappers to dress up like hoes but me and Dee [her friend and rapping partner] won't be wearin' push up bras and tight pants, female rappers who do that are tryin' to compensate for the fact that they don't have any good lyrics."[1] Her words indicate the importance of voice for Boss. They say that to be taken seriously as artists, women must become subjects instead of objects. Boss and Dee's decision to avoid any possibility of objectifying themselves by wearing sexually provocative clothes serves as a sign of the pride they take in claiming their voices.

Also, this aesthetic in part also resists the mainstream. In the mid-1990s, when there was more pressure for female MCs to look "mannish," before Lil' Kim and Foxy Brown heralded hard-edged black girl MC glam, I was watching an episode of the *Ricki Lake Show*, which took as its subject "my sister/wife/friend dresses like a man." Several black and Puerto Rican women on the show wore baggy jeans and athletic attire, for example Nautica, Polo, and Hilfiger, all regular hip hop brands. Facing criticism from the family and the audience, one of the women said she believed the "tight, sexy stuff" was for white women, while her own attire represented a black woman's style. And true enough, the idea of sexiness that the mainstream pumps into our homes through the media and marketing is still largely white and feminine. Even as black Americans maintain a separate sexual aesthetic, white female standards of beauty still haunt black women, so that some African American women have chosen more masculine outfitting as a counter-hegemonic move. The refusal to adhere to grooming or behavior coded as sexually attractive leads to consistent accusations of lesbianism for many women MCs. While it is likely that there are both gay and lesbian MCs in the world of hip hop, the issue here is not the claim's veracity, but rather its heterosexism. It expresses discomfort with the gender transcendence of women MCs, even as such transcendence is often required for them to be taken seriously as artists.

In the era of the sexy female MC, many women now visually look femme, but simultaneously occupy male spaces linguistically. Lil' Kim, for example, often acts out the role of the badman woman. In "Players Anthem," a song in which a variety of MCs from Junior M.A.F.I.A. (Biggie Smalls's crew) rhyme, Lil' Kim appropriates the male space of the player, one analogous to Pam Grier's in the blaxploitation era; she becomes a Foxy Brown (the film character, not the contemporary rapper), a Cleopatra Jones.

> I used to pack Macs in Cadillacs
> Now I pimp gats in the ac's
> Watch my niggas backs

Nines in the stores

Glocks in the bags

Maxing mini markets gettin' money wit the A-rabs

No question confession

Yes it's the lyrical

Bitches squeeze your tits

Niggas grab your genitals

Proteins and minerals

Exclude subliminals

Big mama shoots the game to all you fillies and criminals . . .

Bitches love the way I bust a rhyme

'Cause they all in line

Screamin' "one more time!"

Niggas

Grab your dick if you love hip hop

Bitches rub a dub in the back of the club, straight up.[2]

Lil' Kim is a male player inverted, with cars and purses full of guns, and an audience of women screaming approval. Lil' Kim also concludes the montage song; as the last to rhyme, she is depicted as a definitive player.

Another woman MC, Suga-T, rhymes:

This is the pickup line

I got the big up mind

I'm steppin' to you like a stickup . . .

I be outta control I see what I want and I roll

I get the digits quick

From the honeys they be fly and all that

But right now that's not where my head is at.[3]

Suga, like Lil' Kim, travels back and forth in her occupation of traditionally female and male spaces. In the above lines, she emerges as the sexual subject, as the possessor of the gaze. She thus partakes in a form of subversion canonized by women MCs. Her act proves subversive because video culture and music culture in general so objectify female bodies that to resist it in any way, even so consistently as to create a new paradigm, goes vehemently against the grain. Later in the same song, Suga challenges gender spaces by dancing between traditionally male and female roles: "One arm is on my steerin' wheel and the other arm around my nigga / His pockets fat don't get offended / somebody gotta make it, so somebody gotta spend it / I take it from the boardroom to the boulevard / Trippin' hard I play a nigga like I play a card."[4] She is the woman demanding material things, but she also owns the male physical space—she drives the car with her arm around him, and she locates this empowered and gender-transcendent space as one which women of various social positions can occupy. As she says, she is speaking from the boardroom to the boulevard.

The badwomen (as I will call them from here on) do not simply occupy male spaces, however. They also use their presence to call into question the masculine designation of those spaces, and to at times even offer a feminist critique by using the power vested in these spaces: "Just as hip hop poses a menace to dominant white bourgeois culture, women's participation in its supposedly masculine rituals threatens still another haven of male hegemony."[5]

The trickster and the badman, traditionally male symbols are both critical to the discussion of women appropriating male spaces, as does the trope of freedom as mobility. The trickster/badman of hip hop functions in the midst of the oppressive and chaotic conditions black people experience in American society. His tools and spaces are a consequence of his condition. The "gat" is his weapon; the street and the underground are where he dwells. Cypress Hill rhymes typical badman ghetto realism in "How I Could Just Kill a Man."

> Cause we're like outlaws striding, while suckers are hidin'
> Jump behind the bush when you see me drivin' by
> Hangin' out the window
> With my Magnum takin' out some Putos
> Actin' kinda loco
> I'm just another local kid from the street gettin' paid for my vocals
> Here is something you can't understand
> How I could just kill a man.[6]

They incite fear with metaphoric physical threats. But the badman doesn't merely intimidate, he moves. That mobility is symbolic of his freedom. Rakim rhymed and Eric B. scratched the duo's stratospheric mobility in the following manner:

> So follow me or were you thinkin' you were first
>
> Let's travel at magnificent speeds around the universe
>
> What could ya say as the earth gets further and further away
>
> Planets are small as balls of clay
>
> Astray in the Milky Way
>
> World's outta sight far as the eye can see
>
> Not even a satellite.[7]

Female entrance into the badman or traveling man domain of hip hop might appear radical, but considering black women' music history, particularly in jazz and blues, it seems to come organically. Women such as Ma Rainey, Billie Holiday, Tina Turner, Gladys Knight, and Chaka Khan have, either through style or content, entered artistic spaces gendered as male. Hazel Carby analyzes one of the ways in which women blues singers entered into the domain of male symbolism through lyric content: "What the women Blues singers were able to articulate were the possibilities for movement for the women who have 'ramblin on their minds' and who have intended to 'ease down the line' for they had made it—the power of movement was theirs . . . the train became a contested symbol."[8] Carby describes the female appropriation of the train as a male symbol in the era of the great black migration. The train originally served as a metaphor for men leaving their families behind in their quest for work. And although the image was at times sorrowful, it also symbolized agency, one often limited to men at the beginning because the women had to stay home and take care of the families. Women blues singers, who, unlike most women, as performers had the power to travel, began to open up the symbolism of motion and travel for women through their lyrics. African American literary scholar Robert Stepto documents how slave narratives manifest the establishment of particular tropes later to resonate throughout African American letters, one of which was the intimate association of black male freedom and travel.[9] Born of the stories of male escapes to the North from slavery (it was more likely for a man to attempt to escape for a range of reasons), travel expanded into one of the largest African American literary conventions and, arguably, sociological realities.[10] The act of traveling was the road to liberation as it led the traveler to better work opportunities, freedom from slavery, and escape from corrupt local white authorities. Yet even in the beginning, this male trope saw female "invasion" and contestation, apparent, for example, in the slave narrative of Harriet Jacobs (for whom both the home and road proves important), the 1920s fiction of Nella Larsen, the 1940s work of Zora Neale Hurston, the mythologizing of Harriet Tubman, the traveling abolitionism of Frances Ellen Watkins Harper, various women blues singers, and, currently, in female MCs.[11]

In "Progress of Elimination," Boss repeatedly states in her refrain, "The only way to progress is through elimination." Progress has a double meaning in this song, indicating both motion and life improvement. The character Boss personifies is attempting to escape from some exploitative superiors in her drug dealing operation. Her physical progress to freedom can only be completed through her use of a gun to eliminate those in her way:

> Now I'm surrounded by dead niggas in a haze
> Somehow I have become a slave
> Yassuh Master nossuh Master I work fassa
> Even it means my brain bein' tampered with
> Fuck it
> At least I got rid of the pamper . . .
> Gotta go yeah, gotta go
> The only way to progress is through elimination.[12]

In effect, Boss describes a modern slave escape. Her slavery to the drug market has at least freed her from traditional female oppression (symbolized by "the pamper") and yet now she has to seek control over her own body again by running. Boss uses travel as well as the gun as themes for contesting a male domain. It is possible to draw parallels between the train of blues singers and the gun of modern-day MCs in a multitude of provocative ways. Both are strong phallic images, not only in their material design but also in terms of their power, force, and speed. Both represent technologies from which black men and women were historically restricted. Self-defense and mobility were prohibited during enslavement, and so they subsequently became tools of freedom. When Boss says "I'll put the barrel of my Big Black Gat up to his temple,"[13] she invokes the image of the Big Black Dick and its associations with power and maleness, both of which she now literally and figuratively holds in her hands. There are women in hip hop who challenge the solely male possession of firearms, as there are also both male and female MCs opposed to their use. While we understand the gun's deleterious effects on the black community, it is nevertheless worthwhile to examine the assertion of power that it symbolizes. Yo Yo says, "Have you ever seen a sister straight blow your ass away / don't make my day."[14] Here she refers not just to a gun; with the reference to Dirty Harry, she also claims the sort of worldliness and power found in a white male cop. Weaponry does not simply function as a destructive symbol in her lines: "Come out and check the phat artillery / Harriet Tubman's spirit is still in me," she rhymes, as well as, "Now I'm wanted in every state cause I'm a packer, rapper, jacker, ready for the cracker."[15] Both phrases associate guns with a black liberation strategy.

The expressed potential for female violence does not necessarily have to be read as a "negative" representation of black women as violent additions to brutishly stereotyped black men (although one can make a compelling reading of that sort given the prevalence of gun violence in black communities, which places greater demands on public "role models"). Reading violence as hip hop feminist symbolism works in a fourfold manner. First, it demonstrates how the voice of female violence in imagined nation-building exercises and war games occur within the hip hop community and thus function as an assertion of black female nationalism. Both in language and action then, women fully participate in the battlefront armies. They thus figuratively protect the hood from the white capitalist interlopers, the sellouts, and the culture thieves. They are not passive figures on a pedestal, but active members of the metaphoric armed forces. As Lauryn Hill rhymed, "Yeah in saloons we drink Boones and battle goons til high noon / Bust rap tunes on flat spoons take no shorts like pum pums."[16]

Second, the language of female violence provides the choice of violence over victimization. This might not always be a description of physical violence, but could assume the form of lyrical violence that humiliates and checks a male abuser. In Nikki D.'s song, "You Freak Out," we at the beginning hear the sounds of an obsessive and possessive boyfriend's anger over her socializing, and these quickly turn into the sounds of him hitting her after he hears a male voice on her answering machine. Nikki D. responds:

I'll fuckin' kill you, you know where the fuck I was—

I was out doin' my usual

Shit that girls do

Fucked around and included a nigga or two

Since it was your boys I didn't think that you would mind

But you on some flip shit so here's your biscuit

Turn into a bitch and wanna change the plans

Tell me how a woman is supposed to treat a man

Yeah well somebody give this nigga some room

'Cause I could see this shit bein' over like soon

Follow me wherever I go

Now ain't that cute you little bitch-ass hoe

You always checkin' my beeper and makin' me see a-

Nother side of you but this woman don't need ya

Ridin' my shit won't get you nowheres

Probably a beard and few gray hairs

Get off that bullshit and learn how to come quick

Since you ain't wreckin' it

I want me a new trick.[17]

She uses the kind of language to describe her abuser that men abusively employ against women—*trick, bitch*. She speaks to the man with a furious and empowered voice, and she states her intention to leave the abusive situation. Removing the power that his physical force has over her requires the rage of her tongue. Like Nikki D. on the issue of battery, most women who rhyme about infidelity use first-person narratives for their stories. The discussion of male infidelity among female MCs often rests on "flip the script" scenarios, meaning that they subvert the vulnerable position men have put them in to place the men in that position. The women achieve this by various means, either through an equivalent betrayal of the man, violence against him, or some type of destruction of his possessions. The songs often conclude with moral-of-the-story endings concerning male actions. Boss rhymes:

I'm down with all the shit you're poppin'

Hell fuck naw I don't want to put a stoppin' to your hoe hoppin'

'Cause when you're runnin' the motherfuckin' streets

In between the sheets

Screwin' freak after freak

Boss is straight kickin' in the door at your crib

With enough time to drink the 40 Os and eat a salad

Jack you for your cash and jewelry and all that shit

Then off to the pawn shop to get another phat ass grip

And that's exactly how it is nigga,

I know the fuckin' recipe.[18]

Rather than trying to convince him to be faithful, she uses the opportunity of his betrayal to remind him that, as Lil' Kim said, "payback's a bitch" in "Get Money."[19] Her payback, like Lil' Kim's, occurs in the male space of criminality, through drinking and toting guns. The song is called "Recipe of a Hoe," and Boss saying," I know the fuckin' recipe" refuses to be "hoed."

A third aspect of women's badman mimicry is that it affords a space for rage and frustration in the black female experience, realities often imagined as male in the black community. Many black women—racially oppressed, sexually abused, robbed of gender roles, and overburdened by community responsibility—rarely acknowledge rage. Interestingly, in R & B depictions of black female anger, tongue lashings and clothes burnings abound, while metaphoric violence remains fairly absent. In its place, emotional devastation and heartbreak prevails, tempering the fury. Literature affords us with more examples of violent rage. In Gayl Jones's novel *Eva's Man*, the female heroine, Eva, is imprisoned for killing her lover and biting off his penis. Having suffered years of sexual abuse without any place to speak her pain, she finally acts it out in violence toward men. She first stabs a man who tries to pressure her into a sexual act and then progresses to killing her lover for not loving her enough and treating her like a prostitute. She falls into insanity and envisions herself as the Queen Bee, a character in the novel who works as a prostitute and functions significantly as a symbol of a female feeding off males after they have pleased her. Eva thinks, "The sweet milk in the Queen Bee's breasts has turned to blood."[20] (This compares to Sethe's in Toni Morrison's *Beloved*, whose babies blood mingles with her breast milk after her hauntingly protective murder of her daughter.)[21] Incidentally, this Queen Bee is a self-designation that Lil' Kim has taken on as well, also using the image of a fatal sexual power to describe herself, signaling the perversion of sexuality and motherhood through racial and sexual abuse. As Boss says, the phallocentric claim can be the nail in the proverbial coffin to a black woman's ears: "I wish you would / Come with that dick shit / Fuck you and your manhood."[22] These women decide that they will disallow male impropriety or betrayal as much as lies in their power. Hazel Carby cites this tendency in the work of blues artists as well. There is a parallel between Boss saying in "Diary of a Mad Bitch," in response to male infidelity, "Niggas be creepin' and sneakin' out with a ho every single weekend / but see I'm out to get a grip / but since I let myself grab a gat and get hazardous to a nigga's health,"[23] and Bessie Smith singing in "Black Mountain Blues," "I'm bound for black mountain me and my razor and my gun / I'm gonna shoot him if he stand still and cut him if he run."[24]

Fourth, the use of violent imagery suggests that black women are creating spaces for the depiction of black female instability and insanity, which has historically gone repressed through the construction and role of black women as caretakers and as the backbone of the black community. Although in a popularly commodified medium such as hip hop the line between glorification and tragedy is a thin one, the reality of black women's psychological vulnerability to oppressive conditions is real. In *Beloved*, Morrison addresses this vulnerability in the life of a nineteenth-century woman. Sethe, an escaped slave, murders her child in a desperate attempt to save her (she does not get to the other children) and herself from the continued abuses and degradation of slavery after the Fugitive Slave Act of 1850 brings white captors to her "safe place." She pays for this act with years of isolation before the community comes to her aid to save her from the choking force of the baby ghost who has come back as a young adult to haunt her. The insanity that Boss describes in her lyrics is at times escapist, and yet it smacks of the same type of agency limited to destructive acts as Sethe's, and it merits the same concerns that one of Sethe's community saviors expresses over its brutality: "She understood Sethe's rage in the shed twenty years ago, but not her reaction to it, which Ella thought was prideful, misdirected and Sethe herself too complicated."[25] Similar concerns for violating dominant moral codes and behaving erratically have faced women existing on the edge of black music through the generations.

The escapist part of Boss's work parallels the forty-ounce-beer-drinking, blunt-smoking, lack-of-opportunity narratives of male MCs, and yet their significance is heightened for Boss and other female MCs by the fact that escapism has been severely limited as a black woman's strategy for dealing with the pains of the world. Although I would not want to suggest that hustling and drug scenes have no women participants, the theme of black female escapism is not as widely recognized or accepted as a function of oppression as is that of men. Historically, to make yet another parallel with the female blues, the escapist drug use that led to the tragic deaths of several jazz and blues men and women offered one of the few public spaces open for the discussion of black female decadence neé depression. Lillian Miller in "Dead Drunk Blues" sings, "I'm gonna get drunk Daddy just one more time / . . . 'cause when I'm drunk don't nothin' worry my mind."[26] Boss takes her impropriety and retreats not into a sickroom, but into a street life of illness. Her mother's voice at the beginning of the tape, in agitated response to her daughter's foulmouthed answering message, says that this "gangster stuff" is no way for a young lady who attended Catholic schools, three years of college, and dance lessons to comport herself. In "Diary of a Mad Bitch," Boss details her escape from such constructions, "I just ran out of the house in an outrage / Barreling down the street with a 12-gauge," and she discusses her transformation: "I'm just a good girl gone bad / With a mind filled with agony / That's something that I'll always have / 'Cause my life ain't been nothing but a struggle / Slanging that cocaine / And trying to keep away from the 5-0."[27]

Given the middle-class upbringing she reveals—"I'm tryin to get to Watts but I'm stuck in Baldwin Hills"—we sense that the agony is broader than the economic poverty to which rap anguish is usually attributed, that it concerns complete desperation, with society and its depravity.[28]

> I don't really want to feel
> Like I'm in a daze
> So I smoke and kill just to deal with the ills
> Life is fucked up trip
> My skills ain't payin' bills and its fucking with me and my grip
> I drink that St. Ides shit
> And at the same time drop a wicked rhyme on my naughty nature

'Cause who the fuck cares that I got gray hairs and can't sleep,
Know what I mean?
That's deep.[29]

Such appropriations of male space through violence, unruliness, craziness, and unlawfulness can be represented through the folkloric character of the badman, and hip hop, I would argue, can be credited with the first cultural configuration of the female badman, the badwoman. Although women have used all of the badman's various trappings at one time or another—the defiance of the blues, the male sexual objectification of the comedienne Moms Mabley, the masculinist physical assertiveness of Foxy Brown and other divas of the blaxploitation era, the conspicuous consumption associated with Madame CJ Walker or various blues divas—one is hard pressed to find a historical period in which women have combined these qualities to parallel the "bad nigga" image and his symbolism so exactly.

Despite the strategy of using masculinist aesthetics in women's hip hop, the scene has also witnessed the introduction of certain elements of black female culture that traditionally lend evidence to toughness, in particular, the attitude. Moreover, as the work of Kyra Gaunt in her essay "Translating Double-Dutch to Hip Hop: The Musical Vernacular of Black Girl's Play" illuminates for us, other features of black female culture also appeared in hip hop progressively, including double Dutch rhymes, clap songs, cheers, and the celebration of the hip hop version of the girl next door, the "around the way girl," from the mouths of male artists and the self-characterizations of certain women artists.[30] Nelson George argues that women could have been absent from hip hop and the music would have been no different. But what women have brought to hip hop in terms of black female oral culture is significant. In addition to the occupation of a male space, which grants a certain level of legitimacy to the female MC in the masculinist world of hip hop, black women rappers have also used traditionally black female expressions of "badness" in the form of assertiveness, attitude, and independence in their lyrics. For example, Elysa Gardner notes that "TLC at once scorned the misogyny associated with gangsta rap and openly embraced sex— safe sex, that is. In the video for 'Ain't 2 Proud 2 Beg,' their first hit single, the ladies adorned their trademark baggy-chic b-girl garb with condoms; Left Eye even wore one over her, well, left eye."[31]

In this space, one finds both clearly articulated feminisms as well as complicity with sexist paradigms. On the one hand, within women's roles as badasses, the ideal of an appropriate male partner is often one who trumps the badness of the woman herself. However, one does find voices in which badness most fundamentally becomes a strategy for expressing feminism. As Robin Kelley has argued, "The introduction of new discourses can, and has, proven an important influence on the politics of rap music. Not only have black women rappers played a crucial role in re-shaping attitudes toward women among a substantial segment of the hip hop community, they are also largely responsible for raising the issue of sexism in rap."[32] Early in her part of the song "Get Money," Lil' Kim rhymes,

> Martini and Rossi Asti Spumante
>
> Dom Perignon
>
> So we can get it on
>
> Movado watch tennis for the wrist, nigga
>
> You ain't never seen no ice like this
>
> So now you know what you workin' with handle your business
>
> And keep comin' with that stuff that I like
>
> Light a candle I'm too hot to handle
>
> I see your eyes sizin' up my hips and my thighs
>
> Man I'll do things to you
>
> Vanessa Del Rio'd be shamed to do.[33]

Lil' Kim here takes on the heavily stereotyped image of the hypercritical black woman who requires material advantages in exchange for a romantic partnership with a man. Although this proves a highly problematic construction, popularized by talk shows featuring gold diggers and 1990s T-shirts worn by black women reading "I can't stand a broke ass Nigga" and T-shirts worn by black men reading "I can't stand a begging ass Bitch," it is currently a feature of black female discourse that must be recognized. It is unclear whether this construction is simply one of the myriad of negative images of black women, largely false but latched onto by some black artists out of defiance, a colonized response to mainstream constructions of male value being located in his ability to provide, or black female frustration with the lack of economic opportunity acted out on the male body. Perhaps all of the above holds true. Lil' Kim tells the man to come correct financially, sexually, and romantically. However, later in the song her posturing changes. A relevant aside here is to explain that the song deals with dishonesty and exploitation in a relationship. The first half is rhymed by Biggie Smalls, who describes betrayal by his woman: "My Moschino hoe / My Versace hottie / Come to find out you was fucking everybody."[34] Her intimacy with him makes the betrayal even worse—she knows about all his crimes and scandals. He says, "Because of you I'm on some real fuck a bitch shit." Painfully, for any listener not desensitized to domestic violence, he describes beating this woman who has betrayed him. Lil' Kim, in the second half the song, presents herself as the woman recounting her version of the events. She sets the record straight, explaining that her betrayal was in response to his infidelity and insincerity. She responds to his violent revenge by playing his game and using his tools:

> Me shifty?
> Now you wanna pistol-whip me,
> Pull out your nine while I cock on mine,
> Now what nigga? I ain't got time for this
> So what nigga? I'm not tryin' to hear that shit
> Now you wanna buy me diamonds and Armani suits
> Adrienne Vittadini and Chanel 9 boots
> Things that make up for all the games and the lies
> Oh my God sayin' I apologize
> Is you wit me? How could you ever deceive me?
> Payback's a bitch motherfucker believe me
> Naw I ain't gay this ain't no lesbo flow
> Just a little somethin' to let y'all motherfuckers know.[35]

Seduction remains critical to all "attitude" women's music in hip hop. Antoinette in "Never Get Enough," a song in which her lyrical gifts are woven into her sexiness, and in which she asserts her absolute possession of both, rhymes:

> Guys if you're cool I'll please ya
> But since I gotta big ol' butt I'ma tease ya

With something def that I bring forth

You and yours truly

So let me ring your bell

Inside this place tonight

And my body is yours fellas, right?

Psyche![36]

Roxanne Shante of the Juice Crew in her eighties heyday was the essence of attitude, and yet she could battle with the boys. She emerged as a central participant in the overwhelmingly male battle between the Juice Crew and Boogie Down Productions. In "Have a Nice Day," a dis song directed at those musical rivals, she rhymes:

Me, the S.H.A.N.T.E.

Good-lookin' never tooken female MC

I'm five foot four, maybe a little bigger

Brown skin complexion with a nice figure

Yes the super female that's called Shante

And like Hurricane Annie I'll blow you away

Whenever I'm in a battle yo I don't play

And you bets go about your way and have a nice day . . .

Now I'm not out to dis the whole Boogie Down

Just a featherweight crew from that part of town

You made a little record and then you started frontin'

Tried to dis the Juice Crew but ain't hurt nothin'

Now KRS-One you should go on vacation

With your name soundin' like a wack radio station

And Scott La Rock you should be ashamed

When T La Rock said "It's Yours" he didn't mean his name

So step back peasants poppin' all that junk

Or else BDP will stand for broken down punks

Cause I'm an All-Star just like Julius Erving

and Roxanne Shante is only good for steady serving.[37]

She rejects Boogie Down Production MC KRS-One's assertion that Roxanne Shante "is only good for steady fucking," a trivializing and sexist statement.[38] She says she can serve him and critiques him in the same vein as the men in her crew do. In fact, this appropriative artistic style, like the challenge to gendered spaces described in the previous chapter on the part of men, affords a space for critical engagement that neither falls victim to sexist objectification nor lapses into traditional female roles that potentially limit the freedom of the artist.

Salt-N-Pepa, female rap artists with remarkable longevity, began their career with attitude-style rhymes. In the beginning, they made attitudinal assertions of their strength as women, which over the years have shifted into an explicitly feminist consciousness. At the same time, they transitioned from being hip hop artists to becoming pop artists, later boasting a broad-based crossover appeal, but having lost some of the hardness, roughness, and, arguably, the lyrical dexterity of their earlier days. Some lines from "My Mic Sound Nice," one of the songs from their first album *Hot, Cool, and Vicious*, go as follows:

> It's a fact
> That I will wax
> MCs out there
> Are gonna get taxed
> Rockin' to our funky beat
> I'm a trip so I know you're gonna fall for me
> 'Cause this is the year all men fear
> Female MCs is movin' up here
> Salt-N-Pepa is strictly biz
> You know the color of this
> You know what time it is
> Super is the sound of the boomin' bass
> Nature describes our pretty face
> Turnin' out without out a doubt
> Make no mistake queens is in the house
> Yeah check it out, check check it out.[39]

The heavily punctuated beat matched with strong voices screamed black female attitude. While demanding recognition in the world of hip hop, "This is the year all men fear," they also have a strongly stated female identity, "Queens is in the house," grounded in their authority and their physicality,"Nature describes our pretty face." Their power resides not in brute force, but in a metaphoric seduction, "I'm a trip so I know you're gonna fall for me." Salt-N-Pepa, for a number of years in the 1980s and early 1990s the signature female voices in hip hop, introduced the space of female subjectivity into hip hop discourse. In "I Desire," neither sex nor sexuality emerge as subjects per se, but the position of desiring grants these women power:

> On stage we behave like sizzlin' flame
>
> And oh so cool when we rap you need a sweater
>
> The rhymes so tough you swear they're made of leather
>
> Get the best of your bunch and I bet that we're better
>
> Tell 'em why, Pepa tell 'em why, 'cause I desire."[40]

They desire and are satisfied. For women, the act of choosing proves an emancipatory one. And yet these women here exist in a traditional female space in several ways. First, they participate in a "girlfriend" dialogue between the two of them, and also in interaction with their DJ, Spinderella, in reference to her or to the beats she puts together. They also paired up over the years with the R & B group En Vogue and fellow MC Antoinette. They occupy the traditional space of black female friendship that has a foundation in sharing words of support and emphasis: "Tel 'em why, Pepa tell 'em why, 'cause I desire."

This performance of friendship proved significant because of its infusion into a genre in which women appeared overwhelmingly in battles — Roxanne Shante versus the Real Roxanne versus Sparky D, MC Lyte versus Antoinette, and so on. Yet the battle was clearly not a female-specific phenomenon, just one of the few places where women appeared popularly in hip hop in the early to mid-1980s, until Salt-N-Pepa emerged. Other female duos, Finesse and Synquis, Oaktown's 357, the Cookie Crew, and Dis-N-Dat have all participated in the tradition Salt-N-Pepa epitomized.

In the 1990s, now primarily working as pop artists, Salt-N-Pepa created anthems for collective female identification and assertion, as in "She Thing": "It's a she thing and it's all in me / I can be anything that I want to be / Don't consider me /A minority / Open your eyes / And maybe you'll see."[41] But one wonders how possible it would be to speak with such an explicitly feminist collective consciousness and remain popular within the boundaries of "hip hop," as opposed to "pop" music,

given that Salt-N-Pepa have faced critiqued by some and gained appreciation by others through their transitions, and also given hip hop's discomfort with ideas that seem too clean, too mainstream, and, feminism's
oft-cited tag, "too white." Rather than political consciousness, hip hop
seems to prefer an aggressive self-celebration and empowerment as its
kind of feminism. Take Eve, for example, who in her song "My Bitches"
indicates that the women she is down with are not about to accept any
male impropriety: "My Bitches / My Bitches that'll change the locks /
My Bitches / My Bitches that'll cut up your clothes / My Bitches that'll
steal your stash / My Bitches are bold, my bitches are cold."[42] She indicts
men for their abuses:

My Bitches that take care of they kids
My Bitches
My Bitches that you don't respect
My Bitches
My Bitches that you always neglect
Y'all niggas ain't real
Y'all niggas aint shit![43]

In response to those affronts, she asserts a coldblooded reaction, especially to incarcerated partners: My Bitches / Don't post none of his bail /
My Bitches / My Bitches teach him how he should feel / Don't accept his
calls, don't send him no mail."[44] Finally, she concludes with an uplifting
survivalism:

My Bitches
My Bitches that'll stay in school
My Bitches
My Bitches that can keep a job
My Bitches
My Bitches that can raise they kids
My Bitches are strong
My Bitches'll live![45]

This is one of the few songs in which the subversion of the word *bitch*
from misogynistic slur to feminist identity begins to work, perhaps because of the power of Eve's voice combined with the song's female popu-

list realism. Eve delivers her message in a breathless, almost joyous cadence, located somewhere between a cheer and a battle. It provides a powerful counterpoint to the Jay-Z lines, "Sisters get respect, bitches get what they deserve / Sisters work hard, bitches work your nerves / Sisters hold you down, bitches hold you up / Sister's help you progress, bitches will slow you up / Sisters cook up a meal, play their role with the kids / Bitches in the street with they nose in your biz."[46] Eve rejects the subjugated role of a sister (can we hear echoes of sexist, late 1960s black nationalist gender rhetoric here?) as Jay-Z articulates it, preferring the power of a self-defined bitch.

Much doubt has also been cast on women's authenticity as MCs. With every gifted woman lyricist come accusations that men have written her lyrics. And while it is true that a number of women have had their lyrics written by men, so have a number of male artists, and yet their gender does not immediately call authorship into question. Moreover, the reality of a gender power imbalance in hip hop makes many fail to understand that some of women's badness in hip hop comes in the presence of women who have weathered the storms of the competitive music industry to become power brokers. Speaking of Sylvia Robinson, the founder of Sugar Hill Records, the company responsible for the first rap hit "Rapper's Delight," Tricia Rose writes, "Perhaps there's no better evidence that women hold a righteous place in hip hop's genesis than the fact that it was a female who first thought to cash in on the then underground 'fad.' "[47] She goes on to recognize that Robinson "was soon followed by such prominent female executives as Monica Lynch at Tommy Boy and Carmen Ashurst-Woodard at Def Jam. In contrast to rock, women were firmly established in positions of power in the rap business from the early days."[48] Queen Latifah, Missy Elliot, the late Lisa "Left Eye" Lopes of TLC, and others have distinguished themselves as producers, thus breaking the gendered boundary of composer.

But the authority of women as producers does not necessarily lead to a feminist presence, and neither does the penning of lyrics by women. Even as women producers make headway and several women artists stand among the more popular in the world of hip hop, the landscape for women in hip hop is actually deteriorating. In the last handful of years before the turn of the millennium, the visual image of black women in hip hop rapidly deteriorated into one of widespread sexual objectification and degradation. For years before, hip hop had been accused of misogyny, critics often citing lyrical references to women as bitches and hoes. But it is also true that hip hop often suffered the fate of the scapegoat, being no more misogynistic than American popular culture in general, although perhaps peppered with less polite language. But in the late years of the twentieth century, hip hop took a particularly pernicious turn not only toward sexist assertions but also having a threatening social impact, particularly on black girls and young women.

Visual Images

It seemed to happen suddenly. Every time one turned on BET (Black Entertainment Television) or MTV, one encountered a disturbing music video: Black men rapped surrounded by dozens of black and Latina women dressed in bathing suits, or scantily clad in some other fashion. Video after video proved the same, each one more objectifying than the former. Some took place in strip clubs, some at the pool, at the beach, or in hotel rooms, but the recurrent theme was dozens of half-naked women. The confluence of cultural trends leading to this moment merits more extended scholarly attention than it will receive here, but, in short, it occurred as pornography became increasingly mainstreamed and alluded to in objectifying shows such as *Baywatch*, as the tech boom gave rise to a celebration of consumption and widespread wealth, and as hip hop continued its pattern of shifting dominant foci—from political consciousness to social realism to gangsterism to humor to in this moment, a hedonist conspicuous consumption previously largely associated with Miami Bass music.

The sexist message embraced here proves complex. Its attack on black female identity is multifaceted. First, and most obviously, the women are commodified. They appear in the videos quite explicitly as property, not unlike the luxury cars, Rolex watches, and platinum and diamond medallions also featured. The male stars of the videos do not have access to these legions of women because of charisma or sexual prowess, but rather because they are able to "buy" them due to their wealth. The message is not, "I am a Don Juan," but instead, "I am rich and these are my spoils." Not only are the women commodified, but sex as a whole is.

Moreover the women are often presented as vacuous, doing nothing in the videos but swaying around seductively. Often, they avert their eyes from the camera, allowing the viewer to have a voyeuristic relationship to them. Or they look at the camera, eyes fixed in seductive invitation, mouth slightly open. Any signs of thought, humor, irony, intelligence, anger, or any other emotion, prove extremely rare. Even the manner in which the women dance signals cultural destruction. Black American dance is discursive in that sexuality is usually combined with humor, and that the body is used to converse with other moving bodies. Yet the women who appear in these videos usually dance in a two-dimensional fashion, in a derivative but nonintellectual version of black dance more reminiscent of symbols of pornographic male sexual fantasy than the ritual, conversational, and sexual traditions of black dance. Despite all the gyrations of the video models, their uninterested, wet-lipped languor stands in sharp contrast to (for example) the highly sexualized booty dancing of the Deep South, which features polyrhythmic rear end movement, innuendo, and sexual bravado.

This use of black women in the music videos of male hip hop artists often makes very clear reference to the culture of strip clubs and pornography. Women dance around poles, and porn actresses and exotic dancers are often the stars of the videos, bringing the movement-based symbols of their trades with them. The introduction of porn symbols into music videos is consistent with a larger movement that began in the late 1990s, in which pornographic imagery, discourses, and themes began to enter American popular culture. Powerful examples may be found in the *Howard Stern Show*, E! Entertainment Television, and daytime talk shows. Porn film stars attain mainstream celebrity, exotic dancers are routine talk show guests, and the public face of lesbianism becomes not a matter of the sexual preference of women, but of the sexual consumption and fantasy life of men. The videos discussed here make for an appropriate companion piece to this wider trend. While the music videos are male-centered in that they assume a heterosexual male viewer who will appreciate the images of sexually available young women, it is clear that young women watch them as well. The messages such videos send to young women are instructions on how to be sexy and how to look in order to capture the attention of men with wealth and charisma. Magazines geared toward young women have given instructions on how women should participate in their own objectification for decades, but never before has a genre completely centralized black women in this process.[49]

The beauty ideal for black women presented in these videos is as impossible to achieve as the waif-thin models in *Vogue* magazine are for white women. There is a preference for lighter-complexioned women of color, with long and straight or loosely curled hair. Hair that hangs slick against the head when wet as the model emerges out of a swimming pool (a common video image) is at a premium too. Neither natural tightly curled hair nor most coarse relaxed hair becomes slick, shining, and smooth when wet. It is a beauty ideal that contrasts sharply to the real hair of most black women. When brown-skinned or dark-skinned women appear in the videos, they always have hair that falls well below shoulder length, despite the fact that the average length of black women's natural hair in the United States today is four to six inches, according to Barry Fletcher.[50]

Camera shots linger on very specific types of bodies. The videos have assimilated the African American ideal of a large rotund behind, but the video ideal also features a very small waist, large breasts, and slim shapely legs and arms. Often, while the camera features the faces of lighter-complexioned women, it will linger on the behinds of darker women, implying the same thing as the early 1990s refrain from Sir Mix-A-Lot's "Baby Got Back," "L.A. face with an Oakland booty."[51] That is, the ideal features a "high-status" face combined with a highly sexualized body read by the viewer as the body of a poor or working-class woman.[52] Color is aligned with class, and women are created or valued by how many fantasy elements have been pieced together in their bodies.

While one might argue that the celebration of the rotund behind signals an appreciation of black women's bodies, the image taken as a whole indicates how difficult a beauty ideal this proves to attain for anyone. A small percentage of women, even black women, have such Jessica Rabbit proportions. As journalist Tomika Anderson wrote for *Essence* magazine, "In movies, rap songs and on television, we're told that the attractive, desirable and sexy ladies are the ones with 'junk in their trunks.' And even though this might seem ridiculous, some of us actually listen to (and care about) these obviously misogynistic subliminal messages—just as we are affected by racialized issues like hair texture and skin tone."[53]

Americans have reacted with surprise to abundant social scientific data showing that black girls comprise the social group that scores highest on self-esteem assessments and that they tend to have much better body images than white girls. While these differences in esteem and body image are to a large extent attributable to cultural differences, with black girls having been socialized to see beauty in strong personality characteristics and grooming rather than in particular body types, I believe the media plays a role as well. White girls find themselves inundated with images of beauty impossible for most to attain: sheets of blond hair, waif-thin bodies, large breasts, no cellulite, small but round features, and high cheekbones. Over the years, black women have remained relatively absent from public images of beauty, an exclusion which may have saved black girls from aspiring to impossible ideals. But with the recent explosion of objectified and highly idealized images of black women in music videos, it is quite possible that the body images and even self-esteem of black girls will begin to drop, particularly as they move into adolescence and their bodies come under scrutiny. Many of the music videos feature neighborhood scenes including children. In them, little black girls are beautiful. They laugh, smile, play double Dutch, and more. They are full of personality, and they emerge as cultural celebrations with their hair plaited, twisted, or curled and adorned with colorful ribbons to match their outfits in characteristic black girl grooming style. And yet the adult women generally remain two-dimensional and robbed of personality. Is this what puberty is supposed to hold for these girls?

A Feminist Response?

In such troubling moments, we should all look for a gender-critical voice—in the world, in ourselves. Where do we find a response to this phenomenon that will compellingly argue against such characterizations of black women, where do we find a hip hop feminism? Hip hop has seen a feminist presence since the 1980s in such figures as Salt-N-Pepa, Queen Latifah, and MC Lyte, and hip hop feminism continues to exist despite the widespread objectification of black female bodies. We can find numerous examples of feminist and antisexist songs in hip hop and hip hop soul. Mary J. Blige, Lauryn Hill, Destiny's Child, Missy Elliot, Erykah Badu, and others each have their individual manner of representing black female identity and self-definition.

Alicia Keys, one of the crop of singer-songwriters who fit into the hip hop nation, presents an image that contrasts sharply with the video models. The classically trained pianist who has claimed Biggie Smalls and Jay-Z among her music influences appeared in her first music video for the song "Fallin' " in a manner both stylish and sexy but decidedly not self-exploiting. Her hair in cornrows, wearing a leather jacket and fedora, she sings with visible bluesy emotion. She describes repeatedly falling in love with a man who is not good for her. In the music video, Keys travels by bus to visit the man in prison. This element figures as an important signifier of hip hop sensibilities, as rap music is the one art form that consistently engages with the crisis of black imprisonment and considers imprisoned people as part of its community. As Keys rides in the bus, she gazes at women prisoners working in a field outside the window. They sing the refrain to the song, "I keep on fallin', in and out, of love with you / I never loved someone the way I love you."[54] The women on the bus riding to visit men in prison mirror the women outside of the bus, who are prison laborers. This visual duality comments on the often overlooked problem of black female imprisonment in conversations about the rise of American imprisonment and black imprisonment in particular. It makes reference to two issues facing black women. One is that many black women are the mates of imprisoned men. The second is that many black women wind up in prison because they unwittingly or naively became involved with men participating in illegal activities.[55] The video poignantly alludes to these social ills with a close-up of a stone-faced woman in prison clothing with a single tear rolling down her cheek. Although, like Badu, Keys frequently appeared on her first albums to be narratively enmeshed in a "stand by your man" ethos that propped up male-centered heteronormativity, both of their voices and images offer dramatic feminist moments notable for their departure from objectifying and exploitative depictions.

Singer-songwriter India Arie offers another critical example of a black feminist space in the hip hop world. A young brown-skinned and dreadlocked woman, she burst on the music scene with her song and companion music video "Video" which criticize the image of women in videos. In the refrain she sings, "I'm not your average girl from a video / My body's not built like a supermodel but / I've learned to love myself unconditionally / because I am a queen."[56]

Similar lyrics assert that value is found in intelligence and integrity rather than expensive clothes, liquor, and firearms. The video celebrates

Arie who smiles and dances and pokes fun at the process of selecting girls for music videos. She rides her bicycle into the sunshine with her guitar strapped across her shoulder. Arie refuses to condemn artists who present a sexy image but has stated that she will not wear a skirt above calf length on stage and that she will do nothing that will embarrass her family. Musically, while her sound is folksy soul, she does understand her work as being related to hip hop. "I'm trying to blend acoustic and hip-hop elements," she explains. "I used the most acoustic-sounding drum samples, to have something loud enough to compete with other records, but to keep the realistic, softer feel."[57] Arie understands her work as inflected with hip hop sensibilities, more than with the music's compositional elements. She says: "I don't define hip-hop the way a record company would. The thread that runs though both my music and hip-hop is that it's a very precise expression of my way of life. It's like blues; it's very real and honest output of emotion into a song. Because of that legacy, my generation now has an opportunity to candidly state our opinions. That's what my album is about. I just wanna be me."[58]

Arie's definition of hip hop as honest self-expression is true to the ideology at the heart of the genre at its beginnings, a concept that multitudes of hip hop artists continue to profess to. Yet that element of hip hop stands in tension with the process of celebrity creation. The "honest" words in hip hop exist in a swamp of image making. It does not suffice to examine the clear and simple feminist presences in hip hop; we must consider the murkier ones as well. When it comes to feminist messages, often the words and language of a hip hop song may have feminist content, but the visual image may be implicated in the subjugation of black women. Unlike the individualistic and expressive visuals we have of Arie, Keys, Jill Scott, or Missy Elliot, other artists are often marketed in a manner quite similar to the way in which objectified video models are presented.

Tensions between Texts

Wholesome young stars like Arie and Keys present both strong and respectable images of black womanhood, yet those women who are "sexy" in particular have a much more difficult time carving out a feminist space for themselves. In an earlier piece, "It's My Thang and I'll Swing It the Way that I Feel: Sexual Subjectivity and Black Women Rappers," I argued for the existence of a feminist space in hip hop in which women articulated sexual subjectivity and desire.[59] While I still do believe this is possible, I find it more difficult to achieve now. When the women articulating subjectivity are increasingly presented in visual media as objects rather than subjects, as they are now, their statement to the world is ambiguous at best, and, at worst, the feminist message of their work will become undermined. Joan Morgan reflects on the tension that this presents in her work, which details the conflicts facing a woman with a feminist identity and the erotics of a hip hop market culture: "Am I no longer down for the cause if I admit that while total gender equality is an interesting intellectual concept, it doesn't do a damn thing for me erotically. That, truth be told, men with too many feminist sensibilities have never made my panties wet, at least not like that reformed thug nigga who can make even the most chauvinistic 'wassup baby' feel like a sweet wet tongue darting in and out of your ear."[60] The question is whether the appeal to the erotics of male desire proves too strong to still make the sexy female MC a voice "for the cause."

A musical artist occupies a multitextual space in popular culture. Lyrics, interviews, music, and videos together create a collage, often finely planned, from which an audience is supposed to form impressions. But the texts may conflict with one another. Lil' Kim, the much discussed, critiqued, and condemned nasty-talking bad girl of hip hop, is a master of shock appeal. Her outfits often expose her breasts, her nipples covered by sequined pasties color-coordinated with the rest of her attire. Despite Kim's visual and lyrical vulgarity, many of her critics admit to finding her endearing. Her interviewers know her as sweet-natured and generous. But Lil' Kim stands as a contradiction because while she interviews as a vulnerable and sweet woman, she raps with the hardness adored by her fans. She has an impressive aggressive sexual presence, and she has often articulated a sexual subjectivity through words, along with an in-your-face camera presence. However, as Kim has developed as an entertainer, it has become clear that her image is complicit in the oppressive language of American cinematography in regard to women's sexuality. She has adopted a Pamela-Anderson-in-brown-skin aesthetic, calling on pornographic tropes but losing the subversiveness sometimes apparent in her early career. Andre Leon Talley of *Vogue* magazine noted her transformation from an "around the way girl" with a flat chest, big behind, and jet black (or green, or blue) weave to the celebrity Kim who shows off breast implants and shakes her long blond hair.[61] In her videos, the camera angles exploit her sexuality. In the video for the song "How Many Licks," she appears as a Barbie-type doll, her body parts welded together in a factory. The video stands as an apt metaphor for her self-commodification and use of white female beauty ideals. The video closes off its own possibilities. The doll factory image might have operated as a tongue-in-cheek criticism of image making or white female beauty ideals, but, instead, the video functions as a serious vehicle for Kim to be constructed as beautiful and seductive with blond hair and blue eyes. To be a doll in American popular culture is to be perfect, and she will satisfy many male fantasies as many times as she is replicated. Over several years, Kim has become defined more by her participation in codes of pornographic descriptions of women than by her challenging of concepts of respectability or her explicit sexuality.

It is a delicate balance, but it is important to distinguish between sexual explicitness and internalized sexism. While many who have debated the image of female sexuality have put "explicit" and "self-objectifying" on one side and "respectable" and "covered-up" on the other, I find this a flawed means of categorization. The nature of sexual explicitness proves important to consider, and will become more so as more nuanced images will emerge. There is a creative possibility for liberatory explicitness because it may expand the confines of what women are allowed to say and do. We just need to refer to the history of blues music—one full of raunchy, irreverent, and transgressive women artists—for examples. Yet the overwhelming prevalence of the Madonna/whore dichotomy in American culture means that any woman who uses explicit language or images in her creative expression is in danger of being symbolically cast into the role of whore regardless of what liberatory intentions she may have, particularly if she does not have complete control over her image.

Let us turn to other examples to further explore the tensions between text and visual image in women's hip hop. Eve has emerged as one of the strongest feminist voices in hip hop today. She rhymes against domestic violence and for women's self-definition and self-reliance. She encourages women to hold men in their lives accountable for disrespectful or less-than-loving behavior. Yet the politics of Eve's image are conflicted. She has appeared in music videos for songs on which she has collaborated with male hip hop artists, videos filled with the stock legions of objectified video models. On the one hand, Eve's provocative dress validates the idea of attractiveness exemplified by the models. But the rapper is also distinguished from these women because she is the star. She appears dignified and expressive, while they do not. Her distinction from the other women supports their objectification. She is the exception that makes the rule, and it is her exceptionalism that allows her to have a voice. Similar dynamics have appeared in videos featuring hip hop singer Lil' Mo. In fact, a number of women hip hop artists who claim to be the only woman in their crews, to be the only one who can hang with the fellas, through their exceptionalism make arguments that justify the subjugation of other women, even the majority of women.

Moreover, both Eve and Lil' Kim often speak of the sexual power they have as deriving from their physical attractiveness to men. It is therefore a power granted by male desire, rather than a statement of the power of female sexual desire. While neither artist has completely abandoned the language of empowering female subjectivity in her music, any emphasis on power granted through conventional attractiveness in this media language limits the feminist potential of the music. In one of the songs in which Eve most explicitly expresses desire, "Gotta Man," the desire is rooted in the man's ability to dominate. She describes him as "the only thug in the hood who is wild enough to tame me,"[62] and therefore she is "the shrew," willingly stripped of her defiant power by a sexual union. Instead of using her aggressive tongue to challenge prevailing sexist sexual paradigms, she affirms them by saying that she simply needs a man stronger than most, stronger than she, to bring everything back to normal.

The tensions present in hip hop through the interplay of the visual and the linguistic, and the intertextuality of each medium, are various. Even Lauryn Hill, often seen as the redeemer of hip hop due to her dignified, intellectually challenging, and spiritual lyricism has a complicated image. As a member of the Fugees, she often dressed casually in baggy yet interesting clothes thoroughly rooted in hip hop style. It seems no accident that she became a celebrity, gracing the covers of British GQ, *Harper's Bazaar*, and numerous other magazines, when her sartorial presentation changed. Her skirts got shorter and tighter, her cleavage more pronounced, and her dreadlocks longer. When she began to sport an alternative style that nevertheless garnered mainstream acceptability, she was courted by high-end designers like Armani. As Lauryn's image became more easily absorbable into the language of American beauty culture, her celebrity grew. She even appeared on the cover of *Sophisticates Black Hair Magazine,* a black beauty guide that usually relegates natural hair to a couple of small pictures of women with curly afros or afro weaves, while the vast majority of its photos show women with long straight weaves and relaxers. The hip hop artist was certainly one of the few *Sophisticates* cover models ever to have natural hair, and the only with locks. (Interestingly, the silhouette of the locks was molded into the shape of shoulder-length relaxed hair.) In the issue of British GQ that featured Lauryn as a cover model, journalist Sanjiv writes, "She could be every woman in a way Chaka Khan could only sing about—the decade's biggest new soul arrival with the looks of a supermodel and Hollywood knocking at her door."[63]

In September of 1999, Lauryn appeared on the cover of *Harper's Bazaar.* The article inside discussed her community service projects, and the cover celebrated her model-like beauty. Of course, the cover had something subversive to it. Dark-skinned and kinky-haired Lauryn Hill was beautiful, and the image was ironic. Her locks were styled into the shape of a Farah Fawcett flip, a tongue-in-cheek hybridization at once referencing the seventies heyday of unprocessed afro hair and that era's symbol of white female beauty, Farah Fawcett. The hybrid cover proves analogous to the diverse elements used in the creation of the new in hip hop. Nevertheless, it is important to note that Lauryn became widely attractive when her silhouette—thin body and big hair—matched that of mainstream beauty. So even as the artist has been treated as the symbol of black women's dignity and intelligence in hip hop (and rightfully so given her brilliant lyricism), she too found herself pulled into the sexist world of image making. Although she has made some public appearances since cutting off her long hair, getting rid of the makeup, and returning to baggy clothes, publicity about her has noticeably dropped.[64]

In contrast to Lauryn Hill, Erykah Badu has remained unapologetically committed to the drama of her neo-Afrocentric stylings in her image making, and she therefore has only achieved limited mainstream beauty acceptance. After she shaved her head, doffed her enormous head wrap, and wore a dress shaped like a ball gown (although in reality it was a deconstructed, rough textured "warrior princess," as she called it, work of art), Joan Rivers named her the best-dressed attendee at the 2000 Grammy Awards. Yet she also, rather than simply complimenting her dress or style, said that this was the best Badu had ever looked and that she was an extremely beautiful woman. Rivers appeared to insinuate that the singer was receiving recognition for coming closer to looking "as beautiful as she really is," not for truly being the best dressed. A 2001 *Vogue* article discussed Badu in the context of how ugliness could prove beautiful and how fine the line between the beauty and ugliness was, making reference to her unusual attire, again a sign of how disturbing the beauty industry finds her unwillingness to fit into standard paradigms of female presentation, even as her large hazel eyes and high cheekbones undeniably appeal to individuals in that industry.

I used the examples of Lil' Kim, Eve, Lauryn Hill, and Erykah Badu—all very distinct artists—to draw attention to the kinds of tensions that might exist between a feminist content in hip hop lyrics and the visual image of the artist. I hope these examples encourage readers, as viewers and listeners of popular culture, to become attuned to the multitextual character of the music world and to read as many layers of the media as possible.

The Colonizer and Colonized

In her essay "Language and the Writer," novelist and cultural critic Toni Cade Bambara reminds us that "the creative imagination has been colonized. The global screen has been colonized. And the audience—readers and viewers—is in bondage to an industry. It has the money, the will, the muscle, and the propaganda machine oiled up to keep us all locked up in a delusional system—as to even what America is."[65] Musical artists are cultural actors, but those backed by record labels are hardly independent actors. In music videos and photo layouts, they exist within what Cade Bambara has described as a colonized space, particularly in regard to race and gender. In a context in which a short, tight dress and a camera rolling up the body, lingering on behinds and breasts, holds particular power with regard to gender and personal value, we must ask how powerful words can be that intend to contradict such objectification. How subversive are revolutionary words in a colonized visual world full of traditional gender messages?

In the essay cited above, Cade Bambara asks us to consider the use of metaphors, themes, and other ritualized structures to create meaning in American film. She writes:

> There is the conventional cinema that masks its ideological imperatives as entertainment and normalizes its hegemony with the term "convention," that is to say the cinematic practices—of editing, particular uses of narrative structure, the development of genres, the language of spatial relationships, particular performatory styles of acting—are called conventions because they are represented somehow to be transcendent or universal, when in fact these practices are based on a history of imperialism and violence.[66]

Cade Bambara here speaks specifically of movies, but her observation about the normalization and universalization of conventions that guide interpretation and form part of sexist and racist hegemonic structures applies to the discussion of hip hop as well. Often, language, even aggressive liberatory language, becomes nearly powerless in the face of the powerful visual discourse of music videos.

So then we ask: How should we read these artists who have feminist voices and yet somehow embrace sexist images? If these artists are linguistic proponents of women's power, subjectivity, and black feminism, why do they participate in creating such conflicting visual textual representations? First, it is important to acknowledge that in a society with such strong hegemonies of race, class, gender, and sexuality, virtually all of us, regardless of how committed we are to social justice and critical thinking, remain conflicted beings. We want to be considered attractive, even though we understand how attractiveness is racialized, gendered, and classed in our society, and how the designation often affirms structures of power and domination. Separating out healthy desires to be deemed attractive from those desires for attractiveness that are complicit in our oppression proves challenging. Similarly, we want to be successful, but success is often tied to race, class, gender, and body politics that implicitly affirm the oppression of others. We support the status quo in order to succeed within it, despite our better judgment.

These tensions exist within the artist as much as within the average citizen, and we should therefore err on the side of caution in our judgment of the artists. And even if we remained insensitive to these internal conflicts possibly burdening famous hip hop artists, the artists still should not be considered solely responsible for the tensions between their words and their image. In reality, the "Realness" in popular hip hop and R & B stars is as much an illusion as it is real. Teams construct their public images more often than they do themselves. The incongruous image reflects at least as much (and likely more) a conflict between individuals and interests, that is, the record company's agenda versus the artist's agenda, as an internal conflict within the artist. As critic Joshua Gamson writes: "Celebrity making is clearly . . . an established commercial enterprise made up of highly developed and institutionally linked professions and subindustries such as public relations, entertainment law, celebrity journalism and photography, grooming and training, managing and agenting, novelty sales. As carriers of the central commodity (attention getting capacity), celebrity performers are themselves products."[67] Each artist is a corporate creation, pun intended. And while some artists manage to maintain a good deal of creative control (often those labeled alternative), record companies still have an awareness of the extent to which a consumer market for the "alternative" and the "iconoclastic" exists, so that the space they allow for these kinds of artists still remains somewhat in their control. The construction of celebrity imagery is pervasive. Guy Debord offers a chilling assessment of such star making in a consumer society. He writes:

> The individual who in the service of the spectacle is placed in stardom's spotlight is in fact the opposite of an individual, and as clearly the enemy of the individual in himself as of the individual in others. In entering the spectacle as a model to be identified with, he renounces all autonomy in order himself to identify with the general law of obedience to the course of things. Stars of consumption, though outwardly representing different personality types, actually show each of these types enjoying an equal acccess to the whole realm of consumption and deriving exactly the same satisfaction therefrom.[68]

The insights of Gamson and Debord together assist in this particular examination of gender in hip hop. Gamson's quote demonstrates how the artist shifts from cultural worker to commodity. Instead of simply being an individual who presents songs for consumers to buy or listen to, the image of the celebrity becomes conflated with the person. As consumers, we buy that person (or rather that person's image) in its entirety.

Locating the artist as commodity rather than as creator thus entails far less agency for him or her. Moreover, if the celebrity/commodity's existence is, as Debord suggests, an affirmation of the value of consumer culture, then the sexist imaging of some black female hip hop artists proves even more troubling. The schema is: The creative power of the hip hop artist is usurped by her image and sexualized commodification. This objectification affirms the broader social process of selling black women's bodies through music videos and the concept of black women as sexual commodities in general. However, not all hip hop artists are signed to record labels.

Hip hop has sustained a revolutionary current with respect to consumer culture despite the fact that it has become the most popular music in the United States. This revolutionary current exists in the underground communities of unsigned artists who push forward creative development without corporate involvement. They are cultural workers and artists in the organic sense, and proprietors of their own images. Local underground artists provide a good source when we seek feminist and other politically progressive messages in hip hop.

But even as we understand the power of corporate imaging, we must not fail to consider what the artists can and do continue to own in these difficult circumstances—their copyrighted lyrics. Ownership of lyrics constitutes an asserted property right that competes with the idea that the artist herself (or himself) is "property." For women artists who have written and copyrighted their own lyrics, the lyrics might represent their last area of control, and it may be where we can best find their intended political messages. Looking to the distinction between the copyrighted material, owned by artists and the music videos, owned by record companies, we have some indication of what particular political tensions face a given artist.

We know that the image made by the record company often neutralizes the politics of the artist. While famous persons have a legally cognizable property interest in their public images as a whole, when they consent to making a music video, they grant the record company the use of their image. They allow for the creation of a product that features them as a product, and that in turn encourages the sale of their words and music. Perhaps that web provides a clue as to how artists might regain subversive power through language. If their words are not simply liberatory and progressive but also critically engage, mock, or challenge the very images making the artist into a celebrity, the image may not dwarf them. Instead, the image's meaning might shift, bringing it closer to being owned by the artist. If you can, imagine an artist looking lustily into the camera while narratively critiquing the gaze she is giving you, or discussing the sexism implicit in the dress she is wearing. While this strategy might simply give rise to further conflicted images, there is the distinct possibility that it would force the listener to critically read the image. Certainly in earlier periods of hip hop, groups like A Tribe Called Quest and De La Soul often embedded in their songs strong critiques of the music industry, to which they understood themselves "enslaved" as commodities. Such critiques played a role in their success at being popular, political, and authentic, and they provide a useful model for a feminist voice in hip hop.

Conclusion

Where does the black female self exist in the media soup of image and language? Who owns her identification? Is it articulated more power-fully by the black woman artist, or the producers, publicists, executives, and videographers? Is it possible for the voice of the artist to sound loudest in the din? And what relationship do and should these artists have to the masses of black women and their identities? Are they representatives, belonging to the women, or are they representations of the women, or both?

As a college student, I met the black woman filmmaker Julie Dash. I had recently seen her short film *Illusions* (1983) and her landmark feature *Daughters of the Dust* (1992). Excited by her work, and thrilled to meet her, I gushed about how I wanted to "do what she did." She warned me that if I wrote my movie, I'd better direct it too; otherwise the sub-stance may no longer be intact on completion. In giving me this warn-ing, she was testifying to the degrees of ownership of art, to the inter-action between words and image, and to the importance of black female self-articulation in a colonized medium.

As we categorize artists along lines of positive and negative, good and bad, skilled and stupid, we should pause and reconsider our strategies. Instead of putting them into two or three groups defined by our percep-tions of the artists' morality, politics, or even musical quality and ending our assessment there, we should be reading their presences in the multiple layers on which they exist. The dynamics treated in this chapter make an excellent case for media literacy. It allows us to understand race and gender politics, and to interpret the words, selves, and bodies of women in hip hop.

Mama tell me I am wrong

Is God just another cop

Waitin' to beat my ass if I don't go Pop?

—Tupac Shakur, "Blasphemy"

Ultimately the legitimate potential that hip-hop

artists possess as "urban griots turned Gramscian

intellectuals" is consistently challenged and undermined

by the needs of a transnational economy.

—Mark Anthony Neal, "Critical Noire"

7

Bling Bling . . . and Going Pop

Consumerism and Co-optation in Hip Hop

When I began to write this book, several friends urged me to do it quickly because in their opinion hip hop was dying. The late 1990s witnessed the success of a plethora of MCs with mediocre skills, rhyming primarily about consumerism or murder with mild, watered-down beats and weak production. And yet hip hop also became the most popular musical form in the United States. Even if one were to be more generous about this newer popular rap music, some of which proves aesthetically pleasing even if it does not seem especially good within the standards of evaluation for hip hop heads, there can be no doubt that it constitutes a more simplistic, less innovative, and softened version of original hip hop, meant to cater to a broader listening population, driven and shaped by markets as described in Mark Anthony Neal's work.[1] Yet this still does not signal the death of hip hop. Rather, I believe that hip hop is in the process of reformulating itself in the face of mainstream co-optation of many of its elements and widespread separation from its ideological and cultural context. Co-optation is designated by a repetition of these softened versions until hip hop becomes defined for many (if not most) by those versions instead of by the underground or by those maintaining underground sensibilities. Those of us who love hip hop fear its disintegration into pop, or that it might be "Elvisized," assimilated and recorded in history as its most watered-down and "acceptable" iterations. In anticipation of that demise, many of us have begun to push it away, to separate out "true" hip hop from "fake" simply on the basis of degree of mainstream popularity. But hip hop cannot be defined by that which fails to achieve commercial success. That seems a counterintuitive argument when speaking about popular music. Even those who stay true to the underground want to become popular. De La Soul rhymes about such aspiration to mass appeal:

a male authentic hip-hop only that which fails to achieve (comm. sucess)

> Now this goes out to all area cliques
> Centralized to way out in the sticks
> Remember to keep the De La in the mix,
> Just like log cabin syrup my style is game thick . . .
> Now this goes out to all area cliques
> From manicured lawns to project bricks
> Remember to keep the native tongues in the mix
> Straight butter hits as good as it gets.[2]

In this final chapter, I want to discuss the moral panic within the music, specifically the moral panic created by anxieties about mass production and capitalism and the threat to quality among avid listeners, or hip hop heads. This panic began in part as a coastal anxiety, as a desire for New York to continue to own the music, because the city was constructed as the location where artistry proved more important than the accumulation of wealth. A false construction it was. But more even than that, the panic wanted to assert a kind of progressive politics, and a kind of aesthetic politics too, not unlike the efforts to exert conservative politics through other moral panics the United States has witnessed in recent times. I will argue that while the anxieties about mass production and its threat to quality and the heart of the music are very legitimate, they also prove dangerous for potentially leading to categorizations of hip hop that mimic other divides in American music, and that ultimately do even more to serve the interests of power structures over communities. As David Bry has noted, "New York Hip Hop artists and intelligentsia, ever faithful to the essence of the form—the belief in the purity of hard, non-melodic arrangement and complex, punch-line laden wordplay—had developed a level of snobbery about the subject to match that of the black-turtleneck-and-beret-clad film critics congregating at cafes around NYU."[3]

This phenomenon lends evidence to yet another strand of the tension between living organic cultural roots and the new and interesting shapes they might take on. The following questions arise: How can the aesthetic requirements of and an allegiance to the hip hop community withstand the necessary aspiration of popular artists to have commercial success and make a name for themselves in music? How are the artists to attain mass appeal without sacrificing their cultural or ideological foundations? Lauryn Hill's solo album, *The Miseducation of Lauryn Hill*, provided enormous hope in that direction. She, at the tender age of twenty-four, was the first woman to win four Grammy awards in one year. In 1999, she graced the covers of countless magazines, including the highbrow *Harper's Bazaar* and British GQ. And she did this while dreadlocked, singing and rapping socially conscious and emotionally provocative lyrics, and visibly active in public service. Her compositions make use of the black English of the Northeast and include references to soul and reggae, as well as to black female heroines. She announced the neo–black pride movement for the hip hop generation both in substance and style. Amid a tide of watered-down, ultramaterialistic hip hop in the public eye, she achieved success as a singer and a masterful MC. As she rhymes: "It's funny how money change a situation / miscommunication lead to complication / my emancipation don't fit your equation / I was on the humble you on every station."[4] But she wound up being on as many stations as those who sold out for wealth and fame, and she stood as a testimony to the potential for fluid movement in hip hop, even as numerous die-hard fans anticipated the death of hip hop. And yet the same question emerges for Lauryn as for the others: As hip hop progresses fast and furious, with enormously steep ascents for its stars, how will the artists' skills continue to be cultivated in the way previous generations of African American musicians' have been, a process fundamental to the development of African American music as the most profound modern musico-cultural influence in the world?

The moral panic does not simply respond to forces from without but also to the sensibilities from within hip hop. The threats to hip hop appear both in the form of the dangers of mass production and co-optation by the mainstream and in that of a vapid consumerism fueling and supporting other consumer markets, themselves fueled by artists and video producers. It is fundamental to discuss both when considering what is happening to hip hop. On one level, the moral panic marks an attempt to excise a difficult part of the hip hop self.

Hip hop is a subculture of American music, of American culture, and of black America. And as much as it resists the philosophical and aesthetic pressures of mainstream America, it finds itself in constant conversation with, response to, and a part of Americana. Television, film, lingo, and fashion that one can consider more generally American appear throughout hip hop. The duo Das EFX, for example, continuously integrated popular cultural influences from white America into its lyrics, as well as ones more specific to black America. In hip hop, the use of television images proves important, as does fashion, and both of them stand as symbols of American consumer culture. The designers and labels that young black urban people have tended to favor since the 1970s have been highbrow or distinctly American ones, such as Polo, Tommy Hilfiger, Fila, or Gloria Vanderbilt. In Grand Puba's words, "Girbauds hangin' baggy, Tommy Hilfiger top gear."[5] There were also the odes to sneakers, including "My Adidas" by Run-DMC and "Nike" by Heavy D. Run-DMC rhymed, "The Adidas I possess to one man is rare / Myself homeboy got fifty pair / Got blue and black 'cause I likes to chill / and yellow and green when it's time to get ill / Got a pair that I wear when I'm playin' ball / Put the heel inside, make me ten feet tall."[6] But Heavy D. preferred another brand:

> Nikes I sport 'em
> Out the store I bought 'em
> And on the b-b-b basketball court is where I sport 'em . . .
> They have red ones, yellow ones, green ones too
> White on white, blue on white, just to name a few
> My crew's fully equipped from top to bottom
> Everything Nike makes Heavy D. and the Boyz got 'em.[7]

The acquisition of these stylish status symbols by rappers who created casual chic was matched by the telling of so-called big lies. In traditional black English, this refers to the telling of good bragging stories. The tales of wealth and riches were imaginative, even as heavy "trunk" jewelry hung around the necks of early MCS. Hip hop heads did not fail to recognize that the flow between high fashion and the hood worked in both directions, and that couture designers began copying their styles. I believe it is safe to say that young black people of the early to mid-1990s were responsible for the success of Tommy Hilfiger's clothing label, which was languishing before black youth took up the red, white, and blue loose-fitting preppy styles. But then a transition occurred, subtle perhaps, but quite real. As hip hop became more successful in the mainstream and the artists began to grow very wealthy, conspicuous consumption took on a new meaning for hip hop artists, so that more sophisticated styles became popular, along with more expensive designers. In Mase's words, "I went from Helly Hansen to many mansions."[8]

To be sure, the hip hop version of the Horatio Alger story gives evidence to the music's deep Americanism. Yet some tension arises when a neo–double consciousness, built on identifications with poverty and black Otherness, begins to battle with having "made it" in a big way. The "big lies" now no longer stood as such because the prospect of enormous wealth became a distinct possibility for the hip hop artist. Hip hop artists began to acquire some of the high style and expense of 1960s and 1970s R & B and funk performers. Recall Sly Stone's Halston-designed garments. Biggie's celebration of designers falls right into line: "I put hoes in NY onto DKNY / Miami DC prefer Versace / All Philly hoes down wit Moschino / Every cutie with a booty bought a coogi / Now who's the real Dukey? / Meanin' who's really the shit?"[9] As one critic describes it, "If there is a dominant perception about today's rap superstars among hip-hop's purists, it is that they have squandered the franchise by being obsessed with shaking derrieres, platinum jewelry, fine alcohol, premium weed, pimp culture, gangster rituals, and thug life. Although hip-hop has succeeded far beyond the Bronx of its birth, it has, in the minds of some of its most ardent guardians, lost its soul."[10] Ellis Cashmore even argues that the presence of these elements in hip hop serve white images of black America, racist images that constitute much of the way that what is called black culture enters the mainstream.[11] But we cannot fail to acknowledge here that style has always played a large role in black American culture. Even as their white counterpart hippies engaged in anti-aestheticism, black power followers donned stylish fatigues and combat boots, along with neatly tended afros. Each epoch in black music has had distinct style, from jazz to bebop to blues to doo-wop. And style, particularly that acquired at great expense, has always made for an in-your-face challenge to the powers that be. Let us not forget the Louisiana women of color who, forced to cover their hair, responded with gorgeous tignons, or newly emancipated women throughout the South who purchased parasols and ladies' hats, prompting legislation against such "uppityness." Style is a sign of black humanity and pride, as well as a development within black cultural practice. And an element of that style has always been excess. Think about the women on talk shows today with three-inch airbrushed nails and sculptural hair. Or hearken back to the flamboyance of a Jimi Hendrix, a Patti LaBelle and the Blue Belles, or a Little Richard. Such flamboyance might manifest itself in an extremely unusual sartorial style, as in OutKast's Andre 3000's late 1990s costuming in a blond wig and Mad Max clothing. Or it might manifest itself in capitalistic excess à la boxer Jack Johnson, who in the early twentieth century spent enormous amounts of money on cars, clothes, and white women. Puffy's flashy costumes, parties, and odes to material goods are expressions of both sorts of excessiveness. Despite the badass aspect of Jack Johnsonism, the integration of hip hop into the mainstream means that such ideas become virtually indistinguishable from celebrations of the American capitalist practices integral to the economic devastation of black communities and the enormous wealth disparities in US society that disproportionately affect black people.

> B.I.G.P.O.P.P.A.
>
> No info for the D.E.A.
>
> Federal agent mad 'cause I'm flagrant
>
> Tap my cell and the phone in the basement
>
> My team supreme stay clean
>
> Triple beam lyrical dream I be that
>
> Cat you see at all events bent
>
> Gats in holsters girls on shoulders
>
> Playboy I told ya.[12]

Consumerism and conspicuous consumption have become fundamental elements in hip hop. But rather than simply critique them as crass materialism, I want to consider the pleasures of shopping and dressing and using consumer goods. Consumerism touches on the pleasure derived from the beauty of things, from the adornment of the self. Hip hop consumerism is in part about the use of luxury to express black style. Gadgets also enhance the public self; they declare an importance in being reached. These ideas are rooted in a long tradition of black sartorial expression, where style proves important, and creativity even more so. Status is attached to the goods, not in mimicry of white privilege, but rather in an effort to recast status. Status linked to the body subverts the image of low status associated with black bodies. To adorn oneself marks one as a subject rather than commodity, yet the sartorial or jewel commodity becomes deeply associated with the wearer. The pervasive classism, including the internalized kind, demonstrated by disparaging references to certain aesthetics, sartorial stylistic excesses, and behaviors as "ghetto" lends testimony to this. The kind of excess celebrated elsewhere in American life is deemed disgraceful when associated with poor black people. Insofar as hip hop embraces ghetto sensibilities and ghetto people, it continues to have an important counter-hegemonic force. Much as the crochet cap–wearing and dreadlocked populist Afrocentrist sensibility operates as an affirmation of the black body, those who celebrate the "around the way" people and styles affirm the cultural spaces of the black poor.

Hip hop's extreme consumerism, and the dominance of hip hop in mainstream music culture, can mark a form of subversion. But at what cost does the celebration of those stick-it-to-you "I'm black, from the hood, *and* I wear Versace" values come? Perhaps the critic should just appreciate the achievements of young black people with global popular culture in their hands and understand that hip hop will never simply embrace one set of progressive politics. Numerous talented artists with progressive values remain local, while the excessive and consumerist ones go global. Even if we recognize that hip hop has the potential to revolutionize, it also has the potential to suffer co-optation. It constitutes a community too flexible and too fluid to imagine that it might have one sort of political or social influence. De La Soul rhymes:

> Like the alcohol scenario rap be on the rocks
> Authenticities that missin' and fee they paid to join the flock
> Of MC these niggas stand lower than these
> Dramatized in they eyes as the one to please

When rap kids apply violent pressure

To father, brother, and son for fun say they inflict pain.

R & B niggas lie to mother, sister and daughter to have sex disguised as
    lovin' in the rain

Their words are more hollow than October 31st

What's worse, to see the females switch to sexual mentality that doesn't
    match with their given anatomy

Man they'd rather be hoes like that male MC

And walk around like they got nuts

Or use their tits and ass as a crutch

Man the underground's about not bein' exposed

So you better take your naked ass and put on some clothes.[13]

The demise of the community here is read through glamorized violence
and sexual immorality, both acclaimed in music. Although I hesitate
to align myself with the prescriptive morality assigned to female sexuality, I would agree that the trends De La Soul critiques are disappoint-
ing, although on some level it is apropos of American culture. Isn't it
to be expected that a national culture that reifies mediocrity, sensation,
and flashiness over skill and excellence in everything from movies to
television to literature and music generally would integrate hip hop on
less-than-ideal terms? Heads want hip hop to be more than this, but the
music is of this American culture. No one should read my words as an
indictment of those hip hop artists who have achieved celebrity, because
quite a few of them are good lyricists and DJs. But they do acknowledge
that the bar for skill is much lower in the popular recording industry
context than in the compositional setting. The door remains open for
those who maintain an ethos of staying true to their origins, without
that meaning a celebration of hardness or a denial of the transformation
undergone. As Lauryn Hill reminds us:

Now I'ma get mozzarella like a Rockerfeller

Still be in the Church of Lalibela

Sing hymns a capella

Whether posin' in Maribella couture or collectin' residuals from off
    The Score

Get diplomatic immunity in every ghetto community
    Had opportunity
Went from hood shock to hood chic
But it ain't what you cop it's what you keep.[14]

Here is where the double voice of hip hop becomes not merely important but imperative if it wishes to maintain its constructive uses and
possibilities.

Cognizance of the threat of co-optation, matched with continued ad-
herence to its original aesthetics, ethos, and composition, will assure
the survival of hip hop despite increasing "acceptability." Black language, style, and dance coming from black communities and traditions continue to manifest themselves in all varieties of hip hop. And
the ambivalence of middle America persists as well. As long as young
black hip hop artists continue to contest the boundaries and definitions set forth by race and class, even in politically unhealthy ways,
hip hop will never achieve complete acceptance in American society.
Counter-hegemonic forces are not always ideologically sound, but they
are nonetheless noteworthy. And as long as hip hop remains by and large
counter-hegemonic, there is room within the discourse to battle over
ideas, values, and beliefs while maintaining an internal integrity and,
albeit more fragile the larger it gets, a community.

Nelson George notes that "in its third decade of existence, hip hop's influence is pervasive. While there are signs of weakness — its overwhelming dependence on major corporations for funding, its occasionally glee-
ful celebrations of anti-social tendencies — it shows no signs of heading
for the respirator any time soon."[15] George Lipsitz adds that "whatever
role they serve in the profit making calculations of the music industry,
these expressions also serve as exemplars of post-colonial culture with
direct relevance to the rise of new social movements emerging in response to the imperatives of global capital and its attendant austerity
and oppression."[16] While Lipsitz at times seems too optimistic about
the subaltern potential or stances that hip hop actually takes, at least
with regard to its presence in the United States, he does understand
the political significance of the double voice, the signifying that occurs
in hip hop with regard to the capitalist production of the music. Lipsitz groups hip hop with postcolonial literature and third world cinema,
arguing that all of them "protest against conditions created by the oli-

gopolies who distribute them as commodities for profit. They express painful recognition of cultural displacements, displacements that their very existence accelerates. Yet it is exactly their desire to work through rather than outside of existing structures that defines their utility as a model for contemporary global politics."[17] I agree with this argument to the extent that at worst, hip hop stars appear to engage in what Robin Kelley has called conservative black nationalisms of the production of black wealth, and at best they demonstrate a powerful articulation of the experience of those socioeconomically and politically alienated.[18]

The problem created by mass production and consumerism, both through the lenses of artistic development and community, is that mainstream popularity has led to both a sacrifice of artistry and a limited range of expressions present within the musical community as it is experienced by the majority of hip hop's audience. Braggadocio in visual materialism has displaced impressive literariness. But such a result could easily be anticipated as soon as hip hop obviously warranted profit. The process of late capitalist consumerism includes the creation of formulaic templates that become subject to mass production. The theories of Jacques Attali appropriately describe this phenomenon.[19] One of the first and most influential hip hop scholars, Tricia Rose, criticized Attali for not having the imaginative capacity to understand how repetition could exist outside of capitalist production and commodification.[20] While I agree that on an aesthetic level, hip hop has demonstrated how recorded music, a function of repetition, could in fact display an anti-capitalist aesthetic, Attali got it right on a polito-theoretical level: the repetition of mass production, with the exclusion of the local, has had a destructive impact on hip hop. Bell hooks has demonstrated the danger of repetition for black music.

> All African-American engagement in the performing arts, whether through the staged performance of poetry and plays, or through rap, risks losing its power to disrupt and engage with the specific locations from which it emerges via a process of commodification that requires reproduction in a marketable package. As mass product, live performance can rarely address the local in a meaningful way, because the primacy of addressing the local is sacrificed to the desire to engage a wider audience of paying consumers.[21]

I would alternatively read Attali with an understanding of his appreciation of the local as having primary significance for hip hop because the recorded music comes alive in local public and private space. It is music to be danced to, smoked to, the music of cars and streets, but most powerfully, I would argue, it is music to be deejayed, thereby re-instituting the local relationship between the music and the artist. Attali refers to composition as a stage within the political economy of music that follows capitalist replication and repetition. He uses the term *composition* to refer to the act of putting oneself and one's community back into music locally after it has been mass-produced. He uses the classical black American music, improvisational jazz, as his primary example: "Composition does not prohibit communication. It changes the rules. It makes it a collective creation rather than an exchange of coded messages. To express oneself is to create a code or to plug into a code in the process of being elaborated by the other."[22]

This practice of collective, local creation proved central to the foundation of hip hop. In the initial years, when DJs scratched rhythms over vinyl records, and/or repeatedly played the break beats of already recorded songs, and MCs rhymed over them, hip hop artists were transforming mass-produced recorded music into a vehicle for local participation. Fast-forward to the late 1990s: hip hop has become a several-billion-dollar industry; the majority of hip hop records played no longer exist within a "compositional" framework. Nevertheless, an aesthetic has developed embracing that framework. In the midst of reproduction, the primary level of production and composition is brought into the listener's consciousness. Oftentimes, as part of the recorded music, the MC does microphone checks or engages in a conversational introduction, or the music will contain the sounds of a party or street noise. The prevalence of remixed versions of the same songs—using different beats or additional rhymes, sped up, slowed down, or marked by any number of variations—also forms part of the compositional aesthetic. The audience is constantly aware of the song being worked on and put together over and over again. The ideal of being witness, and hence part of the live production of the reproduction, is aesthetically valued. Sadly, on some level, this simply constitutes an insidious form of capitalism's repetition. It may sound as though we, as listeners, are there, forming part of the production, but by and large, we consume studio music. The imperative of local participation in hip hop has diminished as the sounds of the party are sold to far corners of the globe. An independent MC, Fudge, articulates the following critique of the mainstream consumption of hip hop: "At this point in time hip hop is at its most dismal state of existence / At the place they say hip hop lives[23] they play 2cent rap and the priority of hip hop is called underground / but to me it's simply called hip hop because truthfully that's the only hip hop there is / George Bernard Shaw said in his piece 'Man and Superman' / Hell is full of musical amateurs / Yo Fudge, bring 'em to heaven."[24]

The compositional aesthetic has allowed members of the hip hop nation to lose sight of the damaging effects of capitalist repetition. However, efforts to maintain live composition continue. The DJ remains an important element of parties in young black communities. Whether he or she is adept at mixing records still matters, even if the DJ is not mixing for MCs to rhyme a live performance. And then small venues continue to exist where noncelebrities rhyme, rap, or recite poetry. Often recordings that emerge from these compositional venues reveal a higher level of sophistication in rhyming and deejaying than the average hip hop album. Moreover, local venues that feature spoken word inflected with hip hop, hip hop theater, dance, and other sorts of local production continue to exist and flourish. Community supports the development of art. Attali acknowledged composition's constant threat of co-optation, and to some extent, the assimilation of hip hop has occurred. However, hip hop heads have been unwilling to relinquish the art form to the bosses of capitalist repetition. In the afterword to the English translation of Attali's work, Susan McClary writes the following about this dynamic, speaking with regard to another music form, punk rock: "Even among the most disenfranchised, the values of capitalism are strong and many groups have become absorbed by the recording industry. . . . But while there exists a powerful tendency for industry to contain the noise of some of these groups by packaging it, converting it into style commodity, the strength of the movements is manifested by the seeming spontaneous generation of even more local groups."[25]

That spontaneous generation is the underground in hip hop. Underground artists are those not defined by the co-opting force of mass production, but who see as their primary frame of reference the hip hop community. Primarily, this group consists of artists not signed by major record labels or not receiving much mainstream radio play. A number of artists who have achieved mainstream success still have underground sensibilities about love for the art form and commitment to the hip hop community; they desire material success only while respecting those two principles. On his album *New York Reality Check 101*, constructed as a musical education in "real" hip hop, DJ Premier proclaims, "The underground started hip hop and the underground what's gon' hold the fort down if it ever tried to crumble."[26] The underground maintains the compositional space as hip hop becomes increasingly popular with global communities. As rap has become a staple for advertisement, it provides the artistic and cultural foundation for even the most popularized forms of hip hop. Innovations in style, rhyming, mixing, and production all come out of local compositional spaces. The underground remains firmly rooted within a cultural context that includes interaction, live performance, the art of deejaying, clothing, language, and one that rejects (in practice) the preference of capital over community. (I say in practice because one might be ideologically or artistically bent on the acquisition of capital, rhyme about getting paid and buying commodities, but not be willing to "sell out" the community for it.)

Hip hop has ample opportunity to sustain itself in the face of repetition. It is an art form that has always used repetition for the production of the specific. Attali distinguishes composition from repetition by saying that the network in which knowledge is inscribed in composition is "cartography, local knowledge, the insertion of culture into production and general availability of new tools and instruments."[27] In repetitions, he says on the other hand, it is genealogy, the study of replication, rather than cartography. In contrast, hip hop engages in the insertion of local knowledge and culture into production and yet also uses replication. It reuses commodities, records on wax, and makes them local and new by putting them into a musical collage via sampling or riffing. If any art form is able to sustain a compositional framework, it should be hip hop because its very roots lie in the use of commodity to dislocate commodity. The philosophical democracy at the participatory heart of the art form will continue in the underground, in live venues, people rhyming on the street, in parties, clubs, and dances, in the newer forms of music that constitute variations of hip hop, and even in folks leaning to the side while driving and bopping their heads. What hip hop needs is an appreciation of the local and the popular combined. But the popular space appealed to must remain the space from which hip hop production organically emerged—poor urban black and Latino communities. Places where the arts of dance and deejaying are appreciated, where the underlying aesthetics of black music to which hip hop owes its roots are understood and appreciated. Rather than becoming café music, for hip hop to sustain itself, it must continue to reinvent itself as local music.

Notes

Introduction

1   John Szwed, "The Real Old School," in *The Vibe History of Hip Hop*, ed. Alan Light (New York: Three Rivers Press, 1999), 4.

2   Henry Louis Gates Jr., *The Signifying Monkey: A Theory of Afro-American Literary Criticism* (New York: Oxford University Press, 1988).

3   When I refer to black Americans I am referring to the ethnic group of multigenerational African Americans, largely descended from American slavery.

4   Panel presentation. Harvard Black Law Students Association Annual Spring Conference, April 1996.

5   For her explication of the development of the "politics of respectability," see Evelyn Brooks Higginbottom, *Righteous Discontent: The Women's Movement in the Black Baptists Church, 1880–1920* (Cambridge, MA: Harvard University Press, 1995).

6   Theodor W. Adorno, *Aesthetic Theory*, trans. Robert Hullot-Kentor (Minneapolis: University of Minnesota Press, 1998).

7   De La Soul, "Area," *Bulhoone Mindstate* (Tommy Boy, 1993).

1 Hip Hop's Mama
Originalism and Identity in the Music

1 John Szwed, "The Real Old School," in *The Vibe History of Hip Hop*, ed. Alan Light (New York: Three Rivers Press, 1999), 3.

2 Paul Gilroy, " '. . . To Be Real': The Dissident Forms of Black Expressive Culture," in *Let's Get It On: The Politics of Black Performance*, ed. Catherine Ugwu (London: Institute of Contemporary Arts, 1995), 15.

3 Szwed "The Real Old School," 7.

4 Ibid., 5.

5 Ibid., 6.

6 See Paul Gilroy, *The Black Atlantic, Modernity, and Double Consciousness* (Cambridge: Harvard University Press, 1993).

7 Nancy Guevara, "Women Writin', Rappin', Breakin'," in *Droppin' Science: Critical Essays on Rap Music and Hip Hop Culture*, ed. William Eric Perkins (Philadelphia: Temple University Press, 1996), 50.

8 Mandalit del Barco, "Rap's Latino Sabor," in Perkins, *Droppin' Science*, 69.

9 John Yasin, "Rap in the African-American Music Tradition: Cultural Assertion and Continuity," in *Race and Ideology: Language, Symbolism, and Popular Culture*, ed. Arthur K. Spears (Detroit: Wayne State University Press, 1999), 210.

10 Ibid., 212.

11 Qtd. in Kevin O'Brien Chang and Wayne Chen, *Reggae Routes: The Story of Jamaican Music* (Philadelphia: Temple University Press, 1998), 72.

12 Ibid., 73.

13 Mary Waters, *Black Identities: West Indian Immigrant Dreams and American Realities* (Cambridge: Harvard University Press, 1999).

14 Devon Carbado, "(E)racing the Fourth Amendment," 100 *Michigan Law Review* (March 2002), 946–1044.

15 Mystikal, "Bouncin' Back (Bumpin' Me Against the Wall)" *Tarantula* (Jive Records, 2001).

16 Signifying, in the black oral tradition, refers to a use of language play that enables the speaker to harness power or authority otherwise denied him.

17 Michael Eric Dyson, *Holler If You Hear Me: Searching for Tupac Shakur* (New York: Basic Civitas Books, 2001), 117.

18 Tony Green, "The Dirty South," in Light, *The Vibe History of Hip Hop*, 265.

19 Ibid., 266.

20 Notorious B. I. G., "Going Back to Cali," *Life after Death* (Bad Boy, 1997).

21 OutKast, "Atliens," *Atliens* (LaFace Records, 1996).

22 The Five Percenters were founded by Clarence 13X. The basic teaching of the group, which is largely populated by young black men, has had substantial influences on hip hop, and boasts growing popularity in prison populations, says that once a man has achieved mastery of the self, he becomes God, meaning that he may control his own destiny. Five Percenters refer to men as "Gods" and women as "Earths." They also believe in a numerological system referred to as the Supreme Alphabet and Supreme Mathematics, with each letter and number referring to a religious concept carrying a parable. Teaching through this system is referred to as "dropping science," a term which has gained the broader meaning of saying something of political significance in hip hop.

23 Big Pun, "Still Not a Player," *Capital Punishment* (Loud Records, 1998).

24 Frankie Cutlass, "Puerto Rico," *Politics & Bullsh*t* (Relativity Records, 1997).

25 Yasin, "Rap in the African-American Music Tradition," 221.

26 Houston A. Baker Jr., *Black Studies, Rap, and the Academy* (Chicago: University of Chicago Press, 1993), 62.

27 Neil Strauss, "Rap and Rock," in Light, *The Vibe History of Hip Hop*, 240.

28 Ibid., 248.

29 Joe Wood, "Native Tongues: A Family Affair," in Light, *The Vibe History of Hip Hop*, 191.

30 "Bad niggas" was a term used to designate unruly enslaved people who challenged the physical authority of whites in plantation society. The term carried over into the post-bellum era to describe anti-authoritarian and outlaw blacks.

31 William Eric Perkins, "The Rap Attack," in Perkins, *Droppin' Science*, 20.

32 OutKast, "True Dat (Interlude)," *Southernplayalisticadillacmuzik* (LaFace Records, 1994).

33 Robert Stepto, *Behind the Veil: A Study of Afro-American Narrative* (Urbana: University of Illinois Press, 1979).

34 Albert Murray, *The Blue Devils of Nada: A Contemporary American Approach to Aesthetic Statement* (New York: Pantheon, 1996), 16.

35 Samuel A. Floyd Jr., *The Power of Black Music: Interpreting Its History from Africa to the United States* (New York: Oxford University Press, 1995), 95.

36 Rob Kenner, "Dancehall," in Light, *The Vibe History of Hip Hop*, 352.

37 Charles Johnson, *Being and Race: Black Writing since 1970* (Bloomington: Indiana University Press, 1988), 38.

38 Floyd, *The Power of Black Music*, 229.

39 Ibid., 230.

2 My Mic Sound Nice
Art, Community, and Consciousness

1   bell hooks, "Performance as a Site of Opposition," in *Let's Get It On: The Politics of Black Performance*, ed. Catherine Ugwu (London: Institute of Contemporary Arts, 1995), 210.

2   Clarence Lusane, *Race in the Global Era: African Americans at the Millennium* (Boston: South End, 1997), 86.

3   Michael Eric Dyson, *Holler If You Hear Me: Searching For Tupac Shakur* (New York: Basic Civitas Books, 2001), 158.

4   disChord: A Conference on Contemporary Popular Music, May 9–11, 1997. University of California, Los Angeles.

5   Robin D. G. Kelley, "Kickin' Reality, Kickin' Ballistics: Gangsta Rap and Post-industrial Los Angeles," in *Droppin' Science: Critical Essays on Rap Music and Hip Hop Culture*, ed. William Eric Perkins (Philadelphia: Temple University Press, 1996), 148.

6   Charles Johnson, *Being and Race: Black Writing since 1970* (Bloomington: Indiana University Press, 1988), 28.

7   De La Soul, "I Am, I Be," *Bulhoone Mindstate* (Tommy Boy, 1994).

8   A Tribe Called Quest, "Check the Rhime," *The Low End Theory* (BMG/Jive, 1991).

9   Jadakiss, "It's Time I See You," *Kiss the Game Goodbye* (Ruffryders/Def Jam, 2001).

10   Houston A. Baker Jr., *Black Studies, Rap, and the Academy* (Chicago: University of Chicago Press, 1993), 43.

11   Albert Murray, *The Blue Devils of Nada: A Contemporary American Approach to Aesthetic Statement* (New York: Pantheon, 1996), 13.

12   KRS-One, "Return of the Boom Bap," *Return of the Boom Bap* (BMG/Jive, 1993).

13   Digable Planets, "It's Good to Be Here," *A New Refutation of Time and Space* (EMI, 1991).

14   Digable Planets, "Pacifics (NY Is Red Hot)," *A New Refutation of Time and Space* (EMI, 1991).

15   A. L., "Lyrics," *The Lyricist Lounge Vol. 1* (Priority/Rawkus, 1999).

16   Greg Tate, "Fifteen Arguments in Favor of the Future of Hip Hop," in *The Vibe History of Hip Hop*, ed. Alan Light (New York: Three Rivers Press, 1999), .

17   Junior M.A.F.I.A., "Get Money," *Conspiracy* (WEA/Atlantic, 1995).

18   Jay-Z, "Ain't No Nigga," *Reasonable Doubt* (Priority, 1999).

19   Onyx, "Slam," *Bacdafucup* (Uni/Def Jam, 1993).

20   A Tribe Called Quest, "God Lives Through," *Midnight Marauders* (BMG/

Jive. 1993). Here *Ab* is an abbreviation for Abstract, one of Q-Tip's monikers.

21 Black Star, "Hater Players," *Black Star* (Priority/Rawkus Entertainment, 1999).

22 Meshell Ndegeocello, *Plantation Lullabies* (WEA/Warner Brothers, 1993).

23 Richard Delgado and Jean Stefancic, "Images of the Outsider in American Law and Culture: Can Free Expression Remedy Systemic Social Ills?" in *Critical Race Theory: The Cutting Edge*, ed. Delgado (Philadelphia: Temple University Press, 1995), 220.

24 Ibid., 221.

25 Trinh T. Minh-ha *Woman, Native Other: Writing Postcoloniality and Feminism* (Bloomington: Indiana University Press, 1989), 17.

26 Mel Watkins, *On the Real Side: Laughing, Lying, and Signifying; The Underground Tradition of African-American Humor That Transformed American Culture, From Slavery to Richard Pryor* (New York: Simon and Schuster, 1994), 544–45.

27 Three Times Dope, "Greatest Man Alive," *Original Stylin'* (Arista Records, 1988).

28 Method Man, "M.E.T.H.O.D. Man," *Tical* (Uni/Def Jam, 1994).

29 A Tribe Called Quest, "Can I Kick It?" *People's Instinctive Travels in the Paths of Rhythm* (BMG/Jive, 1990).

30 Eric B. and Rakim, "I Know You Got Soul," *Paid in Full* (Uni/Island, 1987).

31 Jeru the Damaja, "Come Clean," *The Sun Rises in the East* (Uni/Full Frequency Range Records, 1994).

32 Eric B. and Rakim, "Microphone Fiend," *Follow the Leader* (Uni/Universal Records, 1988).

33 Boogie Down Productions, "I'm Still #1" *By Any Means Necessary* (Jive Records, 1988).

34 Eric B. and Rakim, "Eric B. is President," *Paid in Full*.

35 De La Soul, "Big Brother Beat," *Stakes Is High* (Tommy Boy, 1996).

36 MC Lyte, "10% Dis," *Lyte as a Rock* (Atlantic Recording, 1988).

37 The Infamous Mobb Deep, "Quiet Storm," *Murda Muzik* (Loud Records, 1999).

38 OutKast, "Southernplayalisticadillacmuzik," *Southernplayalisticadillacmuzik* (LaFace Records, 1994).

39 Killah Priest, "From Then to Now," *Heavy Mental* (Geffen Records, 1998).

40 Method Man, "Biscuits," *Tical*.

41 Nelson George, *Hip Hop America* (New York: Viking, 1998), viii.

42 Ibid., xi.

3 Stinging Like Tabasco
Structure and Format in Hip Hop Compositions

1   *Closer to Truth*, show 206: "Why do We Make Music and Art?"
   2   Public Enemy, "Timebomb," *Yo Bum Rush the Show* (Def Jam, 1987).
   3   Genius/GZA, "Duel of the Iron Mic," *Liquid Swords* (Uni/Geffen, 1995).
   4   Heltah Skeltah, "The Grate Unknown," *Nocturnal* (Priority, 1996).
   5   MC Lyte "10% Dis," *Light as a Rock* (Atlantic, 1990); Antoinette, "Lights Out, Party Over," *Who's the Boss?* (Next Plateau, 1989).
   6   Samuel A. Floyd Jr., *The Power of Black Music: Interpreting Its History from Africa to the United States* (New York: Oxford University Press, 1995), 95. See also Henry Louis Gates Jr., *The Signifying Monkey: A Theory of Afro-American Literary Criticism* (New York: Oxford University Press, 1988).
   7   Nelson George, *Hip Hop America* (New York: Viking, 1998), 92.
   8   Take for example these lines from Ice Cube which play on the hyper-sexual racist imagery to subvert such ideas: "My skin is my sin, look at my complexion / Section 8 erection great/ Balls like RuPaul and a big fat plank / Get you higher than a Spike Lee joint / See I'm a chicken hawk and I'm hunting chicken and watermelon." Ice Cube, "My Skin is My Sin," *Bootlegs and B Sides* (Priority, 1994).
   9   Floyd, *The Power of Black Music*, 227.
  10   George, *Hip Hop America*, 100.
  11   George, *Hip Hop America*, 101.
  12   Gates, *The Signifying Monkey*, 94.
  13   Ibid., 124.
  14   Ibid., 52.
  15   Robert Stepto, *From Behind the Veil: A Study of Afro-American Narrative* (Urbana: University of Illinois, 1991).
  16   MC Lyte, "Lyte as a Rock," *Lyte as a Rock* (WEA/Atlantic, 1988).
  17   Ibid.
  18   Giovanni's poem includes the lines: "I was born in the Congo / I walked to the fertile crescent and built / The Sphinx / I designed a pyramid so tough that a star / that only glows every hundred years falls / into the center giving divine perfect light / I am bad." Nikki Giovanni, "Ego Trippin'," *Ego Tripping and Other Poems for Children* (Chicago: Chicago Review Press, 1973).
  19   Special Ed, "I Got it Made," *Youngest in Charge* (Profile Records, 1989).
  20   Natural Elements, "Lyrical Tactics," *New York Reality Check 101*, by DJ Premier (Priority Records, 1997).
  21   John Szwed, "The Real Old School," in *The Vibe History of Hip Hop*, ed. Alan Light (New York: Three Rivers Press, 1999), 8.

22 Craig Mack, "Flavor in Ya Ear," *Project: Funk Da World* (BMG/Arista/Bad Boy, 1994).

23 Heavy D and the Boyz, "We Got Our Own Thang," *Big Tyme* (Uni/MCA, 1989).

24 Qtd. in Chairman Mao, "You Spin Me Round (Like a Record Baby): Last Night a DJ Saved Hip Hop" in Light, *The Vibe History of Hip Hop*, 77.

25 Paul Gilroy, " '. . . To Be Real': The Dissident Forms of Black Expressive Culture," in *Let's Get It On: The Politics of Black Performance*, ed. Catherine Ugwu (London: Institute of Contemporary Arts, 1995), 25.

26 Floyd, *The Power of Black Music*, 27–28.

27 Ibid., 56.

28 Houston A. Baker Jr. *Black Studies, Rap, and the Academy* (Chicago: University of Chicago Press, 1993), 89.

29 Theodor W. Adorno, *Aesthetic Theory*, trans. Robert Hullot-Kentor (Minneapolis: University of Minnesota Press, 1998), 57.

30 Eric B. and Rakim, "Follow the Leader," *Follow the Leader* (Uni, 1988).

31 Killah Priest, "Heavy Mental," *Heavy Mental* (Geffen, 1998).

32 Floyd, *The Power of Black Music*, 56.

33 Eric B. and Rakim, "My Melody," *Paid in Full* (Uni/Island, 1987).

34 Kings of Swing, "Nod Your Head to This," *Strategy* (Bum Rush, 1990).

35 Mad Skillz, "The Head-Nodder," *From Where???* (Big Beat, 1996).

36 KRS-One, "Return of the Boom Bap," *Return of the Boom Bap* (BMG/Jive, 1993).

37 Lil' Kim, "Ladies Night: Not Tonight Remix," (Bad Boy, 1997).

38 Joeski Love, "Pee Wee's Dance," (Elektra, 1986).

39 Run-DMC, "Peter Piper," *Raising Hell* (Def Jam, 1986).

40 A Tribe Called Quest, "Check the Rhime," *Low End Theory* (BMG/Jive, 1991).

41 We can imagine an obscene gesture here.

42 EPMD, "Who Killed Jane?" *Business Never Personal* (Def Jam, 1992).

43 Charles Johnson, *Being and Race: Black Writing since 1970* (Bloomington, Indiana University Press, 1988), 50.

44 Boogie Down Productions, "Love's Gonna Getcha," *Edutainment* (Jive, 1990).

45 Dana Dane, "Delancey Street," *Dana Dane with Fame* (Profile Records, 1987).

46 Dana Dane, "Nightmares," *Dana Dane with Fame* (Profile Records, 1987).

47 Genius/GZA, "Duel of the Iron Mic," *Liquid Swords* (Uni/Geffen, 1995).

48 Nas, "It Ain't Hard to Tell," *Illmatic* (Sony/Columbia, 1994).

49 LL Cool J, "I'm Bad," *Bigger and Deffer* (Columbia, 1987).

50 LL Cool J, "Kanday," *Bigger and Deffer.*

51 Lord Taqiq and Peter Gunz, "Déjà vu (Uptown Baby)," *Make it Rain* (Sony, 1998); 2 Pac, "California Love," *All Eyez on Me* (Death Row, 2001); Scarface, "Southside: Houston, Texas," *My Homies* (Rap a Lot, 1998); Boogie Down Productions, "South Bronx," *Criminal Minded* (B-Boy, 1987); Run DMC, "My Adidas," *Raising Hell* (Profile, 1986); Heavy D and the Boyz, "Nike," *Livin' Large* (MCA, 1987).

52 Run-DMC, "Perfection," *Raising Hell.*

53 Nice 'N Smooth, "Hip Hop Junkies," *Ain't a Damn Thing Changed* (Uni/Def Jam, 1991).

54 U.T.F.O., "Roxanne, Roxanne," *U.T.F.O.* (Select Records, 1985); Roxanne Shante, "Roxanne's Revenge, Round One," *Roxanne Shante vs. Sparky D* (Spin Records, 1985); The Real Roxanne, "The Real Roxanne" (Select Records, 1988); Sparky D, "Sparky's Turn (Roxanne You're Through)" (NIA, 1985).

55 MC Shan, "The Bridge," *Down By Law* (Cold Chillin' Records, 1987); Boogie Down Productions, "The Bridge Is Over," *By All Means Necessary* (BMG/Jive, 1988).

56 Poor Righteous Teachers, "Da Rill Shit," *Black Business* (Profile Records, 1993).

57 Eric B. and Rakim, "My Melody," *Paid in Full* 1987.

58 MC Lyte, "Kickin' 4 Brooklyn," *Lyte as a Rock.*

59 Notorious B. I. G., "The What," *Ready to Die* (BMG/Arista/Bad Boy, 1994).

60 Nas, "Represent," *Illmatic.*

61 Mobb Deep, "Start of Your Ending," *The Infamous* (BMG, 1995).

62 Mobb Deep, "Survival of the Fittest," *The Infamous.*

63 Nas, "Life's a Bitch," *Illmatic.*

64 Michael Eric Dyson, *Holler If You Hear Me: Searching For Tupac Shakur* (New York: Basic Civitas Books, 2001), 157.

65 Stevie Wonder, "Village Ghetto Land," *Natural Wonder: Stevie Wonder Live in Concert* (Motown, 1995).

66 Killah Priest, "Fake MCs," *Heavy Mental* (Geffen, 1998).

67 Goodie Mob., "Cell Therapy," *Soul Food* (LaFace Records, 1995).

68 Nas, "Represent," *Illmatic.*

69 Johnson, *Being and Race*, 13.

70 Floyd W. Hayes III, "The Concept of Double Vision in Richard Wright's *The Outsider*: Fragmented Blackness in the Age of Nihilism," in *Existence in Black: An Anthology of Black Existential Philosophy*, ed. Lewis R. Gordon (New York: Routledge, 1997),177.

71 Andrew Ross, *Real Love: In Pursuit of Cultural Justice* (New York: New York University Press, 1998), 74.

72 Scarface, "Don't Testify," *My Homies* (Rap A-Lot Virgin Records, 1998).

73 Ibid.

74 Mobb Deep, "Survival of the Fittest," *The Infamous*.

75 Mobb Deep, "Eye for an Eye," *The Infamous*.

76 Mobb Deep, "Survival of the Fittest," *The Infamous*.

77 Mobb Deep, "Just Step Prelude," *The Infamous*.

78 Mobb Deep, "The Infamous Prelude," *The Infamous*.

79 Digable Planets, "Where I'm From," *Reachin' a New Refutation of Time and Space* (EMI, 1991).

80 Adorno, *Aesthetic Theory*, 19.

81 LL Cool J, "My Rhyme Ain't Done," *Bigger and Deffer*.

4   The Glorious Outlaw
Hip Hop Narratives, American Law, and the Court of Public Opinion

1   Monica Evans, "Stealing Away: Black Women, Outlaw Culture, and the Rhetoric of Rights," in *Critical Race Theory: The Cutting Edge*, ed. Richard Delgado (Philadelphia: Temple University Press, 1995), 503.

2   Cornel West, *Prophesy Deliverance! An Afro-American Revolutionary Christianity* (Philadelphia: Westminster, 1982), 80.

3   Ibid., 85.

4   dream hampton, "Bad Boy," in *The Vibe History of Hip Hop*, ed. Alan Light (New York: Three Rivers Press, 1999), 343.

5   Robin D. G. Kelley, "Kickin' Reality, Kickin' Ballistics: Gangsta Rap and Post-industrial Los Angeles," in *Droppin' Science: Critical Essays on Rap Music and Hip Hop Culture*, ed. William Eric Perkins (Philadelphia: Temple University Press, 1996), 121.

6   As Andrew Ross writes, "the stories and fantasies recounted in music, as in all art forms, are often powerful precisely *because* they are outlawed in daily life, or have no chance of being enacted there."

7   Michael Eric Dyson, *Holler If You Hear Me: Searching for Tupac Shakur* (New York: Basic Civitas Books, 2001), 238.

8   Channel Live, "Mad Izm," *Station Identification* (Capitol Records, 1995); Method Man and Red Man, "How High?" (Def Jam, 1995).

9 · Channel Live, "Mad Izm," *Station Identification* (Capitol Records, 1995).

10 D'Angelo, "Brown Sugar," '*Brown Sugar* (Emd/Capitol, 1995).

11 Redman and Method Man, "How High?" (Def Jam, 1995).

12 KRS-One, "I Can't Wake Up," *Return of the Boom Bap* (BMG/Jive, 1993).

13 Ibid.

14 Snoop Doggy Dogg, "Gin and Juice," *Doggy Style* (Priority, 1993).

15   Mother Superia, "Most of All," *Mother Superia* (Island, 1997).

16   Jody Armour, *Negrophobia and Reasonable Racism: The Hidden Costs of Being Black in America* (New York: New York University, 2000).

17   Nelson George, *Hip Hop America* (New York: Penguin, 1998), 42.

18   Ibid., 49.

19   Homi K. Bhabha, "Of Mimicry and Man: The Ambivalence of Colonial Discourse," *The Location of Culture* (New York: Routledge, 1993).

20   Herman Gray, "Black Masculinity and Visual Culture," in *Black Male: Representations of Masculinity in Contemporary American Art*, ed. Thelma Golden (New York: Whitney Museum of American Art, 1994), 402.

21   Da Lench Mob, "Guerillas in tha Mist," *Guerillas in tha Mist* (Atlantic, 1992).

22   Kelley, "Kickin' Reality, Kickin' Ballistics," 133.

23   See, for example, Richard Delgado, "Storytelling for Oppositionists and Others: A Plea for Narrative," *Mich. L. Rev.* 87 (1989); Alex M. Johnson Jr., "Defending the Use of Narrative and Giving Content to the Voice of Color: Rejecting the Imposition of Process Theory in Legal Scholarship," *Iowa L. Rev.* 79 (1994).

24   Mary Maynard and Jan Winn, "Women, Violence, and Male Power," in Diane Richardson and Victoria Robinson, eds. *Introducing Women's Studies: Feminist Theory and Practice* (New York: Macmillan, 1997).

25   Tricia Rose, *Black Noise: Rap Music and Black Culture in Contemporary America* (Middletown, CT: Wesleyan University Press, 1994), 85.

26   George, *Hip Hop America*, 94.

27   Suzanne McElfresh, "DJs vs. Samplers," in Light, *The Vibe History of Hip Hop*, 171–72.

28   Ibid., 172.

29   Tricia Rose, "Rap Music and the Demonization of Young Black Males," in Golden, *Black Male*, 157.

5   B-Boys, Players, and Preachers
Reading Masculinity

1   Michael Eric Dyson, *Holler if You Hear Me: Searching for Tupac Shakur* (New York: Basic Civitas Books, 2001), 15.

2   Evelyn Brooks Higginbotham, "African American Women's History and the Metalanguage of Race," *Signs* 17, no. 2 (1992): 207.

3   Darrell Dawsey, *Living to Tell about It: Young Black Men in America Speak Their Piece* (New York: Anchor Books, 1996), xii.

4   Patricia Hill Collins, *Black Feminist Thought* (New York: Routledge, 2000).

5   bell hooks, "Feminism Inside: Toward a Black Body Politic," in *Black Male: Representations of Masculinity in Contemporary American Art*, ed. Thelma Golden (New York: Whitney Museum of American Art, 1994), 127.

6   Ibid., 130.

7   Ed Guerrero, "The Black Man on Our Screens and the Empty Space in Representation," in Golden, *Black Male*, 183.

8   Ibid.

9   bell hooks, "Performance as a Site of Opposition," in *Let's Get It On: The Politics of Black Performance*, ed. Catherine Ugwu (London: Institute of Contemporary Arts, 1995), 220.

10 Herman Gray, "Black Masculinity and Visual Culture," in *Golden Black Male*, 175.

11 Channel Live, "Station Identification," *Station Identification* (Capitol, 1995).

12 Keith Murray, "The Most Beautifullest Thing in This World," *The Most Beautifullest Thing in This World* (Zomba Recording, 1994).

13 Michael Eric Dyson, *Holler If You Hear Me: Searching for Tupac Shakur* (New York: Basic Civitas Books, 2001), 234.

14 Ellis Cashmore, *The Black Culture Industry* (New York: Routledge, 1997), 170.

15 "Gangsta Rap in the '90s," in *The Vibe History of Hip Hop*, ed. Alan Light (New York: Three Rivers Press, 1999), 291.

16 Nelson George, *Hip Hop America* (New York: Penguin, 1998), vii.

17 Ibid, 43.

18 George P. Cunningham, "Body Politics: Race, Gender, and the Captive Body," in *Representing Black Men*, ed. Marcellus Blount and Cunningham (New York: Routledge, 1996), 135.

19 Ibid., 144.

20 Dyson, *Holler If You Hear Me*, 182.

21 Notorious B. I. G. "The What," *Ready to Die* (Bad Boy, 1994).

22 George, *Hip Hop America*, 36.

23 Lost Boys, "Jeeps, Lex Coupes, Bimas Benz," *Legal Drug Money* (Uni/Universal, 1995).

24 The Fugees, "Nappy Heads," *Blunted in Reality* (Sony, 1994); Cypress Hill, "Throw Your Set in the Air," *Temples of Boom* (Sony, 1994).

25 Marcellus Blount and George P. Cunningham, "Introduction," in Blount and Cunningham, *Representing Black Men*, xii.

26 "Where Ya At Y'all," *One Million Strong* (Mergela, 1995).

27 Jay-Z, "Friend or Foe," *Reasonable Doubt* (Priority, 1996).

28 Ibid.

29 Ibid.

30 Scarface, "Hustler," *My Homies* (Rap-A-Lot, 1998).

31 Mos Def, "Mathematics," *Black on Both Sides* (Rawkus, 2002).

32 Heavy D. and the Boyz, *Peaceful Journey* (MCA, 1991).

33 Notorious B. I. G., "The Happening," *Ready to Die*.

34 Nine, "Whutcha Want?" *Nine Livez* (Profile Records, 1995).

35 Notorious B. I. G., "Juicy," *Ready to Die*.

36 Lord Finesse, "Speak Ya Peace," *The Awakening* (Penalty Records, 1996).

37 Redman and Method Man, "How High," (Def Jam, 1995).

38 Craig Mack, "Get Down," *Project: Funk Da World* (Arista, 1994).

39 LL Cool J, "Illegal Search," *Mama Said Knock You Out* (Def Jam, 1990).

40 Bone Thugs-N-Harmony, "First of Tha Month," *E. 1999 Eternal* (Ruthless Records, 1995).

41 Ibid.

42 *Lickle* is Jamaican patois for "little."

43 KRS-One, "Sound of Da Police," *Return of the Boom Bap* (BMG/Jive, 1993).

44 "Where Ya At Y'all," *One Million Strong* (Mergela, 1995).

45 Notorious B. I. G., "Juicy," *Ready to Die*.

46 Das EFX, "Freakit," *Straight Up Sewaside* (WEA/Atlantic, 1993).

47 Elizabeth Alexander "Can You Be BLACK and Look at This? Reading the Rodney King Video(s)" in Golden, *Black Male*, 94.

48 Robin D. G. Kelley, "Kickin' Reality, Kickin' Ballistics: Gangsta Rap and Post-industrial Los Angeles," in *Droppin' Science: Critical Essays on Rap Music and Hip Hop Culture*, ed. William Eric Perkins (Philadelphia: Temple University Press, 1996), 137.

49 George, *Hip Hop America* (New York: Penguin, 1998), 131.

50 Cheo Hodari Coker, "N.W.A.," in Light, *The Vibe History of Hip Hop*, 252.

51 Ibid.

52 Hence rhymes like Nas's, "Earlier this year I buried my queen in a casket / Your mother's the closest thing to God you ever have kid." Nas, "Warrior's Song, God's Son," (Columbia).

53 Method Man, "All I Need," *Tical* (Def Jam, 1993).

54 Dawsey, *Living to Tell about It*, 209.

55 Notorious B. I. G., "The What," *Ready to Die*.

56 Method Man, "All I Need," *Tical* (Def Jam, 1994).

57 Ice Cube, "It's a Man's World," *Amerikkkas Most Wanted* (Priority, 1990).

58 Lady of Rage, "Afro Puffs," *Above the Rim* (Priority, 1994).

59 Greg Tate, "Fifteen Arguments in Favor of the Future of Hip Hop," in Light, *The Vibe History of Hip Hop*, 393.

60 Yo Yo, "Bonnie and Clyde Theme," *You Better Ask Somebody* (East West Records, 1993).

61 Notorious B. I. G., "Me and My Bitch" *Ready to Die*.

62 Apache, "Gangsta Bitch," *Apache Ain't Shit* (Tommy Boy 1993).

63 Jay-Z, "Ain't No Nigga," *Reasonable Doubt.*

64 Whodini, "One Love," *Back in Black* (Jive Records, 1986).

65 Black Star, "Brown Skin Lady," *Black Star* (Priority/Rawkus, 1999).

66 William Eric Perkins, "The Rap Attack," in *Droppin' Science: Critical Essays on Rap Music and Hip Hop Culture,* ed. William Eric Perkins (Philadelphia: Temple University Press, 1996), 23.

67 Brand Nubian, "All For One," *One for All* (Electra, 1990).

68 Khrist, "Holy Water," *The Lyricist Lounge* (Rawkus, 1996).

69 Talib Kweli, "Manifesto," *The Lyricist Lounge.*

70 Notorious B.I.G., "Suicidal Thoughts," *Ready to Die* (Bad Boy, 1994).

71 Run-DMC, "Raising Hell," Run DMC *Raising Hell* (Def Jam, 1986).

72 Common, "G.O.D.," *One Day It'll All Make Sense* (Relativity Records, 1997).

73 Ibid.

74 Ibid.

75 Ibid.

6 The Venus Hip Hop and the Pink Ghetto
Negotiating Spaces for Women

1 Boss, interview by, *Art Forum*, June 1993.

2 Junior M.A.F.I.A., "Player's Anthem," *Conspiracy* (Big Beat, 1995).

3 Suga-T, "What's Up Star," *Paper Chasin' (4Eva Hustlin')* (Zomba Recording, 1996).

4 Ibid.

5 Nancy Guevara, "Women Writin', Rappin', Breakin'," in *Droppin' Science: Critical Essays on Rap Music and Hip Hop Culture,* ed. William Eric Perkins (Philadelphia: Temple University Press, 1996), 61.

6 Cypress Hill, "How I Could Just Kill a Man," *Cypress Hill* (Sony, 1991).

7 Eric B. and Rakim, "Follow the Leader," *Follow the Leader* (Uni, 1988).

8 Hazel Carby, "It Jus' Bees Day Way Sometimes: The Sexual Politics of Black Women's Blues," in *Feminisms: An Anthology of Literary Theory and Criticism,* ed. Robin R. Warhol and Diane Price Herndl (New Brunswick, NJ: Rutgers University Press, 1991), 751.

9 Robert Stepto, *From Behind the Veil: A Study of Afro American Narrative* (Urbana: University of Chicago Press, 1991).

10 See Farah Jasmine Griffin, *"Who Set You Flowin'?": The African-American Migration Narrative* (New York: Oxford University Press, 1995).

11 Harriet Jacobs, *Incidents in the Life of a Slave Girl* (New York: Dover Pub-

lishing, 2001 [1861]); Nella Larsen, *The Complete Fiction of Nella Larsen: Passing, Quicksand, and the Stories,* ed. Charles Larson (New York: Anchor, 2001); Valerie Boyd, *Wrapped in Rainbows: The Life of Zora Neale Hurston* (New York: Scribner, 2002).

12 Boss, "Progress of Elimination," *Born Gangstaz* (Sony, 1993).

13 Boss, "Diary of a Mad Bitch," *Born Gangstaz.*

14 Yo Yo, "IBWin Wit My Crewin'," *You Better Ask Somebody* (East West Records, 1993).

15 Yo Yo, "Girl's Got a Gun," *You Better Ask Somebody.*

16 Fugees, "Fugee-La," *The Score* (Sony, 1996).

17 Nikki D., "Freak Out," *Rollin' Wit Tha Flava* (Epic Records, 1993).

18 Boss, "Recipe of a Hoe," *Born Gangstaz.*

19 Junior Mafia, "Get Money," *Conspiracy* (Atlantic, 1996).

20 Gayl Jones, *Eva's Man* (Boston: Beacon Press, 1976), 132.

21 Toni Morrison, *Beloved* (New York: Knopf, 1987).

22 Boss, "Recipe of a Hoe," *Born Gangstaz.*

23 Boss, "Diary of a Mad Bitch," *Born Gangstaz.*

24 Bessie Smith, "Black Mountain Blues," *Bessie Smith: The Complete Recordings,* vol. 4 (Columbia, 1993).

25 Toni Morrison, *Beloved,* 257.

26 Lillian Miller, "Dead Drunk Blues," *I Can't Be Satisfied, Vol.1: Country– Early American Women Blues Singers, Town and Country Classic Recordings from the 1920s* (Yazoo Records, 2000).

27 Boss, "Diary of a Mad Bitch," *Born Gangstaz.*

28 Baldwin Hills is a middle-class black suburb of Los Angeles.

29 Boss, "Deeper," *Born Gangstaz.*

30 Kyra Gaunt, "Translating Double-Dutch to Hip Hop: The Musical Vernacular of Black Girls Play," in Joseph K. Adjaye and Adrianne R. Andrews, eds. *Language, Rhythm, and Sound: Black Popular Cultures into the Twenty First Century* (Pittsburgh: University of Pittsburgh Press, 1997).

31 Elysa Gardner, "Hip Hop Soul," in *The Vibe History of Hip Hop,* ed. Alan Light (New York: Three Rivers Press, 1999), 310.

32 Robin D. G. Kelley, "Kickin' Reality, Kickin' Ballistics: Gangsta Rap and Post-industrial Los Angeles," in *Droppin' Science: Critical Essays on Rap Music and Hip Hop Culture,* ed. William Eric Perkins (Philadelphia: Temple University Press, 1996), 146.

33 Junior Mafia, "Get Money," *Conspiracy* (Atlantic, 1996).

34 Robin D. G. Kelley, "Kickin' Reality, Kickin' Ballistics," 146.

35 Ibid.

36 Antoinette, "Never Get Enough," *Burnin' at 20 Below* (Next Plateau, 1992).

37 Roxanne Shante, "Have a Nice Day," *Cold Chillin': The Juice Crew Story* (Cold Chillin' Records, 1989).

38 Boogie Down Productions, "The Bridge is Over," *Criminal Minded* (B-Boy Records, 1987).

39 Salt-N-Pepa, "My Mic Sound Nice," *Hot, Cool, and Vicious* (Next Plateau, 1985).

40 Salt-N-Pepa, "I Desire," *Hot, Cool, and Vicious*.

41 Salt-N-Pepa, "Ain't Nuthin' but a She Thing," (PGD/Polygram, 1995).

42 Eve, "My Bitches," *RuffRyders First Lady* (Universal Records, 1999).

43 Ibid.

44 Ibid.

45 Ibid.

46 Jay-Z, "Bitches and Sisters," *The Blue Print 2: The Gift and the Curse* (Def Jam, 2002).

47 Rose, "Ladies First," 178; Sugar Hill Gang, "Rapper's Delight" (Sugar Hill Records, 1979).

48 Ibid.

49 The most prominent black women's magazines, *Essence* and *Honey*, as well as *Girl*, geared toward a multicultural audience of adolescent girls, all have an explicitly feminist agenda. Readers of these magazines are not offered articles about how to seduce men or how to appear sexy, the typical fare of such publications as *Cosmopolitan*, YM, and *Glamour*.

50 Barry Fletcher, *Why Black Women are Losing their Hair* (New York: Unity Publishing, 2000), ii.

51 Sir Mix-A-Lot, "Baby Got Back," (Mix a Lot Records 1993).

52 There are many hip hop lyrics that identify the voluptuous body with women who live in housing projects or who come from the hood. Additionally, the assumption that lighter-complexioned black women are of a higher socioeconomic status, or have greater sexual desirability, constitutes a long-standing aspect of black American culture. Although this cultural phenomenon was challenged in the late civil rights era, it flourishes in the images that appear in many television shows, movies, books, and in the tendency of black male celebrities and athletes to choose very light-complexioned spouses if they marry black women.

53 Tomika Anderson, "Nothing Butt the Truth," *Essence*, November 2001, 116.

54 Alicia Keys, "Fallin'" *Songs in A Minor* (BMG/J, 2001).

55 President Clinton pardoned Kendra Smith, the most famous representative of this population, who spent years in prison as the result of her boyfriend's crimes.

56 India Arie, "Video," *Acoustic Soul* (Motown, 2001).

57 India Arie, interview, available at *http://www.mtv.com*.

58 Ibid.

59 Imani Perry, "It's My Thang and I'll Swing It the Way that I Feel: Sexual Subjectivity and Black Women Rappers," in *Race, Class, and Gender in the Media*, ed. Gaul Dines and Jean M. Humez (Thousand Oaks, CA: Sage Press, 1994).

60 Joan Morgan, *When Chickenheads Come Home to Roost: My Life as a Hip-Hop Feminist* (New York: Simon and Schuster, 1999).

61 Andre Leon Talley, "Style Fax," *Vogue* November 1999, 18.

62 Eve, "Gotta Man," *RuffRyders* (Interscope, 2000).

63 Sanjiv, "Queen of the Hill: Lauryn Fugee Finds Her Voice," GQ (UK), October 1998, 188.

64 At the time of the publication of this book, I have found no interviews or articles addressing the reason for Lauryn Hill's second transformation, but it will be interesting to see if she understands it as a rejection of the way in which she was styled in order to be palatable to a widespread audience.

65 Toni Cade Bambara, "Language and the Writer," in *Deep Sightings and Rescue Missions: Fiction, Essays, and Conversations*, ed. Toni Morrison (New York: Pantheon, 1996), 140.

66 Ibid.

67 Joshua Gamson, *Claims to Fame: Celebrity in Contemporary America* (Berkeley: University of California Press, 1994), 64.

68 Guy Debord, *The Society of the Spectacle*, trans. Donald Nicholson-Smith (New York: Zone, 1995), 39.

7   Bling Bling . . . and Going Pop
Consumerism and Co-optation in Hip Hop

1 See Mark Anthony Neal, "Critical Noire: *Like Water for Chocolate*: Common's Recipe for Progressive Hip Hop," *Pop Matters* 5 May 2000, 7; and *What the Music Said: Black Popular Music and Black Public Culture* (New York: Routledge, 1998).

2 De La Soul, "Big Brother Beat," *Stakes is High* (Tommy Boy, 1996).

3 David Bry, "New York State of Mind: The Resurgence of East Coast Hip Hop," in *The Vibe History of Hip Hop*, ed. Alan Light (New York: Three Rivers Press, 1999), 329.

4 Lauryn Hill, "That Thing," *The Miseducation of Lauryn Hill* (Ruffhouse Records, 1998).

5 Mary J. Blige, "What's the 411?" *What's the 411?* (MCA 1992).

6 Run-DMC, "My Adidas," *Raising Hell* (Def Jam, 1986).

7   Heavy D. and the Boyz, "Nike," *Living Large* (MCA, 1988).

8   Puff Daddy and The Family, "Been around the World," *No Way Out* (Bad Boy, 1997).

9   Notorious B. I. G., "Hypnotize," *Life after Death* (Bad Boy, 1997).

10   Michael Eric Dyson, *Holler if You Hear Me: Searching for Tupac Shakur* (New York: Basic Civitas Books, 2001), 108.

11   Ellis Cashmore, *The Black Culture Industry* (New York: Routledge, 1997), 172.

12   Notorious B. I. G., "Mo' Money Mo' Problems," *Life after Death*.

13   De La Soul, "Wonce Again Long Island," *Stakes is High* (Tommy Boy, 1996).

14   Lauryn Hill, "Final Hour," *The Miseduation of Lauryn Hill*.

15   Nelson George, *Hip Hop America* (New York: Penguin, 1998), x.

16   George Lipsitz, *Dangerous Crossroads: Popular Music, Postmodernism, and the Poetics of Place* (London: Verso, 1994), 27.

17   Ibid., 35.

18   Robin D. G. Kelley, "Kickin' Reality, Kickin' Ballistics: Gangsta Rap and Post-industrial Los Angeles," in *Droppin' Science: Critical Essays on Rap Music and Hip Hop Culture*, ed. William Eric Perkins (Philadelphia: Temple University Press, 1996).

19   Jacques Attali, *Noise: The Political Economy of Music*, trans. Brian Massumi (Minneapolis: University of Minnesota Press, 1985).

20   Tricia Rose, *Black Noise: Rap Music in Contemporary America* (Middletown: Wesleyan University Press, 1994).

21   bell hooks, "Performance as a Site of Opposition," in *Let's Get It On: The Politics of Black Performance*, ed. Catherine Ugwu (London: Institute of Contemporary Arts, 1995), 215.

22   Jacques Attali, *Noise: The Political Economy of Music*, trans. Brian Massumi (Minneapolis: University of Minnesota Press, 1985), 142.

23   This is a critique of Black Entertainment Television (BET), which disproportionately often plays hip hop with mainstream appeal and does not tend to give airtime to unknown or so-called underground artists.

24   "L Fudge," *Hip Hop Independent's Day Vol. 1* (Nervous Records, 1998).

25   Susan McClary, "Afterword" in Attali, *Noise*, 143.

26   DJ Premier, *New York Reality Check 101* (Uni/Eureka, 1997).

27   Attali, *Noise*, 147.

Index

Ice-T, 21, 27
"I Cram to Understand You" (MC Lyte), 155
Identity, black: in America, 17, 45; and the everyman, 138–139; female, 175; and feminism, 172–174, 189–190; and gender, 129; and locality, 21–23; male, 118; and media representations, 137–138; and originalism, 9–37; politically charged, 26–27; and wealth, 137–138
"I Desire" (Salt-N-Pepa), 172
"I Got it Made" (Special Ed), 65
"I Know You Got Soul" (Eric B. and Rakim), 52
Illegal activities, 113. *See also* Imprisonment
"Illegal Search" (L L Cool J), 137
Illusions, 189
"I'm Bad" (L L Cool J), 81
"I'm Dreamin" (KRS-One), 105–106
Immigrants, identity of, 17–18
Imprisonment: of hip hop artists, 94–95; images of, 179
Improvisation, 76–77. *See also* Freestyling
"I Need Love" (L L Cool J), 147
The Infamous (Mobb Deep), 145
Infidelity, in lyrics, 163–164
Influences, on hip hop, 12–15, 17, 199
Instruments, absence of, 67–68
Intellectualism, in hip hop, 107
Interaction, of MCs, 74–76
Interpretations, 61–62, 95
Invisibility, theme of, 123
Invisible Man, 123
Islam, 148
"Is There Heaven for a G?" (Tupac Shakur), 151
"Is There Heaven for a Gangster?" (Master P), 96, 151
"It Ain't Hard to Tell" (Nas), 80–81
"It's a Hard-Knock Life," 31

"It's a Man's World" (Ice Cube, Yo Yo), 145
"It's Still Rock and Roll to Me" (Billy Joel), 84
It Takes a Nation of Millions to Hold Us Back, 115
"It Was a Good Day" (Ice Cube), 79–80

Jack B. Nimble, 74
Jacobs, Harriet, 161
Jadakiss, 43
Jamaica, influence of, 13–14, 16, 24
Jamaicans, identity of, 17
James, Rick, 28, 105
Ja Rule, 124
Jay-Z, 31, 146–147, 174, 179
Jazzy Jeff, 70
Jean, Wyclef, 25, 77. *See also* Fugees
Jeru the Damaja, 53
Jim Crow, 27
Jodeci, 35
Joel, Billy, 84
Joeski Love, 73
Johnson, Charles, 41, 94
Johnson, Jack, 196
Jones, Gayl, 164
Juice Crew, 84, 170
Junior M.A.F.I.A., 145, 157.

"Kanday" (L L Cool J), 81–82
Karenga, Ron, 19
Kelley, Robin, 3, 40, 104, 110, 142, 168, 200
Kenner, Rob, 34
Keys, Alicia, 178–179
Khrist, 151
"Kickin' 4 Brooklyn" (MC Lyte), 86
Kid Capri, 65, 70
Kids, 121
Killah Priest, 56, 69, 91
Killing, metaphor of, 60
Kitt, Eartha, 45

54; "I Cram to Understand You,"
155; "Kickin' 4 Brooklyn," 86; "Lyte
as a Rock," 64
MCs, 71–77; critiquing each other, 6;
female (*see* Female hip hop artists);
as the Me in hip hop, 89; as preachers, 153; promoting conspicuous
consumption, 48; regions of, 21–
23; as representing black men,
131; on style, 82–83; as subject
and artist, 38–39; use of murder
metaphors by, 60; West Coast, 21
MC Shan, 84
Media, mainstream, representations
in: of blacks, 120–121, 138; of court,
108–109; of hip hop, 6–7, 93, 95;
of outlaws, 104
Men, black: bodies of, 120; friendship
and, 133; identity of, 118; masculinity of, 124–127; as patriarchs,
119; representation of, 120–122;
sexuality of, 121
Men, imprisoned, images of, 179. *See
also* Imprisonment
Men, white: and black masculinity,
124–127; as consumers of hip hop,
126; as patriarchs, 119
Meritocracy, hip hop as, 7
Metaphor, 59, 64; boxing as, 58–60;
drug dealing as, 104–105; killing
as, 60; murder as, 60; suicide as,
104. *See also* Similes
Method Man, 22, 51, 123, 143; "All I
Need," 143–145; "Bring the Pain,"
56; "How High," 105; use of
"nigga," 143–144
Miami Bass, 62
Milk, 64
Miller, Lilian, 166
Million Man March, 131, 140
Mimicry: by female artists, 159–160,
164, 166–168; thug, 109–111
Minh-ha, Trinh, 50

The Miseducation of Lauryn Hill, 193
Misogynistic, hip hop as, 128–129
Mission Impossible II, 22
Misunderstanding rappers, 50–51
Mobb Deep, 87–88, 97–98, 145
Mobility, as freedom, 159–160
Moms Mabley, 167
"Moral conscience," black people as,
4, 6
Moral panic, in hip hop, 192–194
Morrison, Toni, 164–165
Mos Def, 48, 54, 132–133
Motown, image of, 4
Moynihan, Bill, 112
MTV, 175
Multiple artists per song, appeal
of, 76
Murder, as metaphor, 60–61
Murray, Albert, 33, 43, 142
Murray, Keith, 123
Music: hip hop as, 113–114; as source
of violence, 96
Music, black: and beat boxing, 72;
previous forms of, 57; and sports,
59; tradition of, 33–37
Music, black American: as commer-
cial product, 19; hip hop as, 8,
10–12, 31, 41–42; as political, 16, 29
Musical instruments, absence of,
67–68
"My Adidas" (Run-DMC), 82, 194
"My Bitches" (Eve), 173–174
"My Mic Sounds Nice" (Salt-N-Pepa),
171
"My Rhyme Ain't Done" (L L
Cool J), 99
Mystikal, 95

"Nappy Heads," 130
Narrative, in lyrics, 77–80; about
the law, 102–116; "telling" versus
"being," 91; time frame in, 108
Nas, 28, 80–81, 87, 92, 150

Imani Perry is a professor of Law

at Rutgers University.

Library of Congress Cataloging-in-Publication Data

Perry, Imani
Prophets of the hood : politics and poetics in hip hop / Imani
Perry.
p. cm.
Includes bibliographical references (p.) and index.
ISBN 0-8223-3435-6 (cloth : alk. paper)
ISBN 0-8223-3446-1 (pbk. : alk. paper)
1. Rap (Music)—History and criticism.   2. Rap (Music)—
Political aspects.   3. Hip-hop—Social aspects.   I. Title.
ML3531.P47 2004
782.421649—dc22   2004013136